S0-APO-001

ACTIVE VOICE
    NO ING
        PRESENT TENSE
        NO "WILL"

How to Prepare Managerial Communications

How to Prepare
Managerial
Communications

James W. Jacoby

Revised Edition

of

How to Communicate Policies and Instructions

by

Joseph D. Cooper

The Bureau of National Affairs, Inc., Washington, D.C.

Copyright © 1983
The Bureau of National Affairs, Inc.

Library of Congress Cataloging in Publication Data

Jacoby, James W.
  How to prepare managerial communications.
  Rev. ed. of: How to communicate policies and instructions / Joseph D. Cooper. 1960.
  Bibliography: p.
  Includes index.
  1. Communication in management. I. Cooper, Joseph David, 1917–1975. How to communi-
cate policies and instructions. II. Title.
HD30.3.J32 1982   658.4′5   82-22607
ISBN 0-87179-388-1

Printed in the United States of America
International Standard Book Number: 0-87179-388-1

Foreword

Poorly planned and poorly written manuals, directives, and procedures waste time and money. In large organizations this waste is often substantial, although hard to pinpoint. It shows up in many ways: too high an error rate on forms returned by customers or the field; unnecessary service calls; internal conflicts and bureaucratic infighting; and general confusion among administrators.

Plain language, on the other hand, is both efficient and cost effective. When people don't have to puzzle out the meaning of a poorly written rule, they can do their jobs better and faster. Each of us can confirm this through everyday experience, both at work and at home. How often have we bogged down in completing a task because of poor instructions—whether filling out a form, entering data into a computer terminal, understanding what the head office wants, or assembling a child's toy late on Christmas Eve?

In this book, Jim Jacoby presents a carefully organized and valuable compendium of information on how to plan, organize, design, and write manuals, directives, and procedures; he also provides many helpful checklists and examples.

This foreword considers some of the reasons the problem of poorly planned and written rules continues to plague so many organizations, and then looks at some of the progress currently being made.

The problem continues to exist because of inertia, resistance to change, lack of knowledge, lack of incentive, lack of desire on the part of some lawyers to give up obscure legalese, and lack of proof that plain language is cost effective and efficient. These six reasons make up a formidable list, yet real progress is being made in overcoming these obstacles.

The most dramatic progress is in the area of federal regulations, insurance policies, and other legal forms which consumers must accept as printed. In the Federal Government, the move to use plain language in regulations started with the Ford Administration, received a strong boost from President Carter, and was continued under President Reagan, with a shift in emphasis to cost effective government and reducing the regulatory burden. Some agencies, particularly Social Security and the Federal Communications Commission, have made notable progress in rewriting their regulations in plain language.

Over 20 states now require by law or regulation that insurance policies be written in plain language. The results are dramatic; plain language policies are much easier to understand. Because insurance companies want uniformity in policy forms throughout the country, it seems probable that in a few more years insurance policies will be rewritten in plain language. Five states presently require that other consumer contracts, such as leases and loan forms, be written in plain language. Many organizations, recognizing that plain language is both good business and internally efficient, are converting to plain language without waiting for legislatures to force their hand.

Resistance to change was severe when the plain language movement started. First, the resisters said: "It can't be done. You can't write it in plain language." Then, when people ignored them and did the job, the resisters fell back to another argument: "Why bother? No one ever reads the legalese anyway." Both these objections have been answered. It's worth looking at how this has happened, because the same arguments still reappear from time to time.

The first argument—"It can't be done"—is easy to answer. Enough rules have been rewritten in plain language to make it clear that the job can be done.

The second argument—"Why bother?"—has two answers. Plain language laws were passed and Executive Orders were issued because of a strong feeling that the consumer has a right to receive a legal document that he or she can understand. It's hard to argue seriously with the reasonableness of this view. But the consumer movement is currently not so strong as it was and, furthermore, this answer carries little weight in cases where the user of a set of rules is not an inexperienced consumer. In these cases, the answer is that poorly written rules waste time and money for the organization that creates them—no matter how experienced the user. Plain language is cost effective. Three examples illustrate this point.

Several years ago the Federal Communications Commission rewrote its CB radio regulations in plain language. A well designed question-and-answer format replaced a series of complex regulations written in legalese and scattered throughout many chapters. Before the revision, five people had spent much of their time answering inquiries. After the revision, the inquiries were so few that all five were assigned to other work.

A bank in Connecticut was revising its loan forms to comply with the state's plain language law. The rule for determining the amount the bank returned to the customer, when a loan was prepaid in advance, was buried in a mind-boggling 200-word sentence. At a drafting meeting, the lawyer explained what the sentence really said. The operations manager was alarmed—this wasn't the way loan officers understood the rule or explained it to customers. The computer center manager was even more alarmed because she was sure the computer determined the amount by a third method. To settle the matter, a dummy run was processed through the computer. To everyone's surprise, they found that the computer actually used a fourth method because a programmer had received third-hand instructions he didn't fully understand.

A government agency had a basic form which its public completed each year. About 100,000 organizations were required to do this, yet in one year the agency printed 900,000 copies of the form. Why the waste? The form was printed in two colors, with shading for those areas to be left blank, so that photocopying by the user was not practical. Fill-in areas in some cases were small, requiring either careful typewriter spacing or neat, small handwriting. Because of the form design, users were wasting copies and asking for more. When the design was changed to allow users to photocopy and to allow room for fill-ins, the agency found it could cut down its printing bill substantially.

These examples show three areas in which plain language increased the efficiency of the organization. In the first, employees answering inquiries were freed for other work; in the second, all departments of the bank understood and followed the same rule—the left hand knew what the right hand was doing; in the third, better design saved printing costs.

As you read and use this book, ask yourself how you can increase your organization's efficiency by writing rules in plain language. Look for opportunities to measure or demonstrate by hard evidence the increase in efficiency. Because successful writing is hard work, look for ways to motivate writers of rules to do a better job. The need for clear communication becomes increasingly important as organizations grow and must deal with more complex problems. Each of us must accept the challenge to find ways to develop more efficient communication.

West Hartford, Conn.   *John O. Morris*

Preface

This book is dedicated to all those who are responsible for the mostly thankless task of writing and publishing management communications. Conveying directives and obtaining employee acceptance is their greatest challenge; that any written managerial communications succeed is a reflection of their talents and perseverance.

How to Prepare Managerial Communications is designed to serve both as a "how-to" manual and an up-to-date reference source. It is an outgrowth of a coursebook I prepared several years ago for a University of Minnesota Continuing Education seminar. The coursebook was based, to a large extent, on Joseph D. Cooper's *How to Communicate Policies and Instructions*, published by The Bureau of National Affairs, Inc., in 1960. The present book expands significantly on Cooper's book and provides an in-depth look at the current communications practices of nearly two dozen major corporations.

The structure of the book follows the logical order of the steps required to produce an organizational manual. Following an introductory chapter, the text discusses the initial steps in planning the overall project (Chapter 2); appropriate writing and editing techniques (Chapters 3 and 4); incorporating material into an organizational manual (Chapter 5); review, trial usage, and management approval (Chapter 6); and the production process (Chapter 7). It also covers distribution and updating of publications and eliciting reader feedback (Chapter 8) and includes reference material on graphics (Chapter 9), various types of instructional materials (Chapter 10), and "how-to" documents (Chapter 11).

The appendixes provide helpful information on preparing managerial communications, including a complete style manual, a discussion of plain language laws, a mini guide to procedure writing, examples of specialized manuals, a case study, and available seminars and consulting services. A selected bibliography is also included.

January 1983   *James W. Jacoby*

Acknowledgments

Throughout this two-year-long project, many talented people have contributed ideas, examples, and advice. My thanks to John O. Morris, president of John O. Morris Associates, West Hartford, Conn., for his guidance, critique, and extensive examples, and to McGraw-Hill Book Company, for permission to use several of John's published writings. Roxanne Flett of Hennepin County Administration, Minneapolis, Minn., provided invaluable initial guidance as well as numerous examples from her County Administrative Manual.

Robert Harmon, of Clear Corporate Communications, New York City, developed the American Management Association's questionnaire used in the AMA/MCC Midwest Survey of Administrative Manuals. Management Communications Consultants (MCC) conducted the survey as a Midwest subsample for the AMA's nationwide survey completed late in 1980. I also thank the AMA, which permitted me to use its survey.

Floyd A. Smith of Union Carbide Corporation, New York City, was instrumental in obtaining permission to reprint his excellent UCC Style Manual for Corporate Policies and Procedures.

My heartfelt thanks go to Mary E. Hoeve, communications manager of Control Data Corporation, for her outstanding support and perseverance throughout this entire project as editor, advisor, graphics consultant, and sergeant-at-arms. My thanks also to Sharon J. Ausman, manuscript typist, also of Control Data, whose accuracy, suggestions, and long-standing patience helped complete the book.

Other persons who contributed valuable advice and examples or granted permission to use previously published material include:

Sue A. Berg, Administrator, Control Data Corporation, Minneapolis, Minn.

Elizabeth Berry, Partner, Berry & Associates, Minneapolis, Minn.

Robert B. Campbell, Southern California Edison Company.

Brian M. Cluer, Union Carbide Corporation, New York City.

Daniel J. Fiorino, Chief of Regulations Management Staff, U.S. Environmental Protection Agency, Washington, D.C.

Richard W. Grefe, Director, Continuing Management Education, University of Minnesota, Minneapolis, Minn.

Erwin M. Keithley, University of California, Los Angeles, and Philip J. Schreiner, California State University, Fullerton, Calif.

Gene H. Kreienbrink, postmaster, Minneapolis, Minn., U.S. Postal Service.

Karl C. J. Schricker, Manuals Corporation of America, Setauket, N.Y.

Janice Twohig, Plantronics Zehntel, Bloomington, Minn.

In addition, the following organizations have graciously permitted reprinting of various samples from their administrative and "how-to" communications: Britton & Associates, Corvallis, Ore.; Burlington Northern, Inc., St. Paul, Minn.; Connecticut Law Tribune, Hartford Conn.; Control Data Corporation, Bloomington, Minn.; The Dartnell Corporation, Chicago, Ill.; General Foods, White Plains, N.Y.; Journal of Systems Management, Cleveland, Ohio; McGraw-Hill Book Company, New York, N.Y.; National Micrographics Association, Silver Spring, Md.; The Office, Stamford, Conn.; Onan Company, Minneapolis, Minn.; Russell Manning Communications, Inc., Minneapolis, Minn.; South-Western Publishing Company, Cincinnati, Ohio; State of Minnesota, Fourth Judicial District, District Court of Minnesota; and The Toro Company, Bloomington, Minn.

Table of Contents

1
Introduction

Most organizations recognize the need for written guidance as a basis for effective performance. Many, however, do not fully understand the need for special techniques in communicating policies, procedures, or other management directives. They may, in fact, regard a well-designed instruction system as so much red tape. This chapter provides an overview of the "wide world" of managerial communications. And it presents arguments to convince all levels of management of the value of a well-written, accurate, and up-to-date communications system.

ROLE OF MANAGERIAL COMMUNICATIONS

Managerial communications cover such items as policies, administrative orders, bulletins, regulations, office notices, office and procedural manuals, circulars, memoranda, directives, handbooks, job instructions, administrative routines, standard practice instructions, codes, and releases.

All of these transfer thought among the people within an organization. They convey information regarding official policy and procedures; thus they enable the organization to perform its activities in a specifically intended manner. By establishing the rules of operating conduct, managerial communications serve as guides for measuring performance, eliminate confusion on the part of those who seek guidance, and promote uniformity, consistency, and integration of action.

Organizations that have successfully implemented a communications system are well aware of its value. In a recent survey,[1] 43 companies described the principal advantages as:

[1]AMA/MCC Midwest Survey. The American Management Associations recently conducted a nationwide survey of manual development practices, developed by Robert Harmon of Clear Corporate Communications, New York, N.Y. Management Communications Consultants (MCC) of Minneapolis, Minn., conducted a Midwest subsample of the survey using the AMA questionnaire. MCC is a consulting firm that conducts business communications seminars and provides communications consulting.

- Providing an excellent source of reference and serving as a vehicle for disseminating management communications.

- Encouraging consistency of activities.

- Generating clear lines of authority as well as accountability.

- Enabling company operations to move at a faster pace by allowing executives primarily to handle unusual situations.

- Promoting good human relations by informing employees of what is expected of them.

- Providing information specific to readers' needs, helping to close the communications gap between a home office and a branch, and easing the orientation of new employees.

The study revealed that 80 percent of the companies interviewed currently maintain from one to ten manuals containing policy or procedural information. The types of manuals prepared by these companies are as follows: policy and procedure (79%); procedure (60%); training (51%); and organization (32%).

A study made by Dartnell Corporation in 1978 revealed that two thirds of the companies interviewed had corporate policy manuals (65%) and procedural manuals (68%). Divisional/administrative or operational guides, instructional manuals, and orientation manuals were used to a lesser extent.

Defining Basic Terms

Because there are no standards for managerial communications, organizations define the various terms associated with these publications somewhat differently. In general, policy and procedure terminology should include the following basic elements:

1. Policy—a statement that expresses a basic mode of management.

2. Procedure—a standardized method of performing specified work (a set of how-to-do-it rules).

3. Rule—a statement of a single action, result, or fact.

4. Set of Rules—a collection of related rules.

5. Regulation—a set of rules, frequently of a legal or quasi-legal nature—generally external.

6. Directive—a set of rules relating to an organization's internal operations.

A major midwestern department store explains policies and procedures in the following manner:

"A policy is a guide for carrying out action. It establishes a course of action that has been adopted as expedient to govern the operations of an organization. Thus, it expresses the philosophy, principles, and purposes of the organization, as well as its ideas.

"To differentiate between philosophy, policy, and procedure, use the following examples as guidelines:

"1. Philosophy—The Why

"We believe services to be an important function of our future, and we must constantly upgrade our services to maximize long run potential.

"2. Policy—The What

"On purchases over \$100.01 within our delivery area, there will be no delivery charge to the customer. Any purchase of \$100 or under will require a service charge.

"3. Procedure—The How

"The format followed in writing saleschecks for the previous policy. Also the internal handling necessary for billing of customers and crediting of the parent department."

Union Carbide Corporation, in its style manual for corporate policies and procedures,[2] defines policy and procedure as:

"*Policy:* A continuing directive applying to recurring questions and problems important in setting the limits and directions of managerial actions through which objectives of the enterprise are to be reached.

"*Procedures:* Standardized methods of performing specified work. Procedures implement policies and explain the how by which objectives are obtained."

NEED FOR WELL-DESIGNED COMMUNICATIONS

To be effective, managerial communications must be prepared and released within a systematic framework—called a "directives system." Only in this way can organizations treat related instructions consistently. And only in this way can recipients be sure they have all related items.

[2]See Appendix A.

The Directives System

A directives system provides a formal method of total management control for issuing communications, including planning, organization, writing, editing, publication, distribution, and revision. Directives issued as part of an overall system include any official organizational document that guides, instructs, or informs, including formalized statements of policy and procedure.

The format, coordination, and distribution of written instructions will vary, of course, with the size and complexity of organizations. Where the need for internal communications is infrequent or the rate of change is slight, casual issuance systems may be satisfactory. But large organizations, or active ones, require a logically conceived directives system. With proper planning and execution, a directives system should give the user what is needed and, at the same time, provide each originating office and issuing level with adequate control over those policies and procedures for which it is responsible.

As an example, one major corporation uses several elements of its total directives system to help publicize new or revised policies or procedures. In addition to standard distribution of policies and procedures to specific holders, Control Data Corporation of Minneapolis, Minn., uses its twice-monthly management newsletter to give advance notice of new or modified directives to its total management staff. Either in an interview or a news-story format, the management publication gives relevant background information on the directives, together with the means for and the date of implementation.

Guideposts for an Effective System

In developing an effective directives system, it is important to consider the following guideposts:

Completeness	Only the complete story helps assure that everyone does what management wants. This means complete units of guidance and information for each different type of user.
Clarity	Directives presented in the clearest form save time and energy. Thoughts behind the words and pictures must be so clear that no one misunderstands.
Timeliness	Up-to-date information helps satisfy employee needs and eliminates error.

Simplicity	Simple directives provide an accurate, easy means of reference and help speed operations.
Flexibility	Flexible coverage assures that all organizational levels live within the scope of a directive. Flexible distribution pinpoints those who should receive a directive. Flexibility permits changes without altering the basic directive.
Consistency	With a consistent format, directives are easy to use. Consistent content presentation secures uniformity and reduces misinterpretations.
Dependability	Completely coordinated directives prevent conflicts and overlappings and establish reliability.
Economy	Economical methods for developing directives save the time of writers, reviewers, and approvers. Economical reproduction and distribution save money. Economical methods for maintaining directives save the user's time, energy, and—at times—patience.
Availability	Having directives available to those who need them when they need them helps assure that the job is completed correctly the first time.

When a well-designed directives system has been put into place, both readers and management reap benefits.

Reader Benefits

Training and Indoctrination—For new employees, or old employees on new assignments, written instructions are invaluable in initial orientation and in providing continuing work guides. Employees know what they are expected to do and can have greater confidence in their own performance.

Whenever there is a great influx of new employees, written materials aid in training and reduce "breaking-in" periods considerably. This is invaluable in an expanding organization, particularly in setting up new branch offices.

Employees can visualize the whole process of work operations in relation to their individual tasks. This gives them a sense of participation. On a larger scale, organizational relationships are improved when officers and employees have a mutual understanding of duties and responsibilities.

Communication and Reference—Employers frequently provide their employees with written instructions regarding official policies, procedures, practices, and operating responsibilities. If kept current in a manual, this material constitutes the official handbook. Reference to it eliminates much confusion, error, consultation, correspondence, and loss of time. The manual settles arguments and affords its users a sense of confidence, for they know they are following approved practice.

Management Benefits

Communication Channeling—The most obvious advantage of a directives system to management is having clearly designated and recognized channels of official communication. The status of nonauthenticated publications is not left to conjecture for management or employees.

Organization Control and Planning—If employees are to work together harmoniously, clear-cut divisions of labor must be made so that each will do only his or her assigned task and so that no tasks will be unassigned. By developing a well-designed directives system—such as logically organized manuals of functional statements, operating policies, responsibilities, and procedures—management can:

- Pinpoint responsibility.
- Help prevent repetitive judgments on routine matters.
- Encourage and promote cooperation by delineating work relationships.
- Explain work procedure clearly and concisely.
- Help supervisors and employees in their routine tasks.
- Minimize time needed for orientation.
- Help supervisors play a more positive role and improve operations and productivity.
- Help explain proposed changes, by presenting a plan in writing before it goes into effect.

Standardization—Control of operations depends upon standardization of routines and specification of the manner in which exceptions should be handled. Standard operations can be controlled from headquarters and integrated with other activities, such as home-office control of field operations. Specification of work methods is a prerequisite to fixing work standards and measuring performance. Manuals and standard practice instructions are the vehicles for communicating these instructions.

Value of Audit and Review—The value of an operating manual becomes especially apparent during performance audits. Auditors base examinations and performance appraisals on actual practices and prescribed methods and criteria. They can then identify deviations and unworkable methods for study and possible correction. Financial auditors rely on official written instructions as the primary ruling criteria for audits.

Public Relations Preparation—Manuals and circulars are indispensable for every employee who comes into contact with the public. Because these people are in many ways special public relations representatives, they must know the answers—or where to find them—to a great number of questions. Moreover, increased mobility causes the public to expect the same type of service from branches of the same organization.

TYPICAL PROBLEMS WITH DIRECTIVES SYSTEMS

Directives and instruction systems, unfortunately, are rarely started on a systematic basis. All too often they are built on the ruins of a broken-down structure. The AMA/MCC Midwest Survey cited the following problems with directives and manuals:

1. They are often not written clearly and simply.
2. They are issued too late to meet deadlines or other planning goals.
3. They are garbled or conflict with each other.
4. They are amended and supplemented in confusing ways.
5. They do not reach the employees who need them or are directed toward the wrong audience.

When one major corporation set out to revise its accounting instructions, it listed the following reasons why manuals are not used:

1. The manual is poorly arranged and it is hard to find things in it.
2. It is so complex and wordy that the average employee has trouble understanding it.
3. It is too large, bulky, or heavy for easy use.
4. It is poorly produced and unattractive; hard to read; and hard on the eyes.
5. It is out of date, obsolete.

6. It doesn't fit the job of the employee who is supposed to use it.

7. It is too abstract; it fails to get down to cases.

8. The employee has never been taught why and how to use it.

9. Employees feel that it restricts individual initiative.

Polls of branch offices receiving home office instructions revealed major weaknesses such as:

- Delays in receiving and confusion in beginning to operate under new instructions.

- Issuance of multiple uncoordinated instructions.

- Lack of clarity resulting from weaknesses in language, style, organization of subject matter, and format.

- Insufficient information.

Problems such as these occur primarily because management personnel generally perceive the preparation of instructional issuances as a low-prestige activity. Too often, it is regarded as an editorial task and assigned to personnel with limited backgrounds of creative experience. To overcome these problems, a more disciplined approach is required.

LEGAL RAMIFICATIONS

Prior to 1964, federal law had little impact on management directives, policies, and procedures. Since the enactment of Title VII of the Civil Rights Act of 1964, however, federal, state, and local laws have had an increasing impact on administrative publications.

Legislation affecting managerial communications currently deals with three categories: discriminatory practices, safety practices, and the necessity for clarity. Future legislation will no doubt be more restrictive—not only in these areas but in other areas as well.

Clear-Writing Legislation[3]

Plain language laws are some of the most evident forms of legislation dealing with improved writing of policies, procedures, and how-to directives. These laws are already incorporated into the statutes of Connecticut, Hawaii, Maine, and New York for general consumer transactions,

[3]This section was adapted, with permission, from John O. Morris, "Plain Language Is Winning," *Connecticut Law Tribune,* December 15, 1980. Mr. Morris is the president of John O. Morris Associates, consultants in management communications, West Hartford, Conn., and the author of *Make Yourself Clear* (New York: McGraw-Hill Book Co., 1980).

into the regulations of at least 20 other states for insurance policies, and into the regulations of federal government agencies.

According to John O. Morris, principal drafter of the 1979 Connecticut Plain Language law: ''Its overall purpose is to protect you or me as consumers, in those take-it or leave-it transactions where we have no choice but to accept a printed form contract. Advocates of plain language laws feel the consumer has a right to receive a contract that he or she can understand, free of incomprehensible legalese that may favor the preparer of the contract.''

Users are learning that plain language is good business, according to Morris, for at least three reasons:

- It is good public relations. Users of the plain language forms are pleasantly surprised to find they can understand what they are being required to accept.

- It is efficient. When an organization converts its forms to plain language, employees who must process the forms can understand what they are doing. They need not refer so often to a manual which attempts to translate the legalese into understandable procedures. Therefore forms are processed faster, with fewer mistakes.

- It is legally more sound. Plain language eliminates the awkward, strained sentence constructions which create structural ambiguities that are difficult to see and even more difficult to resolve.[4]

Finally, with an eye to current law and with a feeling for what is likely to become the law, all documents should:

- Be nondiscriminatory, especially with regard to gender.[5]

- Be simple and clear so that readers can understand them.

- Clearly state any hazards created by products.

- Eliminate false or misleading claims about products.

- Be thoroughly reviewed and checked for quality.

---

[4]See Appendix B for information on complying with plain language laws.
[5]See Chapter 3, p. 49.

2

Planning the System

Planning is perhaps the most important element in the development of management communications—yet it is the one area needing the most improvement. The key to effective planning is a thorough understanding of the entire process—from initial thinking about a document all the way through the printing and distribution stages. The development process includes the following:

1. *Project Considerations*—staff responsibilities, project objectives, reader analysis, timing, scheduling, monitoring.
2. *Data Collection*—sources, overcoming resistances, gaining cooperation.
3. *Organization*—outlines, methods, formats.
4. *Writing and Editing*—styles, formats, simplifying complex descriptions, writing in plain English.
5. *Review, Trial Usage, and Approvals*—methods and mechanics.
6. *Production*—typing, graphics, layout, paper, and printing.
7. *Distribution*—techniques, mailing lists, transmittal memos.
8. *Updating*—scheduled, nonscheduled; identification marks.

Proper planning requires that all of these elements be considered in publishing any management communication. The total time involved from start to completion could range from a minimum of a half day for a brief management memo all the way to a year or longer for a major policy and procedure manual. This chapter examines the initial steps: project considerations, data collection, and organization of information.

PROJECT CONSIDERATIONS

Before launching a new project involving publication of an administrative communication, management should determine which staff or organizational unit will be assigned to produce the document. Staff personnel, in turn, should define project objectives, analyze the reader, schedule the project, and establish monitoring controls. Consideration must also be given to potential resistances from other departments within the organization which will be affected by new rules.

Staff Responsibilities

In most cases, planning, promotion, coordination, and final editing of administrative communications are the responsibility of a central communications unit. Actual writing is usually the job of the people most familiar with the work; the mechanical tasks of production, including copy preparation, reproduction, and distribution, usually are the responsibility of office services personnel.

The Central Unit

Functional Statement—The duties of the central communications unit should be spelled out in a statement similar to the following example (which assumes that an organization has both headquarters and field or branch office structures):

The central communications unit:

1. Establishes and maintains manuals and other appropriate media for the dissemination of all policy statements, orders, regulations, operating procedures, and instructions needed to provide essential work guidance: (a) for headquarters personnel; (b) from headquarters to regional and other field offices.
2. Reviews all such policy or procedural materials to assure consistency with the overall pattern, to avoid the issuance of conflicting, incorrect, or irrelevant information, and to assure clarity of presentation and adequacy of details.
3. Reviews proposed releases with appropriate offices, prior to issuance, to determine such factors as legality, timeliness, and feasibility of proposals and their relationship to established or contemplated practices.
4. Identifies differences evident during the clearance process, and refers them for administrative decision where reconcilations of major issues are not achieved.
5. Reviews major areas of policy and procedure and initiates actions to cover deficiencies in existing regulations.
6. Assigns numbers to instructions and identifies cross-referencing requirements.

7. Maintains a procedural library of all instructional releases.
8. Determines and maintains current lists for adequate distribution of procedural materials issued by headquarters.

Operating Charter—In addition to a functional statement, the central communications unit needs its own "charter" or operating regulation. A charter should contain (1) a general statement of purpose, applicability, and definitions; (2) descriptions and definitions of the approved categories of instructional materials; (3) specific statements of responsibility for preparation, clearance, review, approval, and issuance; and (4) a statement of other services or facilities provided by the communications unit.

A definition of regulations and instructions might be worded as follows:

The term "regulations and instructions" shall be understood to mean:

a. Written statements of policy for operating and administrative guidance and use.
b. Statements of specific processes or courses of action to be followed in carrying out such policy.
c. Technical bulletins for the use of employees.
d. Announcements for circulation to staff members.
e. Similar material designed for the instruction, information, or guidance of personnel at headquarters or field offices.

The term shall include policy statements and instructions of general applicability even if the initial method of release is by memo rather than as an integral part of the published series of releases.

The term does not include press releases and information directed to the general public rather than to officers and employees.

Management should encourage preliminary discussion on the anticipated forms of issuance, the desirability of advance approval from other units, and the relationship of the proposed release to existing materials. Discussions should also cover the development of a submission form and supporting documents and the time needed for review, approval, reproduction, and distribution.

The charter of a major manufacturer specifies the following duties of the central management unit:

"Maintain and distribute Corporate-wide Policies and Procedures, Personnel Manager's Policies and the Most Frequently Used Personnel Policies and Procedures (also known as Manager's Manual).

"Provide assistance relative to the format and design of the Corporate-wide Policies and Procedures to attain control and standardization.

"Provide a reference service to a Corporate-wide audience in locating and determining the existence or validity of Policies and Procedures.

"Monitor communication material to ascertain compliance with Corporate Policies and Procedures."

The charter should also (1) specify the role of the management communications unit in reconciling differences, (2) indicate who shall give approval to different categories of materials, and (3) authorize the communications unit to issue any materials which have been approved by affected offices. It may also specify the style standards to be followed in preparing materials for publication.

Project Objectives

Whenever communications are to be prepared, the organization's objectives must be firmly stated. They are necessary for guidance not only in carrying out the project but also in measuring effectiveness when the job is completed. In establishing the objectives, you should determine:

1. What is the purpose of the document? Who issued the assignment? What is the document's function?

2. When will the document be needed and what are the deadlines?

3. Why is it important? What are management's reasons for issuing it?

4. How will it be used? Under what circumstances? Continually on the job? As reference material?

5. Where will it be used? Identify the structure of the organization.

6. Will there be any resistance to your new rules or standards?

7. Who is the reader? What is his or her background, education, and knowledge of your organization, whether business, industry, education, or government?

8. How do you gain reader compliance?

Analyzing Your Reader

Like most people, writers see things from their own vantage point. Because it is easy to produce documents that are self-oriented rather than reader-oriented, material often misses its objective entirely. Therefore, you should write for people—not for machines or organizations. People must be considered for what they know, what they don't know, their level of education, and the intended use of a document.

Try to determine beforehand *all* of the readers of the document. Make a list of the people who will be using it. Try to supply enough information so that the least informed reader will become acquainted with the subject matter and the best informed reader will gain some new information.

Bear in mind that the reader is boss. Each reader decides what, when, and how action is to be taken, regardless of what the instructions say. This varies from organization to organization, depending on internal discipline. For example, new executives learn that they may not expect automatic compliance with their instructions. Officers and employees have their own safe ways of waiting out or slowing down the effect of a new instruction. Sometimes noncompliance may be due to habit and ignorance. Employees resist change in favor of the accustomed order of things. You can do little about this situation; it is primarily a compliance problem.

But you can do something about barriers to understanding. Because instructions are vehicles of change or innovation, readers tend to be automatically predisposed against them. You can minimize this problem by preparing the instructions in a manner which makes them as understandable and usable as possible. For example:

- Be sure to address actual working needs. Avoid any temptation to write the instructions to impress colleagues. Avoid writing for self-protection.

- Be conscious of the differences in background and understanding between you and the reader. For a nontechnical audience, use language and illustrations that are understandable. The same applies to technical instructions addressed to readers who may be technicians *in other fields*. Remember, you generally have more background on the subject than your readers. Therefore, take nothing for granted.

- Inform the reader of the ultimate objective. Readers tend to resent and resist instructions which are vague about their tie-in with a broader situation or procedure.

And most important, cite the benefits that will accrue from performing the instructions. Benefits are fairly easy to express when it comes to safety rules—an employee could have an accident, for example. But in other areas it may be more difficult to express a tangible benefit. Placing yourself in the reader's shoes will help you to understand where "they're coming from." An excellent way to determine this is by interviewing management personnel as you collect your data.

Scheduling and Monitoring the Project

Responsibility for scheduling and monitoring an administrative project is often deferred; management frequently says, "We'll publish it whenever it's ready." And because most writers of administrative communications wear multiple hats, such projects frequently get lowest priority. If a project is worth doing at all, it should be done right the first time. Proper time should be allotted to schedule the total project, from beginning to end. And appropriate procedures should be developed to monitor progress properly. Careful attention to all details in publishing administrative communications is imperative to delivering a quality product, on time and within budget.

To provide adequate management controls over a project of this type, Robert B. Campbell recommends standardizing each activity, using various forms, and then monitoring each step along the way with an overall progress chart. His suggestions include the following,[1]

1. An *assignment page,* which describes the project, names a person as writer, establishes due dates, and lists organizations affected.

2. *A plan of action,* which defines planned milestone activities in chronological order, each with a forecasted completion date. (See Figure 2-1.)

3. *Interview data sheets,* which document detailed information gathered during interviews. Attached to each sheet may be such additional material as related reports, flow charts, and business forms.

4. *Document coordination sheet,* used to transmit drafts of documents to appropriate individuals for review and approval. One copy is retained as a "master" control for recording both sign-offs and responses.

Whether you formally document each step along the way or handle it informally is your decision. Written approvals of administrative communications obviously are mandatory prior to publishing (as indicated in the previous section). But how you handle the overall management of the project is up to you.

---

[1]Adapted with permission from Robert B. Campbell, "Standardizing Procedure Documentation," *Journal of Systems Management,* June 1976, pp. 15–19. Mr. Campbell is an engineering methods analyst for the Southern California Edison Co.

The Plan of Action

1. Subject (specific descriptive title or definitive scope)
2. Milestones

Item		*Completion Date* Target	Actual
a. Hold fact-gathering interviews with the following participants, recording pertinent detail information on individual Interview Sheets:			
	Name *Organization*		
	1. _____ _____	_____	_____
	2. _____ _____	_____	_____
	3. _____ _____	_____	_____
b. Analyze interview information, develop data and search out all necessary data to obtain a clear and unobstructed administrative or operational flow.		_____	_____
c. Write assigned policy, procedure, report, etc., and route through the secretarial process for typing, proofreading, and return.		_____	_____
d. Prepare the Document Transmittal Coordination Sheet, attach to typed document, and arrange reproduction of required number of copies.		_____	_____
e. Route document with attached Coordination Sheet to participants for review and scheduled return.		_____	_____
f. Confirm that coordination review responses are received by the scheduled due date.		_____	_____
g. Examine all comments, judging their validity and appropriateness for incorporation into the document being considered.		_____	_____
h. Rewrite the document draft, incorporating all acceptable comments as received, and route through the secretarial process for typing into final format, proofreading, and return.		_____	_____
i. Process for management approval of publication and distribution of document.		_____	_____
j. Arrange for reproduction and distribution of approved document.		_____	_____

Figure 2–1. The Plan of Action (Courtesy of Robert B. Campbell)

COLLECTING DATA

Before you can begin the writing phase of your project, you must first obtain information on the subject. How much information depends upon the audience for which you are writing. See what has already been published on the same subject, then consult organization files. You may find memoranda or precedents or drafts of other instructions. Studying these materials often gives clues as to why certain provisions were included and others excluded. Other written sources include technical materials in other forms; a reference librarian is an excellent source for help in locating them.

Second, consult key people who are familiar with the subject. They can advise you about what should be included, what should be omitted, and what should be emphasized. Moreover, obtaining their approval during the review cycle is important, and it will be easier if they were participants initially.

Third, thoroughly understand your material; become familiar with the product through actual use.

In defining and limiting a subject, ask yourself: What message or information do I want to convey? Who are my readers and what information do they need? Variations in treatment and informational coverage are obviously necessary in situations which explain or describe:

- Causes of an action.
- Parts of something, including its divisions, members, classes, structure, or composition.
- Results or effects of an action.
- Meanings or characteristics of a situation.
- Purposes, functions, duties, or services.
- How something works or how someone performs.

Data collection includes lengthy and sometimes sensitive interviewing, literature searches, analysis of previous results, and negotiations with individuals about overall policy. Time and effort must be spent in planning and scheduling the data-collection phase.

Typical Resistances

When launching a new instruction program, be prepared to counter resistance from nearly all sides. One exception may be top management, since this staff is often the recipient of many poorly prepared communications. As a result, it looks with favor upon anything that may reduce confusion and congestion. Typical excuses include:

"Our organization is different." Although every organization is different, each organization has a need for communicating operating information and instructions for uniform guidance of those affected. To communicate is common; the differences are in the choice and design of the specific communication needs of individual organizations.

"Our organization is too small." This may be a valid objection, if sincerely offered. It is not a valid objection if the organization is new or expanding, highly complex in its work relationships, highly diverse, undergoing major program changes, or experiencing drastic turnover.

"Our employees learn from the bottom up." An instructional manual represents a broader base of experience than any one person could obtain from immediate supervisors. Dependence upon a trial-and-error learning process diminishes productivity of a company's employees. Written performance guides reflecting past experience abbreviate the time needed for training.

"This project costs too much." Management costs cannot be avoided. An effective instruction program costs money. If avoided as a direct outlay, costs will be hidden in such activities as excessive supervision, longer training periods, correction of errors, duplication of effort, loss of maximum effort, and loss of valuable experience through employee turnover.

"This sounds like a lot of red tape." Red tape is procedure which is *unnecessarily* burdensome. It does not have to be committed to paper to be red tape. Far from introducing red tape, the recording of official practice makes it subject to general scrutiny. The charge of red tape is sometimes made by individuals who prefer to pursue their own objectives without regard to the best interest of the organization.

"This would freeze practices and stifle initiative." This is a possibility, particularly under nonprogressive leadership. It is not necessary to prescribe procedures with excessive detail, nor is it necessary to be bound by previously prescribed practice. In fact, a written record of practice is a most tangible basis for reviewing the need for operational change. Conversely, instructions *do not* have to be narrow and arbitrary. It *is* possible to prescribe latitude for discretion.

"We don't have the time." Unfortunately, the rewards from many desirable management practices are not immediately apparent. The tendency is to focus on the daily operational workload and to brush aside long-range projects as being unprofitable. Sometimes it is simply an inability to organize one's time or to allocate properly between planning

and doing. More often, it is either a resistance to change or a failure to attach importance or priority to the need. Time not invested in the development of a good system is more than offset by the time spent in duplicate and conflicting effort, in the training of new employees, in burdening supervisory and executive staff, and in remedying the consequences of ill-prepared instructions.

"We tried it before and it didn't work." A previous failure does not mean that a new effort also will fail. Universally, the greatest success is achieved when top management gives its full support, particularly in the form of a suitable directive. This may not be enough; frequently it is necessary for management to express intent that ensures full cooperation. This may require memoranda to the top staff requesting cooperation.

Gaining Cooperation From Contributors

During the data-gathering phase you may often need to win the cooperation of officials whose work areas are involved. They can provide skilled personnel to do some of the work on the project if they reassign their people or double up their work assignments. Directives issued from top management may facilitate this but will be inadequate unless participating officials cooperate. Cooperation occurs if these people are really sold on the idea or if they feel it is in their best interests.

Good planning strategy mandates concentrating on favorable aspects. Various approaches include seeking:

1. Key officials in a position to make determinations for operations under their supervision.

2. Operations or activities for which there is a specific need for written documentation or which can be dramatically improved by written communications.

3. Relatively new areas of activity in which resistance is at a minimum.

When you have established a list of contributors, you're ready for the next step: preparing an outline.

PREPARING THE OUTLINE

The natural tendency for most people is to work without an outline. If this is merely impatience to get on with it, it is a false economy, for it will take longer to write without a plan than to invest in the undramatic effort of first developing a written outline. The first draft of an outline is as important, and certainly as difficult to prepare, as the final version. It should be rough, flexible, and amenable to change. The important thing is to get something down in writing to measure against.

Developing an outline is the ideal way of preparing to write because (1) it is easier to move items in an outline from place to place than to rewrite or move written paragraphs; (2) the process of outlining reveals gaps in content; (3) an instruction can be discussed in outline form with the reviewing officer before time is spent (or wasted) on writing; and (4) the final outline can be used as the framework for the table of contents.

After you have gathered all the necessary information, the first step is to list all the ideas that come out of your working materials. The ideas need not be arranged in any special sequence or relationship; in fact, some of them may actually overlap.

The second step is to refine and revise the list, including dropping materials that no longer seem to fit. At this stage you might decide to redefine the subject and purpose. You may find that the original idea of what you wanted to communicate is no longer valid on the basis of actual contact with the material. If you do change the subject and purpose, reexamine each item on the list and test it once more against the new subject and purpose.

Avoid confusing subordinate ideas with large topics or thoughts of which they are a part. You may want to set them aside temporarily until you begin subdividing your outline. Be sure to use concise headings in the outline. A functional verb with a single object is best. Headings should be limited to seven words or fewer; they should not include conjunctions such as "and," "or," or "but."

Allow from one-quarter to one-third of your total writing time to prepare the outline. In fact, even more time may be necessary; completion of the outline may show that you have not allocated enough time for the entire project.

Organization of Information

There are three basic methods of organizing information: (1) work flow (or process) order, (2) functional (or subject matter) order, and (3) a first-things-first order. Base your selection on the arrangement that will best and most easily convey the subject to the reader.

Work-Flow Order—A work-flow or process order (sometimes called chronological sequence) puts ideas in the order that they happen. The more complex the procedure, the more inviting the chronological sequence becomes:

CHAPTER TWO—Making the Bid or No-Bid Decision
      Intelligence Gathering
      Proposal Sampling
      Basic Bid/No-Bid Considerations
      Analysis of Competition
      Proposal Costs
      Making the Decision

Subject-Matter Order—A functional or subject matter sequence simply groups ideas by subject matter. Each idea should be unique and its placement in the outline obvious. The order of these ideas is for reader convenience only:

CHAPTER FOUR—Administrative Policies and Procedures
      Corporate Approval
      Organization Changes
      Conflict of Interest
      Travel
      Memberships and Contributions
      Security
      Record Retention and Protection

First-Things-First Order—A first-things-first sequence is especially useful for large documents used by many levels of personnel. There the most important overall subjects are presented first, followed by lesser levels of detail, and concluding with the procedural sequences themselves. Each level expands upon the preceding level.

For example, rules and explanations are written like a newspaper story. The lead paragraph covers vital information—who, what, why, when, where, and how. Subsequent paragraphs provide more details.

Typical Policy/Procedure Outlines

The opening paragraph of each section of a policy, procedure, or directive is critical, because it tells readers whether or not the section pertains to them. It should be short, clear, and simple, not authoritative or stuffy. The opening (consisting of one or more paragraphs) should answer the questions:

1. *What* is this section all about? What is its purpose? Is this section of interest to a particular reader?

2. *Why* is this section in the document? Why does the organization as a whole need to follow the directives in this section? What organizational policy is fulfilled by this section?

3. *Who* is likely to be interested in this section?

4. *Where* does this section apply in the organization?

5. *How* and by whose authority are its dictates established?

6. *When* does this section become effective within the organization?

7. *Details* follow. Where is the reader going to find these details? Directly following or in a subsequent section? If the reader needs background material to understand this section, where can it be found?

Suggested paragraph headings that pertain to policies, procedures, and directives include the following (not all are necessarily appropriate for any one policy or procedure):[2]

Purpose	State the subject of the policy or the procedure and the need or the reason for its implementation. Objectives may be stated to define the goals of the organization. Background may also be included.
Background	Include key background facts to help the reader, who may be a layperson in this particular subject, to understand the policy or the procedure better.
Policy	State briefly the organizational, divisional, or departmental policy that authorized this procedure.
Objective	Define the goals of the policy/procedure program.
Scope	List the organizations and specific job titles to which this policy/procedure pertains. Define what subject matter it covers.
Authority/ Delegation	Name the originating department or organization that issued the policy. It may also be a specific job title, or a set of rules published by a higher authority.
Effective Date	Specify the date on which this policy/procedure becomes effective.
Procedure	Provide instructions for implementation of the policy. Specify a clear and concise outline of functional steps.

[2]Actual examples of how policies and procedures are organized are provided in Appendix A, "Union Carbide Corporation Style Manual for Policies and Procedures."

Definitions	Include as few formal definitions as possible; most readers find them difficult. Avoid substantive material in the definition, especially when it should be in the actual procedure.
Reference	Provide the department name to whom requests for advice and service should be directed.
Cross Reference	Cite cross references to other policies and procedures.

When you have completed your management plan, begin your writing, keeping in mind effective writing techniques. Chapter 3 focuses on these techniques, while Chapter 4 provides editing tips and proofreading guidelines.

3

Effective Writing Techniques

Most people do not like to read policies and procedures, and fewer still like to write them. But business, industry, educational institutions, and government could not function without them, for they specify how things are to be done and how people are to interact. Whether employees follow written instructions depends largely on their readability—along with management discipline, of course. A major part of this chapter is devoted to a discussion of two primary ways to make directives more readable: (1) selecting an appropriate writing format and (2) following certain basic concepts of directive writing. The remainder of the chapter stresses the importance of using nonsexist language and outlines the advantages of using word processors to simplify the writing and editing processes.

WRITING FORMATS

In preparing policies, most writers use the narrative style of writing. For procedures and instructions, writers generally select the directive style, or some variation such as playscript, question lists, logic writing, or decision charts and tables. This section covers all of these formats and offers guidelines regarding the types of procedures for which each format is most appropriate.[1]

Narrative Writing

Narrative writing is similar to storytelling; it incorporates full sentences in paragraph form, with information presented in chronological order. Writers invariably use this format to describe policies as well as

[1]The guidelines are adapted with permission from Elizabeth Berry, "How to Get Users to Follow Procedures," *Journal of Systems Management*, July 1981, pp. 15–19. A selection guide incorporating all of her recommendations is provided in Table 3–1. Ms. Berry is a partner in the firm, Berry & Associates, Minneapolis, Minn.

concepts, proposals, and research. The following policy statement for records retention of a major corporation is an example of narrative policy writing:

> "Records are to be retained and protected as long as they are needed for normal business operations, and as long as necessary to fulfill the Corporation's obligations to its stockholders, customers, employees, governmental agencies, and to the public. Records are to be retained for the periods of time specified by retention policy, and at the end of this time are to be promptly destroyed."

In procedural writing, the narrative format can cause problems for both the writer and the reader. Writers run the risk of including unnecessary information in describing a process, while readers may overlook specific details when they're not individually listed on separate lines.

Narrative formats are appropriate for procedures only if:

- All steps of the procedure do not exceed 125 words (about half a typewritten page).
- The procedure is a simple, straight-line pattern, without branching, decisions, or yes-and-no questions.
- The procedure has only a few steps.

Directive Writing

For most procedural writing, the directive style provides easier and more accurate communication reception. Directive writing involves the use of step-by-step listings, which are especially effective in presenting a series of actions, results, facts, causes, conditions, or other related items. Safety checklists invariably use a step-by-step listing to assure that the reader will not overlook any one item.

For example, contrast the following recipes. The first is written in cookbook (directive style) form; the second, in narrative form; and the third as a step-by-step listing. The cookbook style is obviously more readable than the accountant's style, but it is not a step-by-step listing. Because most cookbooks combine the various steps of a recipe in a narrative format to save space, many an inexperienced cook has skipped a step and spoiled a dish. Recipes would be more readable if instructions were listed step-by-step rather than written in full sentences.

RECIPE FOR LACY VALENTINE FROSTING

As It Appears in a Cookbook

Bake favorite white cake in layers. Cut each slightly to heart shape. Frost with a white icing. For pink trim, mix 1 cup moist shredded coconut with 8 minced red cherries. Sprinkle over top. Place red cinnamon hearts on sides. Serve on a dainty lace doily.

As an Accountant Might Write It

Lacy valentine cake should be made by carefully observing the following procedures: First, a white cake should be baked in layers. (Note: Any type of cake which falls into this category is satisfactory for this purpose.) Each of these portions should then be cut, in such a manner that the portions resulting therefrom appear to be shaped similar to a heart. Upon the successful completion of this operation, a white icing should be made. Add the pink trim by taking a cup of moist shredded coconut, mincing eight red cherries, and combining these two items into a mixture, which should then be applied evenly over the top of the cake which has been prepared according to the instructions previously given. The cake is now ready for the application of red cinnamon hearts on the side. Thus completed, the cake is ready for consumption. The serving may be accomplished most satisfactorily by application of a lace doily on the cake plate.

As a Step-by-Step Listing

To make a valentine cake with lacy frosting:
1. Bake favorite white cake in layers.
2. Cut each layer slightly to heart shape.
3. Frost them with white icing.
4. Mix one cup moist shredded coconut with eight minced red cherries for the pink trim.
5. Sprinkle mixture over top of cake.
6. Place red cinnamon hearts on sides.
7. Serve on a dainty lace doily.

Guidelines for Directive Writing

In using the directive style, observe the following guidelines:

- *Write the introductory phrase* of the rule as a full sentence, ending with a colon. In a long list, readers lose their way if part of the sentence is in the introduction.

- *List each step on a separate line.* If steps are combined in a narrative sentence, as in the cookbook style, the reader may easily miss a step.
- *Organize the steps* in a sequence logical to the reader. Once again, write for the reader.
- *Write each step as a full sentence* and begin the step with a command verb. In a long list, partial sentences are confusing to the reader.
- *Maintain parallel construction* throughout. For example, if a command verb starts the first two items in the list, it should start all items in the list.
- *Start each entry with an initial capital letter.*
- *Use consistent punctuation.*
- *Separate action steps* in the list from comments, notes, examples, or other explanatory material.

Finally, *avoid repeating lead-in verbs.* Compare this:

1. Formulates, reviews, coordinates, and implements U.S. policy with respect to applications and proposals of foreign governments for loans from the Export-Import Bank, or the International Bank for Reconstruction and Development for whatever purpose.
2. Formulates, reviews, coordinates, and implements U.S. policy with respect to credits or other financial assistance required or requested by foreign governments.
3. Formulates, reviews, coordinates, and implements U.S. policy with respect to general policies on U.S. public and private investments in foreign countries.

With this:

1. Formulates, reviews, coordinates, and implements U.S. policy with respect to:
   a. Applications and proposals of foreign governments for loans from the Export-Import Bank, or the International Bank for Reconstruction and Development for whatever purpose.
   b. Credits or other financial assistance required or requested by foreign governments.
   c. General policies on U.S. public and private investments in foreign countries.

Step-by-step listing is appropriate if the format of the procedure:

- Is a simple, straight-line pattern.
- Has more than five steps.
- Must be contained in the limited space of a label placed on a machine.

- Is performed by one person.

A variation of step-by-step listing incorporates drawings or photographs to clarify the directions of the procedure steps. This variation should be selected if the procedure outlines:

- A complicated assembly task.

- Straight-line operations for technical or complex equipment.

Step-by-step listings are most appropriate when they describe the activities of only one person; if two or more persons are involved, use the "play-script" technique described next.

Playscript Technique

Developed by Leslie H. Matthies,[2] playscript clearly establishes *who* does *what* in a series of chronological events. Compare the following examples of identical instructions. The first is written in narrative style; the second is written in playscript.

Personnel Transfers

The referenced procedure places the responsibility upon the Releasing Department to originate personnel transfers. In order to assist the Releasing Department, a form, "Transfer Request," No. 457, has been made available to all departments. If this form is filled out, it will not only comply with Standard Procedure No. 74, but it will greatly facilitate the review and ultimate placement of personnel who wish to be transferred. At the present time, many requests are coming to Personnel by memo, and on other forms that are either incomplete or inaccurate. A careful use of Form 457 will provide benefits to both the Releasing Department and the Company. As a further aid, the Releasing Department should send both the original and self-carbon of Form 457 to Budgets and Planning. Budgets and Planning then will adjust Company budget and workload records and forward the original and one copy of Form 457 to Personnel. The Personnel Manager then obtains the Receiving Department's supervisor's signature and adds an effective date of transfer to Form 457. Personnel then sends the carbon of Form 457 to the Releasing Department and files the original. The Releasing Department places Form 457 in the personnel record folder and sends the folder to the Receiving Department. Finally the Receiving Department posts the permanent records to reflect the change and files the employee record folder in a locked personnel records cabinet.

[2]Noted business communications author. See Matthies, Leslie H., in the Selected Bibliography.

Personnel Transfers

Responsibility	*Action*
Releasing Department Supervisor	1. Completes Form 457, "Transfers Request," and sends the original and self-carbon to Budgets and Planning.
Budgets and Planning	2. Adjusts budget and work-load records, sends both copies of Form 457 to Personnel.
Personnel	3. Secures Receiving Department's supervisor's signature. 4. Adds effective date of transfer to Form 457 and: a. Sends copy to Releasing Department. b. Files original.
Releasing Department	5. Places Form 457 in Personnel records folder. 6. Sends Personnel records folder to Receiving Department.
Receiving Department	7. Posts permanent records to reflect change. 8. Files employee records folder in locked Personnel records cabinet.

To write in playscript:

1. Divide your page into two vertical columns.

2. Allocate about one third of the page for your left column; list there the title of the person or department performing the action.

3. Reserve the remaining column (right-hand two thirds of the page) for specific action items, numbered separately for each event, and each beginning with a verb in the present tense.[3]

Figure 3-1 illustrates the playscript technique.

Benefits of Playscript

The benefits of using playscript are manyfold. It makes procedures easy to understand and easy to read. It reveals potential duplication in the action and backtracking of action flow. It saves 90 percent of coordination time.

[3]For a comprehensive listing of action verbs, refer to page 46.

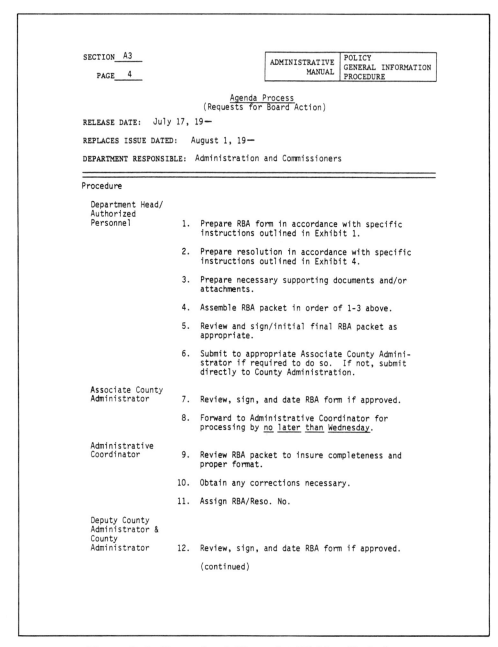

SECTION A3

PAGE 4

ADMINISTRATIVE MANUAL	POLICY GENERAL INFORMATION PROCEDURE

Agenda Process
(Requests for Board Action)

RELEASE DATE: July 17, 19—

REPLACES ISSUE DATED: August 1, 19—

DEPARTMENT RESPONSIBLE: Administration and Commissioners

Procedure

Department Head/
Authorized
Personnel

1. Prepare RBA form in accordance with specific instructions outlined in Exhibit 1.

2. Prepare resolution in accordance with specific instructions outlined in Exhibit 4.

3. Prepare necessary supporting documents and/or attachments.

4. Assemble RBA packet in order of 1-3 above.

5. Review and sign/initial final RBA packet as appropriate.

6. Submit to appropriate Associate County Administrator if required to do so. If not, submit directly to County Administration.

Associate County
Administrator

7. Review, sign, and date RBA form if approved.

8. Forward to Administrative Coordinator for processing by no later than Wednesday.

Administrative
Coordinator

9. Review RBA packet to insure completeness and proper format.

10. Obtain any corrections necessary.

11. Assign RBA/Reso. No.

Deputy County
Administrator &
County
Administrator

12. Review, sign, and date RBA form if approved.

(continued)

Figure 3–1. Example of Playscript Writing Technique
(Courtesy of Hennepin County, Minn.)

For *managers,* playscript indicates whether they are involved in the proposed action. It lets them see the relationship of their department to others in specific team play, and forces decisions on work responsibilities. It brings cloudy areas of responsibility or controversial work to the attention of top management. It makes sense to top management people; they like its simplicity.

For *readers,* playscript focuses attention on the work, not on the words, of a procedure. It increases the enthusiasm of operating people for the system because the plan is clear to them. It explains complex team play simply and provides a uniform format that everybody can understand and follow.

And for *writers,* playscript eliminates nonessential words. It makes it easy to connect the work sequence of various procedures, simplifies making changes, and makes the effect of each proposed change easy to identify. It requires logical sorting of information during the data-gathering process; thus, information that does not make the procedure *proceed* can be rejected immediately.

Select the playscript format if:

- The procedure is a straight-line pattern.
- There is involvement of several users performing different tasks.

Question-List Format

In the question-list format (see example below),[4] readers are guided through a series of instructions based on their response of "yes" or "no" to each question. This format should be selected if:

- Certain decisions must be made before the user can determine what the next step will be.
- The user involves only one person.

SETTING UP A TYPEWRITER
FOR TYPING TASKS

1. Is the typewriter plugged in?
   YES—go to 2.
   NO—plug it in—go to 2.
2. Is the ON button depressed?
   YES—go to 3.
   NO—depress ON button—go to 3.
3. Do you plan to type a letter?
   YES—set margins at 15 and 77—

go to 8.
NO—go to 4.
4. Do you plan to type a report?
   YES—set margins at 12 and 72—
   go to 9.
   NO—go to 5.
5. . . .

---

[4]Adapted from Elizabeth Berry, note 1.

USING LOGIC TO CLARIFY WRITING[5]

Action/Condition Logic

Action/condition logic is another excellent method of writing in an easy-to-read form, especially when your information involves complex rules. To illustrate, let's first review the definition of a rule:

A rule is a statement of one single action, result, or fact, which may be subject to one or more conditions.

If a step or an action is subject to one or more conditions, the writer must understand and use basic principles of logic. Otherwise, the result may be the worst kind of barely intelligible legalese.

For example, the following is an 82-word unpunctuated sentence from a section of the Internal Revenue Code (before the 1969 amendments):

Contributions to an employees' trust made by an employer during a taxable year of the employer which ends within or with a taxable year of the trust for which the trust is not exempt from tax under section 501 (a) shall be included in the gross income of an employee for the taxable year in which the contribution is made to the trust in the case of an employee whose beneficial interest in such contribution is non-forfeitable at the time the contribution is made.

An analysis of this extremely difficult complex sentence reveals that it consists of a statement of one action (or tax result), subject to three conditions. Note that the revised sentence in the following paragraph uses exactly the same words; the changes involve only the sorting out of the action from the conditions, and the listing of the conditions. A few words have been repeated, so that each condition could be worded as a complete sentence. Because no words have been changed, the meaning of the provision remains unchanged. The structure, however, has been greatly simplified through logic.

Contributions to an employees' trust made by an employer shall be included in the gross income of an employee for the taxable year in which the contributions are made, if:
1. The employee's trust is not exempt from tax under section 501 (a) in a particular taxable year of the trust; and
2. Contributions to the trust are made by the employer during a taxable year of the employer which ends within or with such taxable year of the trust; and

[5]This section was adapted from John O. Morris, *Regulations and Procedure Writing;* and John O. Morris, *Make Yourself Clear* (New York: McGraw Hill Book Co., 1980). Copyright © 1980 McGraw-Hill Book Co. Used by permission of the author and McGraw-Hill Book Co.

3. The beneficial interest of the employee in such contributions is nonforfeitable at the time the contributions are made.

To illustrate how to sort out and separate actions from conditions, here is a simpler example of a poorly organized set of rules:

An employee who is eligible for overtime pay and works more than 40 hours in a workweek, shall be paid overtime at the rate of time and a half, but those working more than 40 hours who are not eligible for overtime pay will be credited with compensatory time.

This complex sentence is rewritten as two sentences, each of which states a separate rule or action. Each action is then subject to two conditions. Because the conditions are joined by the word "and," not "or," both conditions must be met in each case. The revised paragraph then reads:

An employee shall be paid overtime pay at the rate of time and a half, if the employee:
1. Is eligible for such overtime, and
2. Works more than 40 hours in a workweek.

An employee shall be credited with compensatory time, if the employee:
1. Is not eligible for overtime, and
2. Works more than 40 hours in a workweek.

In the rewritten versions of the preceding examples, the statement of the action precedes the listing of the conditions. The conditions are indented on the page, to indicate that they are subordinate to the action statement. This is the reverse of the usual order in which a computer operates, and in which people think while solving a problem.

A computer, for example, tests a series of conditions in sequence. If all conditions in the sequence are positive, that is, if they all apply to the particular situation, then the appropriate action follows. This is often referred to as "IF-THEN" logic, because the computer goes from the IF to THEN.

This is the same process by which people think and reach decisions. For example, one night I think about what hour to set my alarm for the morning. I must be at the office by 8:30 a.m.; it usually takes me 45 minutes to rise, dress, and eat breakfast. The drive to work requires an average of 30 minutes. But this morning I need an extra 15 minutes for an errand.

Here is the mental process I might follow: "IF I set my alarm for 7:15; and IF it takes me 45 minutes to dress and eat; and IF I must be at work at 8:30 a.m.; THEN I will be late." After another try, I realize I must set my alarm no later than 7 a.m.

The process just described is one we follow hundreds of times a day in reaching decisions, with far more complicated input than in that simple example, and in far less time than it takes you to read this sentence. And, usually, in thinking through a problem, we go from IF to THEN. But, when the time comes to write the sequence as a rule, the order must be reversed. Conditions are subordinate to actions; hence, the action statement comes first, then, the conditions, indented to show their subordination to the action statement. There is one limited exception—if you have one simple condition and one simple action, you may state the condition first.

You cannot present a series of conditions and subconditions on a page in a clear, readable, step-by-step format if you start the sentence with the word "IF." Examine any series of complex regulations; you will find that some of the most unintelligible sentences are those starting with "IF," and continuing on for too many words, with conditions, subconditions, and actions hopelessly confused.

Cause/Effect Logic

The preceding discussion of action/condition logic is equally appropriate to the logic of cause and effect. The operative word for cause and effect is "because" rather than "if." Cause-and-effect logic looks backward from a point in time; action/condition logic looks forward.

For example, here is the mental process previously described but now shifted in time because I have arrived late at work and am seeking to determine the cause: "BECAUSE I set my alarm for 7:15; and BECAUSE it took me 45 minutes to dress and eat; and BECAUSE I needed 15 minutes extra for the errand; and BECAUSE it took me 30 minutes to drive to work; and BECAUSE I must be at work by 8:30 a.m.; THEREFORE I was late."

If you wish to express a cause-and-effect sequence on paper (this sequence is common in reporting on a problem or making a recommendation), state the effect or result first, then list the causes. The reason for reversing the sequence is the same as that described for action/condition logic.

Guides for Using Action/Condition Logic

Action/condition logic is discussed in detail because the principle is simple and vitally important to clear rule writing; yet many rule writers are not aware of its importance. Use the following guidelines for writing a rule according to action/condition logic:

1. Find and mark the verb for the action statement. (If revising an existing rule, underline the verb. If writing a new rule, write the verb down.)

2. Find and mark the subject for this action verb. (Remember that there is no subject if the verb is a command verb.)

3. Find and mark each ''and'' condition to which the action statement is subject.

4. Find and mark each series of ''or'' conditions to which the action statement is subject. Distinguish carefully between ''and'' conditions, which are cumulative, and ''or'' conditions, which are alternative. Each ''and'' condition must be met, but only one ''or'' condition in a series must be met.

5. Write the action statement as an introductory full sentence, ending with ''if.'' For example, ''This new procedure will work, if:''

6. List the conditions under the action statement, using the guides for step-by-step listing.

7. Show the reader visually that ''or'' conditions are subordinate to ''and'' conditions and that ''and'' conditions are subordinate to the action statement. Do this by indenting, by an appropriate alphanumeric system, or by both.

The following before-and-after example illustrates the use of the guides for action/condition logic. The facts are the same as those presented previously, except for the addition of one series of ''or'' conditions.

Before (written in legalese):

If it is required that I must be at work by 8:30 a.m. and if I set my alarm for 7 a.m. and if I need 15 extra minutes to walk my dog, then I will, provided I require 45 minutes to dress and eat, be late, further provided that I require 30 minutes to drive to work.

After (using action/condition logic):

I will be late to work, if:
    1. I must be at work by 8:30 a.m.; and
    2. I set my alarm for 7 a.m.; and
    3. I require 45 minutes to dress and eat; and
    4. I require 30 minutes to drive to work; and
    5. Either of these conditions apply:
       I need 15 minutes extra for an errand; or
       I need 15 minutes extra to walk my dog.

This example illustrates action/condition logic in a simplified format:

An employee is not entitled to mileage reimbursement, if:
  1. He or she is required to work on a nonscheduled work day and *receives compensation*, and
  2. Travel is from home to the normally assigned work location.

However, an employee may claim reimbursement of the differential mileage if:
  1. He or she is required to work on a nonscheduled work day and *receives compensation*, and
  2. Points of travel are not between home and the normally assigned work location, and
  3. The distance is greater than the distance between home and the normally assigned work location.

Use action/condition or cause/effect logic if:

- Your information involves complex rules, with many branches or decisions.

- There are many "if" conditions followed by "then" actions, or many "because" conditions followed by "therefore" actions.

FLOWCHARTS AND DECISION TABLES

Action/condition logic can also be written in the formats of decision logic tables and narrative flowcharts. Such tables and charts are often used to explain complex rules, sometimes replacing the text, sometimes summarizing the text. The examples shown in Figure 3-2 are simplified versions of an overtime situation. In the horizontal decision table, the format is *if, and if,* and *then*. In the vertical table, the words *condition* and *action* are used, to allow the conditions to be posed as questions. Condition questions are also posed in the narrative flowchart.

"Or" conditions should not be shown in sequence in a decision table; a new rule must be started for each "or" condition. This feature of a decision table is both an advantage and a disadvantage. It forces the writer to sort out the "and" conditions from the "or" conditions, but it also forces the writer to write a new rule for each "or" condition. This can become cumbersome.

Horizontal Decision Table		
If	*And If*	*Then*
1. Employee worked over 40 hours in work week	Employee is eligible for overtime	Pay overtime at time and a half
2. Employee worked over 40 hours in work week	Employee is not eligible for overtime	Credit with compensatory time

Vertical Decision Table

	1.	2.
Condition Did employee work over 40 hours in work week? Is employee eligible for overtime?	Yes Yes	Yes No
Action Pay overtime at time and a half Credit with compensatory time	X	X

Narrative Flowchart

Did employee work over 40 hours in work week?

   ↓   ↓

  Yes   No

   ↓

Is employee eligible for overtime?

   ↓   ↓

  Yes   No

   ↓   ↓

Pay overtime   Credit with
at time and a   compensatory
half   time

Figure 3–2. Three Examples of an Overtime Situation

Further examples of flowcharts and decision tables, and the appropriate times to use them, are discussed in the following section.

Flowcharts[6]

Flowcharts can be used to illustrate any process which can be performed. Their primary purpose is to show *what* is to be done, to present graphically the sequence and flow of an activity. (See Figure 3-3.) They may be used to illustrate procedures if:

- The procedure is *not* straight-line (has branches or decisions).

- The users are familiar with flowcharts.

- The flowcharted procedure will fit on one 8½ x 11 inch page.

- The flowchart can be limited to a few basic symbols.

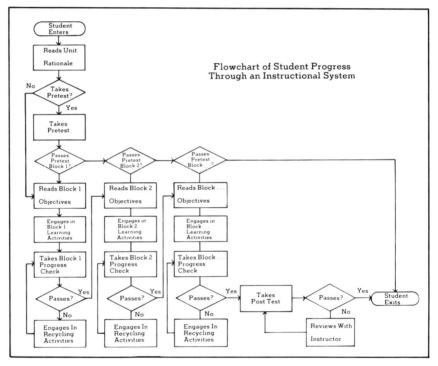

Figure 3–3. Example of a Flowchart (Courtesy of Control Data Corporation)

Narrative Flowcharts

Narrative flowcharts differ from flowcharts in that they do not use complicated diagrams; various steps are presented in narrative or step-by-step blocks. (See Figure 3-4.) They are appropriate if:

[6]The remaining discussion on flowcharts and decision tables and the examples shown in Figures 3-4 and 3-5 are adapted from Elizabeth Berry, note 1.

- The procedure is *not* straight-line (has branches or decisions).
- The procedure usually involves no more than three decisions.
- The user has a nontechnical background.

PROCEDURE FOR RECEIVING JEWELRY ITEMS FOR REPAIR

When the customer brings in the item for repair, the clerk must first check to see if the item was purchased at Apex. The only acceptable verification is: (1) a cancelled check, or (2) a receipt from Apex.

If the item was purchased at Apex:
- Fill out pink receipt
- Place item in envelope
- Staple pink form to envelope
- Give customer white copy

If the item was not purchased at Apex:
- Fill out blue receipt
- Place item in envelope
- Staple blue form to envelope
- Give customer green copy

Enter transaction in log book

Place item in safe

Procedure completed

Figure 3–4. Example of a Narrative Flowchart

Decision Logic Tables

Decision logic tables portray procedures in tabular format, divided into conditions and actions. (See Table 3–1.) Use this format if the procedure:

- Is *not* straight-line (has branches or decisions).
- Involves many "if" conditions, followed by "then" actions.
- Is used to make "on the spot" decisions.

Decision Trees

Decision trees combine elements of the flowchart with the decision logic table. (See Figure 3-5.) The primary difference between decision trees and flowcharts is that decision trees are limited to a few symbols and the decision branching is more obvious. Use the decision tree if:

- The procedure is *not* straight-line (has branches or decisions).
- The procedure involves only a few decisions.
- It is important to show outcomes of the decisions.

Table 3–1. Procedure Format Selection Guide (Decision Logic Table)

User Requirements	Procedure Description						
	Straight-Line — Few steps; less than 125 words	Straight-Line — More than five steps	Straight-Line — Outlining assembly or operation of equipment	Straight-Line — With decisions determining	Branching — With few decisions	Branching — Showing outcomes of decisions	Branching — With many "if" conditions "then" actions
One nontechnical user required to complete procedure	Narrative	Step-by-Step List	Step-by-Step List and Visual Aid	Question List	Decision Tree	Decision Tree; Narrative Flowchart	Decision Logic Table
More than one nontechnical user required to complete procedure	Playscript	Playscript	Playscript with Visual Aid	Narrative Flowchart; Decision Tree	Flowchart; Decision Tree	Decision Tree; Narrative Flowchart	Decision Logic Table
One technical user required to complete procedure	Narrative	Step-by-Step List	Step-by-Step List and Visual Aid	Question List	Flowchart; Decision Tree	Decision Tree; Narrative Flowchart	Decision Logic Table
More than one technical user required to complete procedure	Playscript	Playscript	Playscript with Visual Aid	Narrative Flowchart; Decision Tree	Flowchart; Decision Tree	Decision Tree; Narrative Flowchart	Decision Logic Table

Source: Adapted with permission from Berry, note 1, at p. 24.

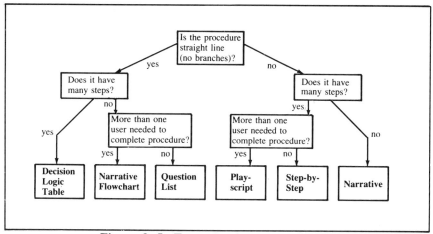

Figure 3–5. Example of a Decision Tree

Combining Illustrative Forms

Sometimes it may be appropriate to combine more than one form into a single chart, such as the illustration in Figure 3–6.

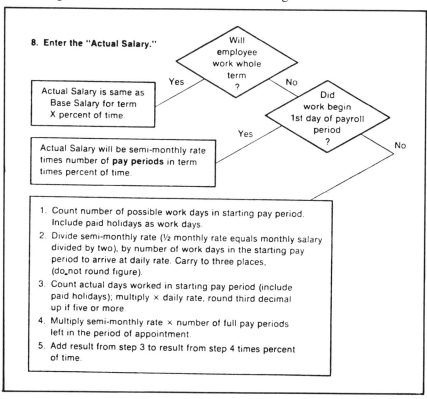

Figure 3–6. Combination Flowchart/Narrative Flowchart/Decision Tree/Step-by-Step Listing From Personnel Manual

BASIC CONCEPTS OF WRITING DIRECTIVES

The general goal of plain English writing is to make writing as understandable to the reader as it can be. To achieve this goal, writers of directives should follow basic principles of style, organization, and context. They should also be aware of the importance of the effective choice of words.

Style

Style is the character of the words, sentences, and paragraphs put down on paper. The important principles of style are:

1. Use short, common, and nontechnical words wherever possible:

   Use rather than *utilize*
   Under rather than *pursuant to*
   Underwater rather than *subaqueous*

2. Cut out deadwood and redundancies:

   Write: One-inch plywood covered this urethane foam.
   Rather than: This urethane foam was covered with plywood of a nominal thickness equal to one inch.

3. Avoid verbs in the passive voice:

   Write: The agency published final regulations on June 19, 19XX.
   Rather than: Final regulations were published by the agency on June 19, 19XX.

4. Use words that refer to definite people and organizations:

   Write: The company requires people who store toxic waste to register it.
   Rather than: Stored toxic waste is subject to registration requirements.

5. Avoid clusters of three or more nouns:

   Write: the pressure at the surface of a body of ground water
   Rather than: ground water body surface pressure

6. Break up overly long sentences:

   Write: The purpose of the requirements in this Subpart is to establish minimum national standards which define the acceptable management of hazardous waste. These standards will apply to owners and operators of facilities which treat, store and dispose of hazardous waste.

Rather than: The purpose of the requirements in this Subpart is to establish minimum national standards defining acceptable hazardous waste management practices applicable to owners and operators of facilities which treat, store and dispose of hazardous waste.

7. Break up a long sentence visually, if you cannot break it up grammatically:

Write: . . . fly ash, bottom ash, or boiler slag that is generated *by:*
1. A utility or industrial boiler,
2. A process steam generator, or
3. A coal gasification or liquefaction unit,
from either:
1. The sole use of fossil fuels, or
Write: 2. The use of fossil fuels in combination with certain other fuels—including refuse-derived fuels from municipal solid waste or any alternative fuel that is not a hazardous waste.
and which is used:
1. In the construction of roads,
2. As a de-icing agent on roads, or
3. As a soil conditioner . . .
Rather than: . . . fly ash, bottom ash, or boiler slag which is generated by a utility or industrial boiler, process steam generator or coal gasification or liquefaction unit from the sole use of fossil fuels or from the use of certain fuels in combination with fossil fuels, including refuse-derived fuels from municipal solid waste or any alternative fuel which is not a hazardous waste and which is used in the construction of roads, as a de-icing agent on roads or as a soil conditioner . . .

8. Make clear what a new paragraph is *about*. Start with a clear topic sentence, a title, or an explicit transitional phrase. For example, in a section about pollution control technology, start a paragraph about the technology in the ferrous metallurgical industries with:

Control technology for ferrous metallurgical industries is constantly improving . . .
Or: Turning to ferrous metallurgical industries . . .
Or: Ferrous metallurgical industries

9. If it is not obvious, make explicit the relationship between a new paragraph and what you have already written, using transitional words. Start your paragraph with phrases such as:

To draw some conclusions . . .
By contrast with earlier cases . . .
The explanation for this . . .
The fifth example . . .

Here are some suggested transitional words:

- *To show cause and effect:* accordingly; as a result; hence; therefore
- *To show exceptions to what has been said:* but; conversely; even though; however; on the contrary; on the other hand; otherwise
- *To indicate time, place, or order:* above all; after all; again; finally; first; further; in summary; meanwhile; next; still; then; too
- *To introduce examples:* for example; for instance; namely; that is

Organization

The organization of your writing is what you identify as its significant parts, and how you arrange them. The principles of organization are:

1. Organize for the needs of your reader. If you are stating what people must do to register their cars:

> *Write:* To register your car, you must:
> a. Apply for insurance.
> b. Apply for plates and pay the excise tax.
> c. Present your car for a safety inspection.
> *Rather than:* A legally registered car is one that has been given a safety inspection, is insured, has plates, and has had its excise tax paid.

2. Choose a principle of organization—the steps to follow, the most important to the least important, the general to the specific—and stick to it. For example, if you are writing about metals, one by one, write everything you have to write about gold all in one place (except for comparisons).

3. Give your reader the "big picture" of what you are writing. Start a chapter on writing in plain English by saying:

> We will discuss these topics:
> - The Goals of Plain English
> - The Symptoms of Unclarity
> - Plain English Resources
> - The Place of Good Writing in Developing a Regulation

4. Reveal your structure both visually and verbally. Use space to set off significant parts and underline titles to reflect your outline.

Context

The context of your writing is the background of knowledge and assumptions the reader must have to understand your instructions. Thus, if you are writing instructions for requesting an economic variance—and your readers may not know what an economic variance is—be sure to explain what the term means in an introduction to your instructions.

Inherent within context is tone. Strictly speaking, quality of tone is not a feature of plain English *per se,* since people can speak plainly and still be as nasty as they like. However, to write in plain English is to try to make life easier for the reader. And most readers can distinguish between those who do and those who do not show them this consideration.

Connotations

Avoid using words that have a negative connotation; virtually every negative word can be restated with a positive word or idea.

Positive Words

ability	correction	loyalty
accuracy	courtesy	pleasure
adjustment	desire (to serve)	right
admirable	diplomacy	service
ambition	distinction	substantial
approval	effective	tact
asset	fair	tactful
assurance	faith	thoughtful
benefit	fortunate	understanding
calm	generous	useful
commendable	glad	welcome
confidence	good	willing
cooperation	happy	wise

Negative Words

apology	hesitant	reluctance
barrier	inconvenience	resistance
biased	inconvenient	sad
blame	lazy	selfish
blunt	liability	sorry
careless	must	suspicion
curt	neglect	tactless
death	negligence	trickery
defeat	never	uncomfortable
deficient	noneffective	uncooperative
disagreement	not	unfair
disaster	problem	unfortunate
dislike	prohibit	unless
failure	refusal	untimely
fault	regret	weak
fear	reject	wrong

Action Verbs

Verbs which precisely define action are just as important as con- notations. These are especially important when writing in playscript. The following verbs were selected because of the frequency with which they appear in functional statements. They have been grouped into three cat- egories: (1) verbs relating to planning, coordination, and collaborative activity; (2) verbs relating to decision making; (3) verbs relating to the execution of work. The groupings under these three headings agree with the primary usage given such verbs. But in some cases, there may be overlapping among these arbitrary groupings.

Some of the verbs are the targets of critics of "gobbledygook." Such criticism relates to the abuse of procedural verbs when they are used excessively or when they do not contribute to the clarity of state- ments. The important thing is that verbs should have a common meaning for both the writer and the reader.

Verbs Relating to Planning and Coordination

advise—to recommend a course of action; to counsel; to give advice to (not simply to tell or inform).

analyze—to study the factors of a situation or problem in detail to deter- mine the solution or outcome.

anticipate—to foresee events, trends, consequences, or problems.

collaborate—to work with and act jointly with others.

consult—to confer; to offer advice; to seek the advice of others.

control—to exercise directing, guiding, or restraining power; to check or regulate; to keep within limits.

coordinate—to bring into common action; to harmonize; to integrate.

correlate—to connect systematically; to establish a mutual or reciprocal relation.

develop—to evolve, promote, or make active a plan, program, or course of action, usually without benefit of prior determination.

evaluate—to appraise; to consider the value of.

examine—to investigate; to scrutinize; to subject to inquiry or inspection; to test by an appropriate method.

formulate—to develop or devise a statement of policy or procedures; to put in a systematic statement, as in a statement of procedure.

initiate—to originate; to introduce in the first instance; to cause or bring to pass by original act, as in originating a plan, policy, or procedure.

participate—to take part in.

plan—to devise or project a method or course of action.

propose—to offer for consideration or adoption; to form or declare a plan or intention.

recommend—to advise or counsel a course of action; to offer or suggest for adoption a course of action.

revise—to rework in order to correct or improve; to make a new, improved, or up-to-date version.

study—to ponder or fix the mind closely upon a subject; to endeavor with thought and planning; to consider attentively.

survey—to determine and delineate the form, extent, or position of a situation (usually in connection with gathering of information).

Verbs Relating to Decision Making

adopt—to take and apply or put into practice; to accept (as a report or a recommendation).

approve—to sanction officially; to accept as satisfactory; to ratify (thereby assuming responsibility).

clear—to obtain the concurrence, dissent, or nondissent of other offices prior to final signature.

determine—to fix conclusively or authoritatively; to decide; to order; to come to a decision concerning, as a result of investigation or reason; to settle; to give a definite direction or impetus to.

direct—to give an order or instruction to; to cause the following of a course of action.

review—to go over or examine deliberately or critically, usually with a view to approval or dissent.

Verbs Relating to the Execution of Work

act—to perform; to do something; to serve or operate in fulfillment of a special function.

administer—to manage or direct the execution, application, or conduct of, as in administering a program.

aid—to help; to further.

arrange—to make preparation for an event; to put in proper order.

assemble—to collect or gather together in a predetermined order; to fit parts together.

assign—to fix, specify, or designate; to prescribe (as in assigning responsibility).

assist—to lend aid; to help; to give support to.

assure—to make certain of.

circulate—to pass into the hands of readers.

collect—to gather or assemble into one body or place, usually for further study or examination.

compile—to collect (information); to compose out of materials from other documents.

conduct—to carry on; to have the direction of; to direct the execution of.

disseminate—to spread information or ideas, usually in the sense of a widespread audience.

distribute—to apportion or deal out, as in distributing literature or mail.

draft—to write or compose papers or documents in rough, preliminary, or final form, usually for clearance and approval by others.

establish—to set up; to institute; to place on a firm basis.

execute—to give effect to; to follow out or through to the end, as a purpose.

exercise—to bring to bear or employ actively, as in exercising authority or influence.

facilitate—to make easy or less difficult, usually by doing something to advance the accomplishment of an act.

forward—to send or transmit onward, usually in the sense of forwarding from one point of activity to another.

furnish—to provide what is necessary for; to supply; to give.

implement—to carry out; to perform acts essential to the execution of a plan or program; to give effect to.

inform—to tell or make known; to communicate knowledge to; to acquaint.

issue—to release or send out; to publish.

maintain—to keep possession of; to hold or keep in any condition; to keep up to date or current, as to maintain records.

notify—to give notice to; to inform or make known.

observe—to inspect or take note of; to pay attention to; to perceive or notice.

obtain—to get hold of by effort; to gain possession of; to acquire; to get; to secure.

operate—to conduct or perform an activity.

perform—to carry out or execute some action; to carry out to the finish; to accomplish.

prepare—to make ready for a particular purpose.

process—to subject to some special treatment; to handle in accordance with a prescribed procedure, as in processing work or requisitions.

provide—to supply for use; to furnish; to take precautionary measures in view of a possible need.

receive—to accept, get, or take what is delivered from another source.

refer—to send or direct to a person or place for action or approval.

release—to set free as in releasing information; to permit at a specified date but not before the publication or dissemination of.

secure—to get possession of; to obtain.

select—to take by preference or choice from among others; to pick out.

stimulate—to impel; to instigate; to urge, usually in the sense of stimulating others who have primary responsibility.

supervise—to oversee for direction; to inspect with authority; to guide and instruct with immediate responsibility for the purpose of performance; to superintend; to lead.

transmit—to send or transfer from one person or place to another.

undertake—to take upon one's self; to engage in; to enter upon.

verify—to prove to be true or accurate; to confirm or substantiate; to check exactness.

AVOIDING SEXIST LANGUAGE[7]

Still another consideration for you as a writer is avoiding sexist language. Some of it is so ingrained that we do not question the usage. The word sexism was coined by analogy to racism, to denote discrimination based on gender. In its original sense, sexism referred to prejudice against the female sex. In a broader sense, the term now indicates any arbitrary stereotyping of males and females on the basis of their gender.

Men and women should be treated primarily as people, and not primarily as members of opposite sexes. Their shared humanity and common attributes should be stressed—not their gender differences. They should be treated with the same respect, dignity, and seriousness. Neither sex should be arbitrarily assigned to a leading or secondary role.

In descriptions of women, a patronizing or girl-watching tone should be avoided, as should sexual innuendos, jokes, and puns:

No	*Yes*
the girls, or the ladies	the women
"I'll have my girl check that."	"I'll have my secretary (or my assistant) check that." Or use the person's name.
lady lawyer; lady doctor	lawyer, doctor—A woman may be identified simply through the choice of pronouns: "The lawyer made her summation to the jury."
authoress; poetess	author; poet
suffragette; usherette; aviatrix	suffragist; usher; aviator

Try to avoid gender modifiers altogether. When you must modify, use woman or female: "a course on women writers," or "the airline's first female pilot."

---

[7]Adapted with permission from "Guidelines for Equal Treatment of the Sexes in McGraw-Hill Book Company Publications."

The word man has long been used not only to denote a person of male gender but also generically to denote humanity at large. To many people today, however, the word man has become so closely associated with the first meaning (a male human being) that they consider it no longer broad enough to be applied to any person or to human beings as a whole. In deference to this position, alternative expressions should be used in place of man (or derivative constructions used generically to signify humanity at large) whenever such substitutions can be made without producing an awkward or artificial construction. In cases where man-words must be used, special efforts should be made to ensure that pictures and other devices make explicit that such references include women.

No	*Yes*
mankind	humanity; human beings; human race; people
If a man drove 50 miles at 55 mph . . .	If a person (or driver) drove 50 miles at 55 mph . . .
the best man for the job	the best person (or candidate) for the job
manmade	artificial; synthetic; manufactured; constructed; of human origin
manpower	human power; human energy; labor; workers; work force

The English language lacks a generic singular pronoun signifying he or she, and therefore it has been customary and grammatically sanctioned to use masculine pronouns in expressions such as "one . . . he," "anyone . . . he," and "each child opens his book." Nevertheless, avoid whenever possible the pronouns he, him, and his in reference to a hypothetical person. Various alternatives may be considered:

- Reword to eliminate unnecessary gender pronouns:

No	*Yes*
The average American drinks his coffee black.	The average American drinks black coffee.

- Recast into the plural:

Most Americans drink their coffee black.

- Replace the masculine pronoun with one, you, he or she, her or his, as appropriate. (Use he or she and its variations sparingly to avoid clumsy prose.)

• Alternate male and female expressions and examples.

• To avoid severe problems of repetition or inept wording, it sometimes may be best to use the generic "he" freely, but to add, in the preface and as often as necessary in the text, emphatic statements to the effect that the masculine pronouns are being used for succinctness and are intended to refer to both females and males.

Whenever possible, occupational terms ending in man should be replaced by terms that can include members of either sex (unless they refer to a particular person) and job titles should be nonsexist:

No	*Yes*
businessman	business executive; business manager
fireman	fire fighter
mailman	mail carrier; letter carrier
salesman	sales representative; salesperson; sales clerk
insurance man	insurance agent
camerman	camera operator
foreman	supervisor
steward; purser; stewardess	flight attendant
policeman; policewoman	police officer
maid; houseboy	house or office cleaner; servant

Language that assumes all readers are male should be avoided:

No	*Yes*
you and your wife	you and your spouse
when you shave in the morning	when you brush your teeth (or bathe) in the morning

Unnecessary reference to or emphasis on a woman's marital status should be avoided. Whether married or not, a woman may be referred to by the name by which she chooses to be known, whether her name is her original name or her married name.

ADVANTAGES OF WORD PROCESSING

One final note on writing. The most efficient method of transferring thoughts to paper is dictation, either into a tape recorder for later transcription, or directly by telephone into a "word processing" system. Modern word processing machines, such as memory typewriters and text editors, eliminate the necessity for retyping entire pages for simple editing corrections, or for more extensive changes necessitated by approval cycles.

Dictation is faster than writing longhand—up to four times faster for most people. The human being can speak 120 words per minute, but can write only 30. Furthermore, the resulting document is more conversational. It reflects more how you talk than how you write. And we tend to speak more clearly and simply than we write. But dictation doesn't come easily to everyone; good planning and outlining are mandatory to achieving efficient dictation. Some writers may simply send handwritten copy or even rough draft typed copy to a word processing center or to a combined secretarial staff equipped with automatic typewriters or word processing equipment.

More sophisticated word processing equipment displays transcribed information on a video screen for editing and revision. With this system, a document may be received by telephone dictation (on a cassette tape from a dictating machine); the information can be stored for later playback and transcription. Then, as the word processing operator transcribes, the information is displayed on the video screen. The operator may edit the document according to preestablished style and format, with the final result printed error-free at speeds of 300 words per minute.

Another capability of word processing is storage and retrieval of previously recorded material. Because of its speed, the system can locate stored data in a matter of seconds, move copy from one area to another, enter and merge new information into an existing document, and delete material.

4

Editing to Meet
Reader Challenges

After each section of writing is complete, or upon completion of an entire project, it is imperative that the copy be edited, either by the writer or by someone assigned to an editing function—preferably both. In addition, it is advisable to test the readability of sample paragraphs of the copy, as described in the second part of this chapter.

EDITING AND REVISING COPY

Revision is as much an art as original writing. If you write and revise your own copy, you should, if possible, allow sufficient time to elapse between the two processes. Time lends a perspective. In the heat of writing, your work may seem brilliantly clear, but after a period of time, many gaps, inconsistencies, or language faults should become apparent. Figure 4-1 provides an excellent checklist for anyone who writes business communications; the checklist identifies 20 efficient writing principles that may be isolated and scored. The following techniques should also be helpful during the editing and revision process.

Editing Quick Tips

What's the best way to edit? First, assume the reader's identity. What are his or her expectations, education, background, and knowledge of the business, industry, or profession? Second, review the specific purpose of the document. And, finally, read each policy, procedure, or instruction *four* times:

- First, for *structure*—Is its construction consistent with the type of information being conveyed and its purpose?

53

EDITOR'S CHECKLIST FOR EFFICIENT WRITING

A written business communication is efficient, if it does what the writer wants, in the way the writer wants, with a minimum of time-wasting misunderstanding and frustration.

The Checklist identifies 20 principles for efficient writing which can be isolated and scored. It then asks a question for each principle.

Use this checklist as you edit your own or someone else's writing, to identify specific strengths or weaknesses of the writing.

First, score it for each of the writing principles. (If a question doesn't apply to the writing you are scoring, don't score it.)

Next, total your score. This is the overall efficiency score for this writing. The lower the score, the better. This score gives you a broad measure of the quality of the writing. For example, a score of 18 or over suggests the need for vigorous editing; a score of 8 or under suggests that only minor editing is needed.

Then, if you are reviewing your own writing, concentrate your editing on those questions you scored "2" or "1." If you are reviewing someone else's writing, use the completed checklist to help focus attention on those areas which most need editing.

Scoring columns (0, 1, 2):
- 0 — OK: no further editing needed
- 1 — Adequate: editing desirable, not essential
- 2 — Poor: further editing essential

1. Is the objective correctly and clearly stated?

2. Does the writing respond to audience needs?
3. Is the audience motivated to act?

4. Are the facts accurate and complete?

Structure of ideas
5. Is the writing well-organized?
6. Is the organization visible?
7. Is there a summary up front?
8. Is listing used, whenever possible?
9. Are layout and format well-designed?

Structure of sentences
10. Are long sentences avoided? (average words: under 25)
11. Are long paragraphs avoided? (average words: under 75)
12. Are simple, direct sentences used?
13. Is it well-punctuated?

Choice of the right words
14. Are strong, active verbs used?
15. Are everyday words preferred? (average syllables: under 160 per 100 words)
16. Are useless words vigorously pruned?

Structured formats
17. *Rules:* Does the writing clearly separate actions from conditions?
18. *Status Reports:* Does it clearly highlight key findings?
19. *Problem Solving:* Does it clearly state the problem/objective/issue, background, findings/options (pro & con), recommendations and action?
20. *Sales:* Does it clearly state their needs, your capabilities, and the benefits to them?

© Copyright 1980 John O. Morris Associates, West Hartford, CT 06107

Figure 4–1a. **Editor's Checklist for Efficient Writing** (Reprinted With Permission of John O. Morris)

EXPLANATION OF CHECKLIST QUESTIONS

1 Is the objective clearly and correctly stated?

Does the writer know his or her purpose in writing? Is this shown to the reader?

> Question 1 is always the starting point. Clear writing requires clear thinking first.

2 Does the writing respond to audience needs?
3 Is the audience motivated to act?

Who are all the audiences this communication may reach? What are the needs of each audience?

> Don't overlook the broader audience of non-experts, particularly senior management.

Does the writing motivate the various audiences to act in the way the writer wants? Is it logical, persuasive, interesting? Is the tone appropriate? Or is it likely to turn off those whom the writer most wants action from?

4 Are the facts accurate and complete?

Are there obvious errors or omissions that irritate the reader or interfere with effective presentation of ideas?

> This is the only question that is directed primarily at the substance of the writing.

5 Is the writing well-organized?
6 Is the organization visible?
7 Is there a summary up front?
8 Is listing used, whenever possible?
9 Are layout and format well-designed?

These five questions relate to the structure of ideas.

Are the ideas presented in a sequence that is logical to the reader? Are the first and second level ideas clearly identified?

Does the writer visibly organize ideas by using descriptive headings, a table of contents (for a longer communication), and a numbering or lettering system (for a set of rules or long report)?

Is there a summary up front of those key facts every reader wants to know promptly?

Does the writer consistently present in listing format each series of facts, conditions, findings, recommendations or options, etc.?

Is layout and format well-designed, so that the arrangement of type and white space on the page is pleasing to the eye, logical, and efficiently designed to help the reader quickly find the message?

10 Are long sentences avoided?
  (average words: under 25)
11 Are long paragraphs avoided?
  (average words: under 75)
12 Are simple, direct sentences used?
13 Is it well-punctuated?

These four questions relate to the structure of sentences.

How many text lines, on the average, are sentences and paragraphs?

> This quick test helps you estimate sentence and paragraph length, assuming ten words per line on a typical typed page.
>
> Long sentences and paragraphs are the wrong

format for business writing. Usually they are poorly-structured and difficult to understand.

Does the writer use simple, direct sentences that start with the main idea, stated in subject-verb-object order?

Are commas or other punctuation marks used appropriately, to show the reader when and how long to pause?

14 Are strong, active verbs used?
15 Are everyday words preferred?
  (average syllables:
  under 160 per 100 words)
16 Are useless words vigorously pruned?

These three questions relate to the choice of the right words.

Is the passive voice avoided? Do the verbs carry the weight of the sentence?

Are everyday words used that will communicate their meaning to the widest audience? Or is there unnecessary use of inhouse jargon, legalese, gobbledygook and technical words?

> An average syllable count of 1.6 helps cut down the unfamiliar words, which usually have more syllables.

Are useless words pruned so that they will not clutter the writing and distract the reader?

17 Rules: Does the writing clearly separate actions from conditions?
18 Status Reports: Does it clearly highlight key findings?
19 Problem Solving: Does it clearly state the problem/objective/issue, background, findings/options (pro & con), recommendations and action?
20 Sales: Does it clearly state their needs, your capabilities, and the benefits to them?

These four questions relate to structured formats for four types of communications.

Complex rules are almost always made up of the statement of an action or result, subject to one or more conditions. The best structure is to list the action first, as a full sentence, and then follow with conditions, as full sentences.

A status report states facts. It does not recommend or require action. The busy reader wants a summary up front; the best format is a series of highlights presented as a list.

Problem-solving reports and proposals require a series of standard headings to efficiently present key facts up front. The reader wants a concise statement of the problem, objective or issue; followed by a brief background statement; then a list of findings or options, with pros and cons for each option; then the recommendation; and finally the action. After this, if needed, detailed discussion may follow.

In a sales communication, look for a clear statement of the needs of the various audiences, the capabilities of the writer and his or her organization to meet these needs, and the benefits to the various audiences of having these needs met.

Figure 4–1b. Editor's Checklist for Efficient Writing (Cont'd)

- Second, for *logic*—Does the writing make sense? Is there a logical flow from start to finish?

- Third, for *grammar and punctuation*—These are self-evident but also as important as all other factors. For whenever there is a slip, a reader falls into a ''mechanical trap'' and inadvertently looks for other potential errors before resuming where reading was left off.

- And fourth, for *understanding*—Can the reader now perform what is asked, or fully understand what you have written, *the first time through?* An important measurement of good writing is that a reader should be able to understand the message at the first reading.

Seven Symptoms of Unclarity

There are at least seven signs of trouble you can see for yourself— as you look at what you've written, as you try to read it, and as you try to explain it informally:

As You Look

1. You cannot see any signs of structure at all—just line after line of prose.

2. You cannot pick out the significant parts, or easily find your main points.

As You Read

3. You have trouble remembering what was already read.

4. You have trouble keeping track of where you are—so that if you have to stop, it's hard to come back and find your place.

5. You cannot skim or read quickly with any understanding.

As You Explain

6. You cannot give an overview, or identify your main points.

7. You have to depart significantly from what you have written, in style, in organization, or in context.

If any of these seven statements are true, you can be virtually certain that your readers will find it hard work to make their way through what you have written. To improve your writing, you must edit heavily, using a style guide such as those published by the Government Printing Office, the University of Chicago, or the Associated Press.[1]

---

[1] See Selected Bibliography.

The following principles, which provide an almost mechanical procedure for editing, should also help.

The Concession Theory of Editing

The Concession Theory of Editing[2] is a device for using other people to help you find places where you should make changes. Under this theory, you change something you have written—concede and rewrite—if it misleads someone. It does no good to swear on a stack of grammar books, or trace an intricate path to the meaning, if someone cannot follow what you have written. Material in draft form is fluid; treat it that way and change it often.

One easy way to apply the Concession Theory is to use it to find ambiguous phrases. Writers rarely realize that something they have written can mean something different to their audience, because only one of the two meanings stands out for the writer—just not for the reader. Take a simple four-letter word such as lead. Is that "leed" or "ledd"? Anyone who wrote a heading like *Lead Recommendations* or phrases like *lead standard* or *lead agency* would have no trouble, but even a knowledgeable reader could go chasing a wild goose if the context did not make them completely clear.

Changes to clarify an ambiguous word or two are easy, of course. The next step is to extend the concessions to phrases, sentences, and paragraphs. Remember, if you let the reactions of people around you direct you to what you need to change, you can make those changes while the document is still under your control. Certainly that is preferable to having other people, with a different perspective, come along and "clarify" it to meet their own preconceptions.

In other words, use the Concession Theory in group writing, when other people are reviewing and questioning your material. Liberally applying the Concession Theory—realizing that there are always other ways to get the point across—will help you to avoid "I'm right, you're wrong" confrontations. Using the Concession Theory you can say, "Let's change it to make the point clearer."

The Red Flag Approach to Editing

The Red Flag Approach says that there are certain constructions (marked with imaginary red flags) that you should examine in more detail. Two primary concerns are passive voice and multiple nouns.

---

[2]The material in "The Concession Theory of Editing" and "The Red Flag Approach to Editing" is adapted from *Be a Better Writer—A Manual for EPA Employees*, U.S. Environmental Protection Agency, March 1980.

Passive Voice—Although the passive voice is a prime contributor to an impersonal writing style, it can also be acceptable, in moderation. The Red Flag Approach can help you determine whether individual instances of the passive voice are necessary or not.

Here is how the Red Flag for passives works. Consider the following sentence, then follow four steps:

> The study will be completed by this department within six months.

Step 1. Find the "-ed" verb. (A past participle; in this case, "completed.")

Step 2. Find what follows the word *by*. (If it's not there, supply it. In the example, "this department" follows *by* and is the actor in the sentence).

Step 3. Recast the sentence in the active voice. (Ordinarily, there is no need to write anything down yet—this is a mental exercise and good practice.)

> This department will complete the study within six months.

Step 4. Test whether the sentence is better in the active voice (often the right choice) or whether it should stay in the passive.

That decision in Step 4, however, is still open to judgment. Three additional questions may help you decide: (1) Are the transitions evident? (2) Is the actor clear? (3) Is the active sentence balanced?

1. *Are the transitions evident?*—The beginning of a sentence is often the place for a transition, a phrase that reinforces your organization. Suppose you are writing something about the Clean Air Act and have used a quotation from the Act, mentioning energy requirements, as your organizing principle. You spend several paragraphs on other topics. Then, starting your next paragraph, you write:

> Energy requirements were included in the model the five agencies in the Task Force on Energy will use to project the effects of the new standards.

Try the test: (1) red flag at "included;" (2) no "by," but probably the five agencies, etc., included the requirements; (3) consider the alternative:

> The five agencies in the Task Force on Energy included energy requirements in the model they will use to project the effects of the new standards.

Here the balance may tip toward the passive, because using it causes the paragraph to begin with a transitional phrase "Energy requirements," picking up the language in your organizing paragraph. In this example, placement of transitions may take precedence over the normal tendency to put more sentences in the active voice.

2. *Is the actor clear?*—Every time a Red Flag pops up in connection with a passive, a second flag should pop up when you search for the "by" phrase and can't find one. Ask yourself what phrase you should add to complete the sentence. On a few occasions, the actor is (a) totally redundant, (b) refers to everyone, or (c) refers to people you cannot name. For example:

(a) The Task Force report was prepared during the last two weeks.
(b) It is generally accepted that aerobic digestion is less sensitive to upsets than anaerobic digestion.
(c) The samples were washed, then titrated at pH 3.

Example (a) is acceptable as a passive if the task force really prepared the report. The example is misleading, however, if a contractor had prepared the report—and the passive is back at work hiding *who* did *what*. In example (b), the sentence says (as the word generally hints) that everyone accepts a fact about aerobic digestion. These general statements are acceptable without an actor. In example (c), your answer to "Who did it?" should be "Who cares?" In restricted cases like this example, when you're sure that nobody cares, the passive is again acceptable.

3. *Is the active sentence balanced?*—Sometimes, after you have reconstructed the active sentence corresponding to the passive you wrote originally, you will find that you prefer the passive because it simply sounds better. Fine. You've considered the alternative, and that is the point of the Red Flag Approach.

Noun Sandwiches—Some nominals are a necessary evil in most writing on technical subjects. How could people write without

resource recovery
land use planning
waste treatment

But when you find nominals and other words stacked up—sandwiched together—more than two deep, it is time for caution. Take an example:

Direct product design regulations

In this case, four words are stacked up without any little words to help group them together. Recast the phrase, supplying *for, the,* and *of:*

Direct regulations for the design of products.

Or, better, use an "-ing" form for one of the nominals.

Direct regulations for designing products.

Then ask yourself whether the original or either of the two options sounds best and is the easiest for your reader to understand.

Try the following rule of thumb for unpacking these constructions:

Unpack three-word noun sandwiches for the first few references, then allow them to stand together. Always unpack four-word sandwiches.

(After all, who ever heard of a sandwich that went bread-meat-bread-meat?)

The reason for the rule of thumb is familiarity. As people work with complex concepts, they begin to use larger and larger chunks of words to describe them. They pronounce those chunks easily and understand them well. When you have reached the stage where you process four-word sandwiches comfortably, however, you have lost the public. They must superimpose emphasis and grouping on the long phrase, and that takes time and increases frustration. Give your readers a break.

HINTS FOR PROOFREADING

Proofreading is an art. Most material never needs the exacting, meticulous review that professional proofreaders can provide. (See Figure 4-2 for a list of editorial and proofreading marks.) But it never hurts to know some tricks, because random typos can be embarrassing: "Container deposits are more than the public can beer." Here are five practical suggestions to help in proofreading:[3]

1. Never be ashamed to go to the dictionary. If a word looks strange, check it. Try this rule of thumb: if you really needed to consult the dictionary in only 20 percent of the cases when you actually did, you are using it appropriately.

2. Sound out long words. Long words are tricky: if they start right and end right, we skip over what is in the middle. To counteract that tendency, sound out all the vowels; for example, make fluoride come out as "flew-oh-ride."

---

[3] Adapted from *Be a Better Writer—A Manual for EPA Employees*, note 2.

Mark Used	Correction Indicated	Example of Mark Used Within Copy
ℛ	Delete	When inn the course
(ℛ)	Delete and close up	When in thre course
⌒	Close up, no space	space⊃borne capsule
⧣	Leave space	performedwithin
(⧣)	Close up to one space	When ⧣ in the
⊏	Move to left	⊏ with the machine
⊐	Move to right	With the machine ⊐
⊓	Move up	With ⊓the machine
⊔	Move down	With ⊔the machine
⊗	Replace imperfect type	C[o]mputer
¶	Make new paragraph	building. ¶ The module
No ¶ or ⊋	Run into same paragraph	side effects. ↰ The language is then
(sp)	Spell out	75% of the survey
≡	Capitalize	united States
/	Place in lower case	a Writer was
⁄‾	Capitalize first letter	RØBERT FREDERICK
∧,	Insert comma	camera∧film and other
∨	Insert apostrophe or single quote	managements intention
∨" "∨	Insert quotation marks	entitled∨Physical Characteristics∨
∧	Insert period	radio∧ Thus, the
∧:	Insert colon	the following∧move right, move left
∧;	Insert semicolon	control∧this would include
∧ ( ) ∧	Insert parentheses	criteria∧similar to the preceding∧
∧?	Insert question mark	ask "When will it stop∧"
∧	Insert hyphen	heavy∧duty equipment
‾	Underscore	the word exception
∨	Set as subscript	A∨3
∧	Set as superscript	10∧8
⊓⊔	Transpose letters or words	for following the
stet	Restore word crossed out, ignore correction	anticipated slippages stet
↶	Insert omitted material*	When the became Ⓐ
⟲	Move to position indicated	impedance∧too high became
‖ ═	Align	‖Color Telephone ‖Display

*When lengthy material is to be added, use a circled letter (Ⓐ) and attach separate page.

Figure 4–2.   Editorial and Proofreading Marks

3. Reread lines containing an error. It is human nature to pounce on mistakes; it is also human nature to make two mistakes close together. Rereading lines containing errors helps break these all-too-human tendencies.

4. Read backward to break content. Use this technique for solo proofreading, when the material must be exceptionally error free. Read the material once from top to bottom (this is useful for catching singular subjects with plural verbs and for spotting dropped minor words such as "not"). Then grit your teeth and read backward. You will not understand what you are reading, but you will be sure the words are spelled right.

5. Have two people read to each other. This is the best method, especially if the one who worked from the draft copy now reads the typescript.

MEASURING READABILITY

Determining the relationship between writing style and reading comprehension has been the object of many studies. Numerous tests for measuring the effect of long sentences, big words, and abstract ideas on understanding have been developed. Among the early researchers during the 1940s were Robert Gunning and Rudolph Flesch; the methods they developed are discussed next.[4]

Gunning's Fog Index

The Fog Index produces a score representing the approximate number of years of schooling an individual must have to read a prose passage with ease and understanding. The higher the score, the more difficult the passage is to read. To use the Fog Index, select a sample of at least 100 words and follow these steps:

1. Calculate the average number of words per sentence, treating independent clauses as separate sentences. (For example, treat semicolons as periods.)

2. Count the number of polysyllables (words of three syllables or more) per 100 words. Ignore capitalized words, compound words made up of simple words (such as "insofar"), and words made into three syllables by adding "ed" or "es" (such as created or trespasses).

---

[4]See Robert Gunning, *The Technique of Clear Writing* (New York: McGraw-Hill Book Co., rev. 1968), and Rudolph Flesch, *The Art of Readable Writing* (New York: Harper & Row, 1974).

3. Add these two factors (average sentence length and number of polysyllables) together and multiply their sum by 0.4. The result, with decimal digits dropped, gives an estimate of the "grade level" required to read the material. For example, a document with a Fog Index of 8.3 requires an eighth grade education. A Fog Index of 8 or 9 requires junior high school readers; an index of 11 or 12 requires high school graduates; and 13 or 14, college graduates. Any passage that tests higher than 17 is assigned a Fog Index of 17 plus.

Flesch's Reading Ease Formula

The Reading Ease Formula also counts the number of words per sentence and the number of polysyllables per word to produce an overall reading level score. Unlike the Fog Index, however, a high score under the Reading Ease Formula indicates ease of readability and comprehension rather than difficulty. All of the insurance language laws use this formula as a basic objective test. According to John O. Morris, "The Flesch test was never designed for this purpose. But it has been adopted by state insurance commissioners and the insurance industry because it provides a measurable standard that eliminates much argument as to what is and is not plain language. Computers now do the actual counting."

Clear River Test

In contrast to the Fog Index and the Reading Ease Formula, the Clear River Test, developed by John O. Morris,[5] does not produce a composite or average score. As Morris explains: "Rather, it shows whether a particular piece of writing is exceptionally high, thus unreadable, on any one or more of four items tested."

The Clear River Test measures the number of words per sentence, words per punctuated pause, words per paragraph, and syllables per 100 words. This test suggests the following as safe maximum scores, on the average, for business and government writing:

- 25 words per sentence
- 12 words per punctuated pause
- 75 words per paragraph
- 150 syllables per 100 words

[5]Excerpted from John O. Morris, *Make Yourself Clear*. Copyright © 1980, McGraw-Hill Book Co. Used with the permission of McGraw-Hill Book Co.

As described by Morris:

"The point of the Clear River Test (or of any readability test) is simply this: If your message does not materially exceed the suggested safe limit for any of the four items, then you have placed no unnecessary obstacles between your audience and you. But when a written message scores notably high in any one or more of these four items, you have placed unnecessary obstacles between your reader and you. Your message is written at a readability level higher than the level comfortable for most people. This means that you can expect your audience to have difficulty with your message; thus you face the danger that your message will not get through, and therefore you will not accomplish your purpose.

"The Clear River Test is not a precise mathematical test. In measuring readability, such a test would be burdensome to use and probably pointless. Rather, the test provides a quick simple rule of thumb to help any writer or reviewer identify writing which is unnecessarily difficult and complex. It therefore uses several shortcuts to make the counting less burdensome; with a little practice, a sample of writing can be tested in 10 minutes."

To make the Clear River Test:

1. Choose a sample in which the line lengths remain consistent and calculate the average number of words per line. (Try for a sample size of 10 paragraphs with limited use of numerals, abbreviations, proper names or dialogue.)
2. Count the number of lines in the first 10 sentences of the sample.
3. Multiply these two to give an estimate of the number of words per line. Then divide by 10 to get the average number of words per sentence.
4. Count the number of punctuated pauses in the first 10 sentences— in other words, the number of times a reader pauses for clarity. Divide the average number of words per punctuated pause by the estimated number of words.
5. Isolate 10 paragraphs of the sample. Count the number of lines in 10 paragraphs; multiply by the average number of words per line; and divide by 10 to get the average number of words per paragraph.
6. Isolate 100 words of the sample and count syllables.

Automated Readability Tests

Because of the numerous "Plain English" laws recently enacted by many states, several computer services organizations have begun offering automated readability tests. Some companies have developed their own computer programs for such analysis.

One typical program is Britton & Associates, Inc. "Readability Analysis System,"[6] offered through Business Information Services of Control Data Corporation. The Readability Analysis System determines the highest grade level at which a publication will be understood. The program analyzes sample passages and applies readability formulas such as Fry, Dale-Chall, and Flesch. Specific documents for analysis include books, standardized tests, business contracts, technical manuals, and government information documents. Figure 4-3 provides an example of a typical computer-readability analysis.

---

[6]Developed and copyrighted by Britton & Associates, Inc., of Corvallis, Ore.

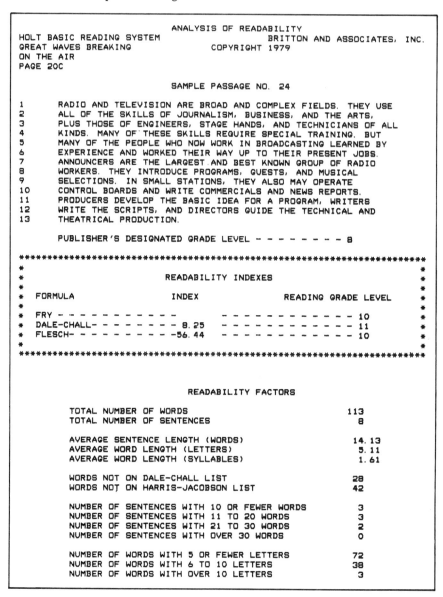

```
                        ANALYSIS OF READABILITY
HOLT BASIC READING SYSTEM               BRITTON AND ASSOCIATES, INC.
GREAT WAVES BREAKING            COPYRIGHT 1979
ON THE AIR
PAGE 20C


                       SAMPLE PASSAGE NO. 24

 1      RADIO AND TELEVISION ARE BROAD AND COMPLEX FIELDS. THEY USE
 2      ALL OF THE SKILLS OF JOURNALISM, BUSINESS, AND THE ARTS,
 3      PLUS THOSE OF ENGINEERS, STAGE HANDS, AND TECHNICIANS OF ALL
 4      KINDS. MANY OF THESE SKILLS REQUIRE SPECIAL TRAINING. BUT
 5      MANY OF THE PEOPLE WHO NOW WORK IN BROADCASTING LEARNED BY
 6      EXPERIENCE AND WORKED THEIR WAY UP TO THEIR PRESENT JOBS.
 7      ANNOUNCERS ARE THE LARGEST AND BEST KNOWN GROUP OF RADIO
 8      WORKERS. THEY INTRODUCE PROGRAMS, GUESTS, AND MUSICAL
 9      SELECTIONS. IN SMALL STATIONS, THEY ALSO MAY OPERATE
10      CONTROL BOARDS AND WRITE COMMERCIALS AND NEWS REPORTS.
11      PRODUCERS DEVELOP THE BASIC IDEA FOR A PROGRAM, WRITERS
12      WRITE THE SCRIPTS, AND DIRECTORS GUIDE THE TECHNICAL AND
13      THEATRICAL PRODUCTION.

        PUBLISHER'S DESIGNATED GRADE LEVEL - - - - - - - - 8

***********************************************************************
*                                                                     *
*                       READABILITY INDEXES                           *
*                                                                     *
*  FORMULA                INDEX                READING GRADE LEVEL     *
*                                                                     *
*  FRY - - - - - - - - - - -      - - - - - - - - - - - - 10          *
*  DALE-CHALL- - - - - - - 8.25   - - - - - - - - - - - - 11          *
*  FLESCH- - - - - - - - -56.44   - - - - - - - - - - - - 10          *
*                                                                     *
***********************************************************************



                       READABILITY FACTORS

        TOTAL NUMBER OF WORDS                       113
        TOTAL NUMBER OF SENTENCES                     8

        AVERAGE SENTENCE LENGTH (WORDS)            14.13
        AVERAGE WORD LENGTH (LETTERS)               5.11
        AVERAGE WORD LENGTH (SYLLABLES)             1.61

        WORDS NOT ON DALE-CHALL LIST                 28
        WORDS NOT ON HARRIS-JACOBSON LIST            42

        NUMBER OF SENTENCES WITH 10 OR FEWER WORDS    3
        NUMBER OF SENTENCES WITH 11 TO 20 WORDS       3
        NUMBER OF SENTENCES WITH 21 TO 30 WORDS       2
        NUMBER OF SENTENCES WITH OVER 30 WORDS        0

        NUMBER OF WORDS WITH 5 OR FEWER LETTERS      72
        NUMBER OF WORDS WITH 6 TO 10 LETTERS         38
        NUMBER OF WORDS WITH OVER 10 LETTERS          3
```

Figure 4–3.   A Computer Readability Analysis (Courtesy of Britton & Associates)

5

Developing an Effective Organizational Manual

This chapter examines the elements involved in the mechanical side of producing an organizational manual: the principles of loose-leaf manual design, selecting a numbering system, and designing an effective page layout.

PRINCIPLES OF LOOSE-LEAF MANUAL DESIGN

A loose-leaf manual is in a constant state of revision. The challenge is in assuring that it retains all of the cohesiveness and reference facility of a bound book. In a permanently bound manual, the text is identified by the title page, table of contents, numbered chapters, numbered pages, and an index. In a loose-leaf manual, the only constants are the title page and the chapter numbers. Because pages are being added, deleted, or replaced, they should be numbered and dated in special ways.[1]

Guiding elements in the design of a loose-leaf manual are:

Ease of reference—attained through logical organization; tables of contents; indexing; schematic numbering of volumes, chapters, and sections; and page identification.

Ease of revision—accomplished through a loose-leaf format, with additions, substitutions, and deletions of pages.

Readability—achieved through suitable typography; ample spacing; judicious use of headings; use of short paragraphs; and indentation. Readability is also improved through use of appropriate illustrations.

[1]See "Page Design," p. 85.

67

Physical Specifications

Size. The size of a manual is governed by how it will be used by the reader, the extent to which forms and other letter-size illustrations need to be included, and the size of other manuals in the same series.

For office or desk use, letter size is standard: 8-1/2 × 11 inches. This permits the inclusion of standard letter-size forms. It is also most convenient for office duplicating equipment. For shop or vehicle use, as well as some office or executive use, half-size pages, either 5-1/2 × 8-1/2 inches or 6 × 9 inches, are often used.

Binders. The standard three-ring loose-leaf binder is commonly used. If the amount of material dictates using one larger than one-inch capacity, it should be specifically designed to prevent tearing. A series of binders may be necessary if one alone is too bulky.

The pages of the binder should lie flat when the binder is open so that new material can be inserted and old material deleted quickly. Convenience in using a loose-leaf binder is very important, for awkwardly made binders discourage prompt insertion of pages.

The binder should be sturdy, to permit its continuing use without deterioration either of the cover or of the ring or prong mechanisms. If the binder is to be used for desk or drawer use, a medium weight and quality may be satisfactory. But if it is to be used by traveling personnel or by shop hands or if it is to be used continuously, a heavy-duty binder should be chosen. If the binder is to be stored in an upright position, it should be of stiff construction; otherwise it may be either stiff or flexible.

A common problem with loose-leaf binders is tearing of the beginning and end sheets. Page lifters—protective inserts which are punched with the same hole spacing as the sheets of paper but with the holes offset in such a manner that the front and end pages are actually lifted into place before the cover of the binder is closed—will prevent the pages from tearing.

Cover—The cover design should be coordinated with the manual contents. The subject of the manual should be readily apparent, but the word "manual" need not be the most prominent part of the caption. If the manual is one of a series, make its individual caption most prominent, with series identification secondary.

Cover colors may be varied to distinguish one from others. Very light colors afford maximum contrast with the print, but they also soil easily. Some intermediate choices are light gray, buff, light salmon, light green, and light blue.

Tabs and Dividers. The main parts of a manual should be separated for quick reader access through use of tabs and dividers. The tabs should give a short title index to the contents of the manual. The dividers can include a table of contents for that portion of the manual.[2]

Note that binders should be ordered early enough to ensure delivery when needed. Depending upon the type selected, it can take up to two months to have them produced.

Paper—An audience's overall impression of a printed piece may depend largely on the paper used. If used correctly, it can enhance all of the other graphic elements and processes used; if used incorrectly, it can diminish desired results. The finest paper available may not be the best choice. Other factors which have impact include strength, weight, bulk, color, opacity, and texture. Above all, the paper selected should be available for future use in updating. This may well be the determining factor in the final selection.

Paper should be strong, so that the holes will not tear in the loose-leaf binder. The need for strength depends on the amount of use and the conditions of use. Strength may be increased by using a heavier paper or by using better quality paper. The latter costs more, of course, but may balance overall costs in the end.

Weight and thickness must be considered. Obviously, the thicker the paper, the more room it will take in a loose-leaf binder. Paper is very, very heavy. If you are forced to go to a larger binder, the added weight will tend to discourage the user from picking it up for an occasional reference. If the materials are to be mailed in any substantial quantities, weight will increase mailing costs.

Paper selection is also governed by the printing process which you are to use. If you are printing by offset process, a wide variety of paper surfaces can be used. But don't assume that just any paper will be satisfactory; papers will vary in their ability to take and hold ink. Some will hold solid areas better than others.

A good, dead white, opaque paper is to be preferred, particularly if it is to be printed on both sides. Avoid calendered or other fancy surfaces; the paper surface should enable the reader to make pen or pencil notations if necessary. Colored pages may be used for special exhibits, inserts, dividers, tables of contents, etc. When color is used, it should be of light tint, so as not to interfere with readability.

---

[2]Appendix A provides excellent specifications for binder and divider tabs on pages 176 through 178.

MEMO

TO: MANAGEMENT

FROM:

SUBJECT: Policies and Procedures

         success depends on the company's most important asset, its employees.

The Management Group of our company can best fulfill its obligations to our employees and the company only if each member understands the nature and scope of his or her own job responsibilities and gains an appreciation for the job responsibilities of all others. To that end this manual has been prepared and distributed.

With new   Functional Organizations being established at locations other than   , it is my intention to closely parallel all operations, not only in organizational structure, but also in operating practices and procedures.

In order to assist management personnel in:

- Defining the division's specifications for conducting business
- Administering those objectives in a uniform manner for the benefit of our employees

the need to have written and current Policies and Procedures as a part of our efficient Management Policy is:

- A recognized necessity
- A means of fulfilling our company's commitment to leadership in management as well as in industry

The Policies and Procedures contained herein are a guarantee that personnel at all   locations are working with the same plan and are in compliance with Corporate requirements.

Management is urged to contribute suggestions for the improvement of **existing** Policies and Procedures and to keep the media in this manual current. Current media will:

- Eliminate many job-transition problems being experienced during our division's rapid growth
- Encourage each manager assuming a new job to always review the organization's objectives, and perhaps find newer and better methods of getting the job done

Economically,   is now able to distribute this new type of manual to every member of   Management. All Policies and Procedures will be maintained in a computerized form, permitting inexpensive periodic updating and annual replacement of the entire manual, making the manual a more vital tool in defining our divisional operations.

Figure 5–1. Transmittal Memo (Policies and Procedures Manual of a Major Manufacturer)

Arrangement

A manual is usually arranged in the following manner:

1. Front matter
    a. Cover
    b. Title page
    c. Transmittal memo (or preface)
    d. Maintenance checklists
    e. Revision notices
    f. Plan of the manual
    g. Table of contents/list of illustrations
    h. Index
2. Individual chapters
3. Appendices

The *transmittal memo* officially establishes the manual. Brief and to the point, it should be signed by the officer who usually has authority over all of the subjects covered by the manual. The letter should be more than a mere statement—it should set the tone of management attitude. It may also be part of the preface or the foreword, or incorporated into the first transmittal notice, which is not bound permanently into the manual. If there is overlapping of this material with the plan of the manual, consider combining the two. (See Figures 5-1 and 5-2.)

Maintenance checklists give the user a handy means of keeping track of all revisions. By checking them off as they are received, the user can detect any missing notices.

Revision notices transmit new pages or page changes. These notices are sometimes filed in the manual itself for a period of time so that the user can check back on any explanations the notices may contain. Sometimes the notices are used as receipts to be returned to the manual control center.[3]

The *plan of the manual* should include a brief explanation of how to use the document. A more detailed explanation can be included at a later point. (See Figures 5-3 and 5-4.)

The *table of contents* is a directory of the manual's content. In a logically ordered manual, the major headings tell briefly where to locate any subject. Subheadings pinpoint classifications. (See Figure 5-5.) The

---

[3]See ''Revision Notices,'' Chapter 8, p. 114.

PREFACE

GENERAL

This manual contains Policies and Procedures that specify how and by whom certain divisional business functions are to be conducted. Policy 0100 describes in more detail the purpose and origins of this media.

Some of the publications herein implement   Corporate Policy or Procedure requirements, while others specify unique divisional practices as negotiated by persons or organizations affected, or as directed by Division management. All require approval by the Cognizant Manager to whom publication requirements are addressed.

The manual and the publications it contains are distributed by the Policies and Procedures Department at

The role of the manual as a Division business practice standard will be realized only if the persons and organizations to whom its requirements and guidelines are addressed know about and comply with them.

The value of the manual content will be adequate only if it covers the current needs and conditions of the functions covered.

Management personnel at all levels are responsible for:

- Reviewing new and revised manual publications as they are issued.

- Assuring that operations under their control are conducted in accordance with the applicable published requirements.

- Prompting both removal of those publications containing obsolete material and the correction of out-of-date or faulty content.

The Policies and Procedures Department should be contacted regarding needed actions of this nature (see back cover of this manual).

TRANSMITTAL RECORD SHEET

The Transmittal Record (located on the inside cover of this manual) is used to record each new addition and/or revision publication you receive for insertion into your manual. Each addition and/or revision published will be assigned a transmittal number, beginning with the number one and continuing sequentially until the manual is re-published at the beginning of each new calendar year.

REVISION NOTICES

Revisions to this manual will occur on an "as needed" basis at first, due to the extensive manual update task which must be accomplished. Each revision notice you receive, how-ever, will list all the current additions, deletions and revisions to the manual and will include the appropriate transmittal number for proper recording procedures.

ii

Figure 5–2. Preface (Policies and Procedures Manual of a Major Manufacturer)

MANAGEMENT GUIDE

No.100.01

GENERAL INTRODUCTION

SECTION:

PURPOSE OF THE MANAGEMENT GUIDE

The   Management Guide is published as a central reference source for current and future policies of   . Implementation of these policies by all members of   Management will provide uniformity of action in handling situations that occur repetitively in conducting Company business. The Guide does not provide detailed instructions for implementing all these policies. In many instances, such procedural information will be found in the manuals and bulletins issued by the various corporate departments, operating divisions, groups, and profit centers. Policies issued by operating divisions, groups and profit centers must conform with all   policies.

The Management Guide also functions as a catalog of Corporate Services that are provided to the Company. A Corporate Services section is organized by department and indicates the individual to be contacted regarding specific services.

Additional corporate policy statements will be issued from time to time as releases to the Beatrice Management Guide.

ALL CURRENT AND FUTURE POLICIES CONTAINED IN THE GUIDE, REGARDLESS OF SIGNATURE, HAVE THE FULL AUTHORIZATION AND SUPPORT OF THE CHIEF CORPORATE OFFICER AND CHIEF EXECUTIVE OFFICER OF   .

If you are not certain as to the applicability of a policy or the propriety of any particular practice, do not decide the matter yourself. You should contact your immediate supervisor, the Corporate Law Department or the Corporate Planning and Procedures Department for assistance and guidance.

DATE: Original Guide

PAGE 1   OF 1

Figure 5–3. Purpose of the Manual (Management Guide of a Major Food Processor)

MANAGEMENT GUIDE

No. 100.02

GENERAL INTRODUCTION	SECTION: ORGANIZATION OF THE MANAGEMENT GUIDE

The ▓▓▓▓ Management Guide is divided into the following sections:

100 - General Introduction — Summary of organization and purpose of the Guide including the table of contents.

200 - Management Directives — Major policy statements that are reflective of legal, social and/or moral responsibilities. Any employee who violates these Directives will be subject to appropriate disciplinary action.

310 - Administrative Policies — Policies primarily concerned with administrative matters relating to employees or outside parties.

330 - Financial Policies — Policies primarily concerned with accounting and financial data.

350 - Operational Policies — Policies primarily concerning plant operations and products.

400 - Corporate Services — Summary of services available to the Company from the Corporate Office.

900 - Transmittal Letters — Cover sheets accompanying all re-leases for the Guide - to be filed in numerical sequence.

Each release for the Guide is assigned a five digit control number for filing purposes. The first two digits identify the tabbed sections within the Guide. The third digit is reserved for subsection identi-fication. The fourth and fifth digits identify the individual releases within each subsection.

For purposes of simplicity the term "Original Guide" has been inserted next to the word "DATE" at the bottom of each page contained in the initial distribution of the Guide. New policies will be issued from time to time and will be effective on the first day of the month following their release which will be shown at the bottom of the page.

DATE: Original Guide   PAGE 1   OF 1

Figure 5–4. Organization of the Manual (Management Guide of a Major Food Processor)

MANAGEMENT GUIDE

No. 100.00

GENERAL INTRODUCTION

SECTION:

TABLE OF CONTENTS

100.   Introduction

    100.00   Table of Contents
    100.01   Purpose of the Management Guide
    100.02   Organization of the Management Guide
    100.03   Distribution of the Management Guide
    100.04   Procedures For Approval of Releases to the Management Guide

200.   Management Directives

    200.00   Index of Management Directives
    200.01   Responsibility of Management
    200.02   Antitrust Compliance
    200.03   Equal Employment Opportunity
    200.04   Occupational Safety and Health
    200.05   Conflict of Interest
    200.06   Illegal and Improper Use of Company Funds and Assets
    200.07   Improper Accounting Practices
    200.08   Announcements of Acquisitions, Mergers and Divestitures
    200.09   Release and Use of Inside Information
    200.10   Proposed Legislation

310.   Administrative Policy Sections

    310.00   Index of Administrative Policies
    311.00   Employee Benefits
    312.00   Insurance
    313.00   Personnel
    314.00   Industrial Relations
    315.00   Law
    316.00   Corporate Development
    317.00   Public Relations

330.   Financial Policy Sections

    330.00   Index of Financial Policies
    331.00   Accounting
    332.00   Auditing
    333.00   Tax
    334.00   Treasury

DATE: Original Guide   PAGE 1   OF 2

Figure 5–5. Table of Contents Showing Page Numbers Incorporated Into Overall Numbering Scheme (Management Guide of a Major Food Processor)

INDEX OF POLICIES AND PROCEDURES

Title	Number	Page
Accounting, Functional Area Specifications	N3 -0000	3-1
Accounts Receivable Age Profile	N4 -8300-1	4-17
Advance Deviation Request Processing	N5 -8200-1	5-143
Advance Vacation Pay	N3 -0900-1	3-26
Affirmative Action	N6 -0001	6-3
Age Profile, Accounts Receivable	N4 -8300-1	4-17
Aprons, Shop	N7 -0400	7-13
Artwork, Printed Circuit Board	N10-1800-1	10-68
Assemblers	N9 -0010	9-4
Selection, Training and Placement	N9 -0010-1	9-6
Assemblies, Purchased		
Changes To Piece Parts or Sub-Assemblies	N10-3300-1	10-106
Assemblies, Stock Level	N5 -8800	5-192
Establishing	N5 -8800-1	5-193
Processing SRO Requirements Through Stockroom	N5 -8800-4	5-198
Shipments From ARCs To Rec/Pre-Pack	N5 -8800-6	5-201
Shipments From ARCs To Stock (A, S, N, G)	N5 -8800-5	5-199
Shipments From Satellite Facilities To (A, S, N, G)	N5 -8800-3	5-197
Shipments From Satellite Facilities To Receiving (N)	N5 -8800-7	5-202
Tracking	N5 -8800-2	5-195
Assembly Area Responsibility Codes (ARCs)	N3 -7000	3-53
ARC List	N3 -7000-1	
Assembly Shipments		
ARCs To Stock	N5 -2103-1	5-77
Satellite Facilities To Stock and ARCs	N5 -2102-1	5-76
Audits		
Stock Status Error Report	N5 -1000-5	5-59
Authority To Ship Usage	N5 -0610-1	5-50
Automatic DIP Insertion System	N10-3000	10-90
Processing ECOs	N10-3000-2	10-93
Processing New Releases	N10-3000-1	10-92
Requesting a Paper Drive Tape	N10-3000-3	10-94
Updating Division Unique File	N10-3000-4	10-94
Backorder		
Edit and Update Error Messages	N5 -1000-4	5-57
Processing Through Material Services	N5 -0500-2	5-46
Bill of Material	N10-0400	10-29
Bogus	N5 -9000-1	5-214
Modular Structuring	N10-0010	10-7
Processing Engineering Documentation Release	N10-0400-1	10-31
Processing Request	N10-0400-2	10-34
Bogus Assemblies		
Establishing	N5 -9000	5-213
Processing Engineering Change Orders	N5 -9000-2	5-215
Bogus Bill of Material	N5 -9000-1	5-214
Burden Material		
Adjusting Quantities	N10-0800-1	10-58
Processing Traveling Stock Requisitions	N5 -8101-5	5-119
Burn-In, Circuit Card	N9 -8500-1	9-72
Business Software Charter	N1 -0600	1-7
Business Travel and Meetings	N3 -6411	3-47
Luncheon Cash Advance	N3 -6411-3	3-52
Reimbursement	N3 -6411-2	3-50
Travel Advances	N3 -6411-1	3-49
Travel Reservations	N3 -6411-1	3-49
Calendar, Fiscal Year	N3 -0100	3-4
Camera Pass	N2 -0003	2-6
Capital Equipment		
Consigning Surplus For Trade-In Credit	N5 -8401-1	5-165
Disposing of Surplus	N5 -8400-6	5-158
Requirements, Preparing and Forecasting	N3 -4000-1	3-28
Transfer Between Divisions/Plants	N5 -8401-2	5-167
Capital Expenditure Authorization, Request For	N9 -4000-1	9-27
Challenge Sheets		

IND-1

Figure 5–6. Index Listing Both Policy/Procedure Numbers and Page Numbers (Policies and Procedures Manual of a Major Manufacturer)

table of contents can be detailed, provided that it does not add too much to the bulk of the manual. If it is very detailed, precede it with a summary table of contents. The complete table of contents may be at the beginning of the manual or a separate table of contents can be inserted before each separate chapter.

List all *tables and illustrations* in the front matter. Tables are rows and columns of information; illustrations (or figures) are everything else, such as photographs, drawings, charts, and computer printouts.

The *index* is an alphabetical guide to specific subjects discussed in the text. Because of its importance as a reference tool, the index should be placed at the end of the front matter section rather than at the traditional end-of-the-book location.

Considerable skill is required in preparing an index. An indexer must be able to relate to readers, anticipating the names or descriptions under which they will look for specific information. (See Figure 5-6.) The usual technique is to proceed through the text and identify each subject of possible references, sometimes called a "key word," determine how to describe each item, then list it several different ways: (1) by itself; (2) as a cross-reference to another listing; or (3) as a subtopic under a major listing. Success of an index is measured by the average time it takes for a reader to get to a desired paragraph anywhere in the document. Today's standards call for a *maximum of 90 seconds* to reach one's goal!

The *Keyword-in-Context* (KWIC) index, a unique method of indexing, involves the use of all principal words of a subject heading or chapter title (see Figure 5-7). (A principal word includes everything in the heading or title except short "to be" verbs, articles ("a," "an," and "the"), and prepositions.) The KWIC index lists each full title or heading as many times as there are principal words, within each principal word's alphabetical listing. This permits subject retrieval through the use of "key words."

To use this index, read down the center of the listing. The key word appears in its correct place in the title, with the other words appearing in their proper place to the left or right of the key word. Figure 5-8 illustrates how the title "A Review of Future Administrative Systems" would be listed under various letter headings in a KWIC index.

Keyword-in-Context Index

A

	A-V Microfiche: A New Approach To The Use Of	77-0274
Microforms and the	Academic Library	76-0391
User	Acceptance	76-0420
In Indexing Costs Through Use Of High Speed Rand	Access Microfiche	77-0481
Effective	Access To The Periodical Literature: A National	77-0412
Manual Storage and Retrieval/	Accessories and Supplies	76-0436
Microfilming General Books Of	Account: Complying With IRS Revenue Procedure 76-43	77-0240
Replacement for Slides in a University Elementary	Accounting Course	77-0102
a Replacement for Slides in A University Elementary	Accounting Course	78-0012
	Accounting Records And VAT On Microfilm	73-0244
	Accounting Records And VAT On Microfilm	73-0245
	Accounting Records And VAT On Microfilm	73-0246
	Accounts Payable System	76-0409
PH4.106-1977 Specification For Photographic Grade	Acetic Acid CH3COOH, 28% Solution	77-0342
PH4.100-1977 Specification for Photographic Grade	Acetic Acid, Glacial, CH3COOH	77-0406
The	Acquisition Of Library Microforms	77-0217
The	Acquisition Of Library Microforms: Part II	77-0218
An	Acquisitions Up-Date For Government Publications	77-0377
	Administrative Integration of Microformated Government	77-0375
A Review of Future	Administrative Systems	76-0390
Automated Document Storage And Retrieval System	(ADSTAR) System Procurement Request For Proposal	77-0438
	Advanced Mail Systems Scanner Technology, Second Annual	76-0506
	Advanced Technical Data Study (U)	75-0378
Engineering 35 mm Aperture Card System and	Advantages In The Total Concept	76-0385
	AFIPS Conference Proceedings, Volume 46, 1977 National	77-0401
Micrographics Council: Concern of Government	Agencies In Micrographics	77-0141
Evaluation of the	Agfa-Gevaert LF101 Microfiche Reader	77-0414
Evaluation of Full-Size COM Microfiche Readers:	Agfa-Gevaert LF303; Microphax Mini-Cat TN; Microscot	77-0404
	Airline Puts Long Lookup Times to Flight With Microfilm	77-0298
	Alaska on Film	77-0118
	All About Microfilm Cameras	77-0094
	All About Micrographics	76-0572
Computer Assisted Drafting At	Allis-Chalmers Switchgear Division	76-0387
	Alphanumeric COM's - A Comparison	77-0085
	Alphanumeric COM's: A Comparison	77-0145
A Study Of Microfiche As An	Alternative To The Reserve Room Function	74-0293
	Amendment of Microfilm Images By The Hokushin	77-0462
Systems	Analysis and Design	76-0445
Economic	Analysis And Micrographics	77-0242
Microfilm Data Systems &	Analysis Design	73-0218
Sampling A Job	Analysis Questionnaire In Microfilm Production	77-0471
	Annual Review of Information Science and Technology Volume	77-0411
	ANSI PH2.39-1977 Method Of Measuring The	77-0345
	ANSI PH3.37-1977 Method For The Determination Of	77-0338
	ANSI PH3.74-1977 Method Of Testing Image Distortion	77-0346
	ANSI PH4.100-1977 Specification for Photographic Grade	77-0406
	ANSI PH4.101-1977 Specification for Photographic Grade	77-0407
	ANSI PH4.106-1977 Specification For Photographic Grade	77-0342
	ANSI PH4.106-1977 Specification For Photographic Grade	77-0344
	ANSI PH4.176-1977 Specifications For Photographic	77-0337
	ANSI PH4.205-1977 Specification For Photographic Grade	77-0343
	ANSI PH4.225-1977 Specification For Photographic Grade	77-0336
	ANSI PH4.226-1977 Specification For Photographic Grade	77-0333
	ANSI PH4.300-1977 Specification for Photographic Grade	77-0334
	ANSI PH4.303-1977 Specification For Photographic Grade	77-0335
	ANSI PH4.39-1977 Spectrophotometric Determination Of	77-0347
	ANSI/NMA MS12-1977, Method for Measuring the Screen	77-0093
Engineering Drawin Information With Microfilm	Aperture Card System	73-0221
Engineering 35 mm	Aperture Card System and Advantages In The Total	76-0385
	Aperture Cards And Reprographics	77-0170
Color Micrographics: Experimental Design and	Application In a Regional School District	76-0402
More to COM Than Economy—Just Count the	Applications	77-0070
Fitting Microfilm Technology to	Applications	77-0089
Personal Learning Package PLP2-COM: Systems and	Applications	77-0090
	Applications Of Graphic COM To Creation Of Drawings	73-0226
Microfilming Maps,	Architectural And Constructional Drawings	73-0238
	Archival Considerations In Microfilming Public Records	76-0417
4331: Photography - Processed Photographic Film for	Archival Records - Silver-Gelatin Type on Cellulose Ester	77-0105
Microforms In Libraries and	Archives	73-0228
An Evaluation of Information Collected From National	Archives	76-0494

75

Figure 5–7. First Page of a Key Word-in-Context (KWIC) Index (Courtesy of National Micrographics Association)

	A	
A Review of Future	Administrative Systems	76–0390*
	F	
A Review of	Future Administrative Systems	76–0390
	R	
A	Review of Future Administrative Systems	76–0390
	S	
A Review of Future Administrative	Systems	76–0390

*Number at right is index code of National Micrographics Association; first two digits represent publication year; last four digits represent sequential numbering of the document.

Figure 5–8. KWIC Index Placement of Entry With Four Key Words (Courtesy of National Micrographics Association)

You can subdivide a manual into *volumes, chapters, titles,* or *parts.* Generally, the term ''volume'' is used when there are physically separate binders; the term ''chapter'' denotes the major divisions of a book, manual, or handbook. Each chapter within a single binder should be separated from the others by a tab divider.

Individual *forms, exhibits,* and *illustrations* should be included directly with related parts of the text. A convenient way of numbering exhibits is to assign the number of the text material in which the exhibit is referenced. When forms are grouped together and away from explanatory text, the reader has to look in two different places.

Separate *appendixes,* either at the end of a chapter or at the end of the whole manual, provide reference material which cannot be integrated with the text. A list of forms is an appropriate appendix. The list may show all current forms, in numerical sequence, their titles, and the references to their use in the manual. Another appropriate appendix is a glossary—an alphabetical listing of key terms used in the text, with accompanying definitions. (See Figure 5-9.)

To help you determine whether particular material should be included in the text, or moved to the appendixes, use these three tests:

1. *Is the material ''necessary'' or ''nice''?* If it is important to your explanation, retain it within the text. If it is nice to know, but doesn't add substantially to your primary information, cite its existence and refer the reader to a specific appendix for details.

a

abandonment
Leaving without intending to return. This occurs when one spouse leaves another or a tenant abandons his premises, etc.

abatement
Deduction from the full amount of a claim, frequently occurs when the funds used for payments do not cover the claims. Each claim gets a proportional share.

abet
To aid, help or assist.

abstract of title
A list of deeds and other documents outlining the history of title to land.

accessory
A person who assists in an illegal act.

accomplice
A partner in an illegal act.

acknowledgment
An admission under oath that you performed a particular act.

acquittal
In criminal law, someone charged with an offense is acquitted when set free by court decision.

action
A lawsuit.

ad damnum
In pleading, "To the damage." The technical name of plaintiff's claimed money loss or damages.

additur
A court order applied when a jury verdict is too small giving the defendant a choice between a higher award or a new trial.

adjudication
Giving or pronouncing a judgment or decree. Also, the judgment given.

ad litem
Acting for this purpose only. For instance, a guardian ad litem usually represents a minor child for a specified purpose.

VII-1

Figure 5–9. First Page of the Glossary of a Court Employee's Orientation Manual (Courtesy of the State of Minnesota, Fourth Judicial District, District Court of Minnesota)

2. *Is it too technical?* If your material provides technical information not specifically needed by the reader of a particular section of text, relegate it to an appendix. But be sure to "call out" the reference within the text.

3. *Is it bulky?* Repetitive forms, lengthy examples, backup information, and computer printouts in quantity should all be confined to the appendixes to prevent the reader from turning page after page to get to the next portion of text.

SELECTING A NUMBERING SYSTEM

The next step in developing a manual is to select a numbering system for the individual chapters of the text.

Simple Alphabetical-Numerical

The simplest numbering system uses Arabic numbers in sequence, such as 1, 2, 3, and 4. Sometimes the more formal I, II, III, IV are used. Generally, combinations of Roman and Arabic numerals are used, alternately with upper and lower case letters, in the following sequence:

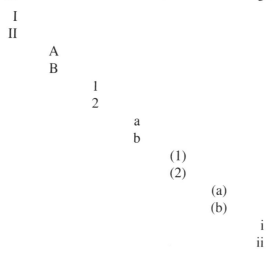

Other numbering systems are used for elaborate, extensive, or complex information, particularly that published in loose-leaf form. A simple arrangement is to assign blocks of numbers to several subjects and then to number individual instructions in sequence within these blocks. For example, 1000, 2000, 3000, and 4000. Within each block, it would be 1001, 1002, 1003, and 1004 in sequence up to 1999.

A further refinement is subdividing the blocks into 100s. For example, 1100, 1200, 1300, and 1400. Within each, the numbering would be 1101, 1102, 1103, and 1104, up to 1199. These numbers are used only to identify an instruction unit. The separate parts of subdivisions of the instruction unit are subnumbered by using the previously described alphabetical-numerical sequence or by additional numerals, such as 3103-1, 3103-2, etc., or 3103.1, 3103.2, etc. In these cases the number following the hyphen or period is the internal section number.

The use of block numbering for broad subject-classification may have countless variations. One system assigns a single digit to each of the major headings of an instruction, as 1, 2, 3, 4, etc., then adding digits as the material is subdivided. For example:

$$
\begin{array}{l}
1 \\
2 \\
3 \\
4
\end{array}
\longrightarrow
\left\{
\begin{array}{l}
3.1 \\
3.2 \\
3.3 \\
3.4
\end{array}
\right.
\longrightarrow
\left\{
\begin{array}{l}
3.3.1 \\
3.3.2 \\
3.3.3 \\
3.3.4
\end{array}
\right.
\longrightarrow
\left\{
\begin{array}{l}
3.3.3.1 \\
3.3.3.2 \\
3.3.3.3 \\
3.3.3.4
\end{array}
\right.
\longrightarrow
\left\{
\begin{array}{l}
3.3.3.3.1 \\
3.3.3.3.2 \\
3.3.3.3.3 \\
3.3.3.3.4
\end{array}
\right.
$$

This process can be continued indefinitely.

Open and Closed Numbering Systems

An open-end numbering system places no restrictions on the numbers of chapters in a manual or on the numbers of subdivisions in a single instruction. Thus, major headings in an instruction can be numbered from I to VIII or from I to XXV. The chief disadvantage of this system is that overlapping and confusion can result, particularly when making revisions or additions. Another disadvantage is that the reader's convenience of reference is reduced as the number of chapter headings increases.

The closed decimal system, which incorporates the basic concept of the well-known Dewey decimal system, limits all breakdowns of any one heading to a maximum of nine topical breakdowns and one general breakdown. Any of these breakdowns can be subdivided in turn, but in no case can there be any more than nine subdivisions of equivalent stature. The chief advantage of this system is that it compels the logical ordering and interrelating of information. By forcing additions or revisions to be made only at their logical places, conflicts or differences must be resolved. The very limitation of the system forces the grouping of related matter.

If your objective is merely to provide numbers for written material, use any open system; but if you need subject matter control with maximum flexibility for *internal* expansion, use the 100 or 1000 closed system.

Implementing the 100 or 1000 (Closed) System

To outline and number according to the 100 or 1000 system:

1. Devise a master subject outline. For each major topic, assign hundred-numbers 100 through 900, as needed. These are chapters of a single volume. In a multi-volume series, major subjects could be numbered I, II, III, IV, etc., and then subdivided.

2. Similarly, subdivide each chapter into subchapters to which ten numbers 10 through 90 are assigned, such as 110, 120, 130, etc.

3. Subdivide each subchapter into digit-numbers, by substituting a digit 1 through 9, as needed, for the zero. Thus 120 would be divided into 121, 122, 123, 124, etc.

4. Further subdivide by adding a decimal point followed by a series 1 through 9, continuing until three decimal digits are added, as in 123.451. Use a, b, c, d and (1), (2), (3), (4) sequences for final subdivision.

The following example illustrates the 100 system:

Chapter*	Subchapter	Section	Subsection	Paragraph	Paragraph
100	110	121	123.1	123.41	123.451
200	120	122	123.2	123.42	123.452
300	130	123	123.3	123.43	123.453
400	140	124	123.4	123.44	123.454
500	150	125	123.5	123.45	123.455
600	160	126	123.6	123.46	123.456
700	170	127	123.7	123.47	123.457
800	180	128	123.8	123.48	123.458
900	190	129	123.9	123.49	123.459

*Text references to a chapter would be to Chapter 1, 2, 3, etc., rather than to Chapter 100, 200, 300.

Figures 5-10 and 5-11 illustrate the operation of the closed decimal system.

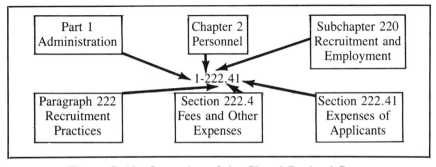

Figure 5–10. Operation of the Closed Decimal System

Contents—110 Employee & Labor Relations Manual

CONTENTS

Issue 3, 1-22--

Figure 5–11. A Three-Digit Numbering System—Contents Overview (Courtesy of the U.S. Postal Service)

Once you have selected a numbering system best suited to your document's specific needs, the next challenge is to develop an attractive, functional page.

PAGE DESIGN

Identification

In a loose-leaf manual, pages cannot follow a strict arithmetic sequence, because additions and deletions disturb the previous sequences. In place of ordinary page numbers, a well-designed manual uses the first or last text number on the page as the page identifier. (See Figure 5-12.)

Because pages are replaced, the reader must also be able to know whether the page is a current one. Therefore, date each page; if it is a revision page, show both the original and the revision dates. To help the reader locate a subject quickly, print the manual title and chapter, or other identifying captions, at the head or the foot of the page.

Pages ordinarily should be printed on both sides for economy and to minimize bulk in the manual. New chapters and subchapters usually begin on right-hand pages. In this way, the beginning of each subject has a distinct appearance, rather than being backed up to the end of a substantially different subject.

Layout

Page layout often ignores the most basic principles of readability; this is particularly true of procedural documentation. Yet proper layout helps to assure that the reader's attention will be drawn particularly to the meanings of each page. (Figures 5-13 through 5-16 illustrate various layouts of policies and procedures.)

There are basically three types of readers of technical communications: those who are methodical; those who skim; and those who read randomly. Methodical readers read all copy and take time to read any charts, graphs, and tables. Skim readers partially read a document but look for important items only. Random readers usually read the first paragraph and may or may not read subsequent paragraphs; it is difficult to predetermine the focus of random readers.

With this in mind, target your message toward skim readers, using the following guidelines to help maintain their interest:

• *Use white space.* The area on which no printing appears on the page is crucial. A lack of white space—involving narrow margins, or no

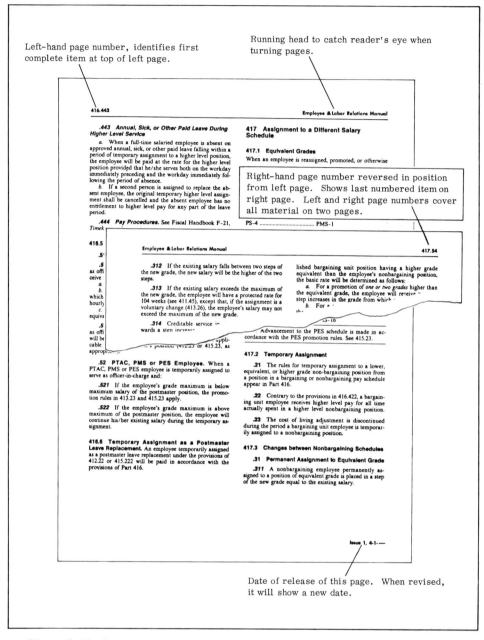

Figure 5–12. Design of a Loose-Leaf Page (Courtesy of the U.S. Postal Service)

	NO. C1:00:01
POLICY & PROCEDURE	REV.
	DATE 8/—
	PAGE 3 of 5

PUBLICATION STANDARDS FOR POLICIES AND PROCEDURES

PURPOSE

It is the purpose of this procedure to outline the steps required to publish   policies and procedures.

SCOPE

This policy and procedure is to be implemented for Operations.

POLICY

Only policies and procedures processed in accordance with methods set forth in this procedure will be included in the Policy and Procedure Manual.

PROCEDURE

Responsibility		Action
REQUESTOR	1.	Completes rough draft using suggested format (Attachment A) of documentation with necessary exhibits and form completion requirements.
	2.	Reviews with supervisor for preliminary approval.
SUPERVISOR	3.	Initials and dates approved rough draft.
REQUESTOR	4.	Completes Documentation Request form. (See Attachment B)
	5.	Forwards Documentation Request with rough draft to: Policy and Procedure Administrator,
POLICY AND PROCEDURE ADMINISTRATOR	6.	Reviews documentation for adherence to publishing standards.
	7.	Forwards draft to Senior Word Processing Secretary and/or artist for completion of finished draft.

Figure 5–13. Policy and Procedure Page Layout (Divisional Manual of a Major Manufacturer)

PERSONNEL POLICIES AND PROCEDURES
A — Introduction

1. INTRODUCTION

- This Personnel Policies and Procedures Manual reflects an up-dating of GF's present philosophy for managing. It recognizes the changing environmental influences on managerial values, concepts and organizational behavior. The mission for Personnel and the approach to human resources reflect concern for people as well as achievement of a successful and profitable business.

  The manual is written with reference to United States laws and regulations. It is intended that International and Canadian Units apply it with the adjustments necessary for their own operations. Domestic subsidiary units should conform to this manual, making necesary adjustments with the approval of the Personnel Policy Committee.

2. PURPOSE

Personnel Mission

- The mission of the Personnel function is "To lead the organization in the management of its people in their work so GF will prosper and grow and employees will achieve their goals with satisfaction."

GF Creed

- GF is committed to building a work environment in which people can enjoy high standards of health, express their needs, and develop and apply their skills productively through meaningful work to achieve personal and company goals. Therefore . . . .

  GF Management Believes Employees:

  - Want and are entitled to meaningful work and an opportunity to achieve.

  - Want to and will be recognized on the basis of their performance and potential without discrimination.

  - Should be compensated on the basis of performance and results.

  - Need and are entitled to feedback on quality of their performance.

  - Should be informed promptly about company matters which concern them.

Page 1   October 19—

Figure 5–14. Page Layout of a Personnel Policies and Procedures Manual
(Courtesy of General Foods Corporation)

VII
PERSONAL TIME, HOLIDAYS, AND VACATIONS

Time-off policies are influenced by the needs of employees, business requirements, and current practices in the business community. Because these influences change, our time-off practices are periodically adjusted.

THE PERSONAL TIME PROGRAM

Time away from work which is not Sick Leave or Vacation is reported as Personal Time. The Vacation Program, which permits accrued time and use of time in units as small as one half day, will usually meet the needs of most employees. However, Personal Time is available to all salaried employees, subject to the qualifications below:

• UNPAID—Unpaid personal time up to two weeks for one absence may be granted by a Department Head or his or her designated representative. This decision will take into consideration the work schedule of the department and the attendance and performance of the employee. Unpaid personal time over two weeks for one absence requires advance Personnel-Administration Department approval. Unpaid personal time cannot exceed four consecutive weeks.

★• PAID—ENTITLEMENT

Required short-term (up to 4 weeks) Military Service—Up to five days per calendar year.

Duty as a Municipal Election Official—Up to one day.

Jury Duty—The necessary time away from the office.

Citizenship Papers—Up to one day.

Court Attendance As A Witness, Plaintiff or Defendant—Up to one day.

Pall Bearer—Up to one day.

Wedding Of A Relative—Up to one day.

Funeral Of A Relative—For death in the immediate family, the Company will pay for any absence up to a maximum of three days. "Immediate Family" includes (in addition to spouse) only the brother, sister, parent, child or child's spouse, of employee or employee's spouse. For death of other members of an employee's or spouse's family, the Company will pay up to one day.

Only the necessary time away from work for the above causes will be paid for, up to the maximums. If time beyond the limit is needed, vacation or unpaid personal time may be used.

★• PAID—DISCRETIONARY

Apart from the above, absences of two days or less to meet unusual or emergency needs of an employee may be paid for at the discretion of a Department Head or his or her designated representative. This decision will take into consideration the reason for the absence, the employee's attendance record (including paid personal time previously granted), performance, and the availability of current or accrued vacation.

Discretionary paid time may not be granted in conjunction with paid or unpaid Sick Leave, Vacation, Unpaid Personal Time, or Entitlement Paid Personal Time.

When time away from work is more than two consecutive days, no part of the absence may be paid for under this Discretionary section.

Departments are responsible for reporting all Personal Time absences of one half day or more (except time spent on Jury Duty), paid or unpaid, in the same manner as Sick Leave absences.

THE PERSONAL PASS PRIVILEGE

The Personal Pass privilege provides time off when the purpose is wholly personal and requires only an hour or two.

This policy also applies to time off for participation in Club activities.

I. Generally, the pass privilege provides for an absence from the office of an hour or less. If an employee attends a wedding or a funeral, up to two hours may be permitted.

Each department is authorized to grant this time off, and is responsible for its control.

II. When the time off is overstayed, and an employee is absent for a full work session, it is

Figure 5–15. Page Layout of a Supervisor's Handbook (A Major Insurance Company)

A 84

ATTENDANCE

I. POLICY

Employees are expected to be regular in attendance and prompt in reporting for work. Promptness and regularity are factors in earning promotions and merit increases.

Excused absences, with or without pay, may be granted to employees in accordance with practices below.

Employees are not paid for avoidable and unexcused absences. Continued unauthorized or excessive absences are considered cause for disciplinary action.

II. PRACTICES

A. RECORDING ATTENDANCE

Exceptional weather or conditions beyond employee's control may cause occasional tardiness. Such cases are dealt with fairly.

1. SALARIED EMPLOYEES

   a. All employees not exempt from the overtime provisions of the Fair Labor Standards Act must record their daily attendance and hours worked on Time Reports provided for this purpose. Instructions for preparation appear on the Time Report (7261▓▓▓).

   b. For control purposes, a record of employees' attendance is kept by a time checker. In the absence of a time checker, each department head should furnish the office or the personnel manager with a memorandum of attendance of the employees under the department head's direction.

2. WAGE EMPLOYEES

   a. Where time clocks are provided, employees register their own time on a clock card as they enter and leave the plant. Employees are not permitted to punch the time clock card more than 10 minutes before the regular starting time, and they must punch out within 10 minutes after the regular quitting time. In case overtime work is authorized, the employee must punch out within 10 minutes after the completion of such overtime. This will effect substantial agreement between the time indicated on the clock card and the record of account distribution of time worked, which is approved by the supervisor and is used as the basic record for payroll computations.

   b. Where time clocks are not provided, the employee is required to record by hand the hours worked on a facsimile clock card or daily time slip. This card or slip is turned in to the time clerk for comparison with the supervisor's records of hours worked or is approved by the supervisor.

   c. Normally, any employee coming to work more than 10 minutes late will start work only on the next quarter hour and will be paid accordingly.

B. REPORTING ABSENCES

1. Each supervisor should make certain that employees understand they must notify the supervisor promptly whenever they will be absent for any reason.

2. If an employee is absent without notice, the absence should be promptly investigated by the supervisor.

C. EXCUSED ABSENCE

1. ILLNESS OR INJURY

   See Sick Leave S 40

2. PERSONAL

   Employees with good attendance records may be allowed reasonable time off for moving, weddings, funerals, special religious holidays, medical treatment, and other important personal needs that cannot be handled outside of working hours.

1-1- –

Figure 5–16. Page Layout of a Personnel Policies and Procedures Manual
(A Major Food Processor)

space between paragraphs or lists—is an affront to the reader and produces an unfriendly atmosphere. The cost of paper is almost always less than the cost of a reader's time. Very rarely should it be a determining factor in producing a readable document.

- *Limit line length to 65 (typewritten) characters.* Studies have shown that normal eye movement makes it difficult to easily scan a width of more than 5 to 5½ inches.

- *Block-indent various levels of information.* This helps readers to grasp information quickly and to picture relationships among different elements.

- *Limit paragraph length to seven or eight lines.*

- *Use headings.* Headings serve a dual purpose. Aside from breaking up the monotony of the page, headings provide a running index to the contents of the text. Varying the typography of headings shows the relative importance of material.

- *Use illustrations.*

- *Stay away from fine print or photographic reduction.* Both are offensive and automatically cut down on readability.

Readability is also affected by the style, arrangement, or appearance of typeset matter. When designing *text* material avoid ultra bold type, expanded type, condensed type, or light type. Other guidelines include the following:

- Very heavy typefaces tend to create a depressing mood.
- Script typefaces have a light and somewhat social appearance.
- Italics are less straightforward than Roman and are viewed as less businesslike.
- Very light types convey a mood of "fun."
- Tables of figures and statistics can be produced most effectively in sans serif typefaces.

The longer the line length, the larger the typeface should be. However, 12-point type is the largest which should be used in text material, with 10 point the most readable of all.

Typefaces can be mixed for highlighting purposes but not merely to provide variety. Boldface or italics should be used only briefly to highlight parts of a message. Some graphics designers advocate using no more than two typefaces per page; others say two typefaces plus variations—boldface and italic—can be used.

6

Review, Trial Usage, and Approvals

A final check for authenticity, prior to preparing draft material for the printer, involves three steps: document review, trial usage, and approvals. At this stage, an ounce of prevention is worth a pound of cure, especially when the ailment could be incorrect or misleading data, incomplete data, or unworkable data. Failure to correct any of these elements could result in expensive reprinting and shipping costs, as well as loss of time.

THE REVIEW CYCLE

The first step is the review cycle, a procedure for obtaining confirmation of information provided by primary sources. The review cycle is necessary to coordinate viewpoints and to resolve differences at subordinate levels. During this procedure you will receive additional ideas from reviewers, including some suggestions you may not have anticipated.

Consideration for the review cycle should actually begin early in the preparation and planning process. One person should be made responsible not only for writing a given document in the first place but also for revising and fine-tuning it later. If at all possible, this person should be identified on all versions of the document—both to acknowledge authorship and to identify responsibility. If you avoid anonymity in document production, you will gain consistency and efficiency throughout the various writing, editing, review, and approval cycles of your project.

In planning for the review process, consider the following guidelines:

- Writers and reviewers should agree beforehand about *areas of responsibility*. Is the overall organization of the document up for grabs? Or is the review process just to confirm accuracy of the draft?

- *Schedules* should include adequate time for review and correction. Perhaps as much as 50 percent of total project elapsed time should be set aside for this purpose.

- *Outlines* should be reviewed and approved before the actual writing begins. And these outlines should be more or less frozen before documentation production is well under way.

- The *review process* should be in two steps: the first for overall organization and content and the second for detail.

Ideally, the review process should involve only the writer and those who provided the information. Reviewers should discuss all changes with the writer, and explain why the changes need to be made. Reviewers should focus on accuracy, not on style. Style is a matter of personal preference; as long as the reader's interests and objectives are being served, style should not be a matter for concern. Comments should be positive; the writer should be told what was done correctly as well as what needs to be changed.

After all primary data sources have reviewed your document and their changes have been incorporated, you can mark the text "final draft." The next step is making sure that what you've written actually works.

TRIAL USAGE

One of the most overlooked activities in the total scheme of publishing a management communication is trial usage. Just a simple walkthrough of a new directive, procedure, or "how-to" description by a non-involved employee, or even a writer's spouse or friend, could save countless dollars that are often spent to correct incomplete, ambiguous, or incorrect information. And these dollars are lost not only in printing of corrected pages but also in additional postage for mailing and wasted time by recipients in updating their documents.

To verify that your information "works," ask your trial usage "guinea pig" to read and perform each step precisely as written. If something goes wrong along the way, or is unclear or ambiguous, this test should reveal the shortcoming; thus you can provide the needed "fix" prior to the embarrassment of having a high-level approval person catch it—or even worse, a reader—after it's been published. By incorporating trial usage into your standard review and approval cycles, you ensure:

- Workability—your reader can do what it says, the first time through.

- Understanding—all meanings are clear, with no ambiguities.
- Completeness—every step is included.
- Time and cost savings—no need for recall.

Following a successful walk-through, you're ready for the final step in this sequence—approvals.

APPROVALS

Obtaining approvals—agreement of those responsible for information dissemination—is one of the most difficult aspects of the instruction-preparing process. The objectives of approval are to:

1. Refer proposed policy and procedural materials to interested officials whose comments contribute to the formulation of effective proposals.
2. Assure top officers that full staff input is represented in materials submitted.
3. Submit any unresolved differences for top level determination.

Apart from the importance of obtaining the actual constructive views and suggestions of other people in the organization, the approval process enables you to obtain their acquiescence to the new policies or procedures. New directives which are released to those who must abide by them are not accepted quite as readily as when they are the results of participation by those people through their representative officers. This is a very important consideration which should be understood by management long before the writing process begins.

Approval Systems

The three most prevalent methods of obtaining approval are conference, sequential, and concurrent. Whichever approval method you select depends upon the necessity for reaching responsible organizations quickly and obtaining their views with a minimum of delay. Each is applicable in specific circumstances.

Conference Approval—Approval of materials through conference is suggested when the subjects are complex or involve significant new policy. The conference brings out useful information that does not occur through written approval. It brings conflicts into focus and in some cases serves as a means for resolving them. The usual disadvantages of conferences apply: (1) they are time consuming; (2) participants are frequently not prepared for discussion; (3) individual personalities, particularly those of top executives, tend to dominate; and (4) nothing seems to be accomplished.

To a great extent, these disadvantages can be overcome. A skillful conference leader can keep the discussion on track, avoid debates over language, and restrict the conference to substance alone. In addition, discussion drafts can be sent to all participants for review prior to the conference. (Too much time should not be allowed, since materials may be forgotten or set aside.) After the conference, a draft of agreed-upon material can be prepared for formal written approval; conflicts which were unresolved can be presented as alternatives.

Sequence Approval—Another commonly used method is to circulate one copy of a proposal in sequence from one name to the next on the list of approval officers. Each person approves or comments as appropriate. If time is not important, the sequence method has the advantage of collecting all approvals on a single approval form for ready references.

This technique, however, has four disadvantages. First, the method is time consuming. Second, the sense of responsibility of each recipient is weakened; those listed at the top may rely on subsequent approvals, while those listed toward the bottom may assume that adequate review has already been made. Third, when approval comments are made, those yet to make approval tend to rule on the comments rather than to concentrate on the original material. Fourth, the same process must be repeated when materials require reapproval.

Concurrent Written Approval—When timing is important, an individual copy of the proposed material can be sent concurrently to each of the organizational units, with reasonable time limits indicated for review and return. This has the advantages of speed and of fixing individual responsibility; its disadvantage is the creation of a bulky approval file.

Approval Mechanics

Do not send materials automatically to a standard approval list. For example, an approval delay with legal counsel is not warranted unless the legal interests of the organization are clearly involved. Approval must be obtained from those having a bona fide interest in the proposed material if they (1) would take some form of action as a result; (2) would be affected by the adoption of the proposed policy or procedure; (3) are technical authorities on the subject matter involved; or (4) are administratively or legally responsible for making a review.

Developing an Approval Document—Material to be distributed should be typewritten, with double or triple spacing and ample margins to allow room for written comments. An approval document should allow space for:

1. The organizational unit name to which it is being addressed and the name of each person responsible for approval.
2. Transmittal date.
3. Identification of transmitted material.
4. The name, room number, and telephone number of the person who wrote the material.
5. Special remarks, such as the reason for proposing the material; perhaps a synopsis of the material; relationship to other materials; the materials to be superseded, supplemented, or revised; a description of any attachments; and the names of the units involved in approving the proposal.
6. The deadline for returning the material.
7. Approval action and signature.

If possible, deliver approval material by hand; it saves time and precludes a claim that the material was lost in the mail.

Establishing Deadlines—Set a deadline for returning the material that allows enough time for adequate review but is short enough to discourage any tendency to set it aside. The deadline provision of the transmittal might read as follows: ''Please return this material with your action no later than the date specified. If not received by that date, concurrence will be assumed, unless arrangements have been made for additional time.''

Request the return of all copies regardless of whether the reviewer approved, disapproved, modified, or indicated no comment. Confirm by memorandum any extensions of time for approval that are granted and include a polite reminder that action must continue regardless of whether there is approval compliance.

Approval Factors—Approvals should be confined to substance rather than words, and then within the limits of responsibility. Unless the document requires legal wording, the writing is the responsibility of the drafting manager. This minimizes the potential areas of dispute. If there are differences, the central staff manager should assume this responsibility.

When approval comments are received, consider the following:

1. Are comments in line with the responsibility of the office making them or are they gratuitous?

2. Are the comments relevant, significant, and accurate?

3. Are the suggestions for inclusion sufficiently detailed or too detailed?

4. Are the remarks authoritative?

Next, decide on the treatment of these comments, being careful to insert only those items which are relevant. If there are conflicting suggestions, either obtain agreement among the differing parties—through conference or direct negotiation—or, as a last choice, present the matter for a decision by a higher decision-making level. If a draft of material is substantially changed as a result of approval, obtain approval again. In this case, approval should be obtained only from those offices having a functional interest in the specific changes or new material.[1]

When your "final draft" is truly final, you're ready to go to the production process, covered in the next chapter.

[1]An example of one company's method of obtaining final approval on a typeset document using a proof copy form is shown in Figure 7-4, Chapter 7, p. 107.

7

The Production Process

Most of the hard word is now over. The material has been written, edited, and approved. And now you're ready for the final steps: copy preparation and printing.

PREPARING COPY FOR REPRODUCTION

In many instances typewritten copy is just as acceptable as typeset text as long as the completed document accurately presents the facts in a logical and orderly manner and the pages are neat and attractive. Type-written copy is generally reproduced on standard letter-sized sheets. For small quantities, documents may be photocopied, printed on a small in-house machine, or sent outside to a quick-service economy printer. Pages are then assembled with a single or double staple or punched to go into a loose-leaf binder.

Typing Tips

In preparing typewritten copy for reproduction, the following items should be considered:

Paper—Paper should be white, unlined bond (8-1/2 × 11 inches), of substantial weight, and typed on only one side. Duplicated copies must be easy to read; unreadable copy is of little use of anyone.

Margins—Guide sheets can be used to help the typist set margins. One kind is preprinted in nonreproducible blue ink. Material is typed right over the blue and, when the sheet is printed or photocopied, the blue disappears, leaving only the typed material. Another type (see Special Guide Sheet[1] in Figure 7-1) is ruled with a dark pen; the ruled guide is placed behind each blank sheet to be typed. To use the Special Guide Sheet, follow these directions:

1. The short line at the top right and the short line at the bottom of the sheet indicate the positions of the page number. When the page number appears at the top of the page, the top of the number should touch the short line. When the page number appears at the bottom of the page, the bottom of the number should touch the line. These lines are 1/2 inch from the top and the bottom of the sheet.

2. The vertical rule at the left indicates the left margin of the copy; it is 1-1/2 inches from the left edge of the page. This margin includes 1/2 inch for binding.

3. The vertical rule at the right indicates the right margin of the copy; it is one inch from the right edge of the page. The right margin should be as even as possible. Not more than two or three letters should extend beyond this right vertical line. It is acceptable to divide words between appropriate syllables, but the trend is to avoid this whenever possible. Avoid having more than two consecutive lines end with a hyphenated word; never end a page with a hyphenated word. Do not syllabicate for one- or two-letter syllables at the beginning or end of a word.

4. The two horizontal lines at the top, one inch and two inches, respectively, from the top edge of the paper, indicate the upper margins for the copy. The lower of these two lines is used only for the first page of a part of the document, such as a preface, a memo of transmittal, a table of contents, or a chapter. The upper margin is for the second and subsequent pages of a part. The typed letters should touch but not extend above the appropriate margin.

A typing guide for differing levels of headings is shown in Figure 7-2.

Spacing—Single spacing is the rule for typing final documents.

Pagination—Each page of the document except the title page should be numbered. Lower case Roman numbers are used for preliminary pages; Arabic numbers are used for pages in the body of the document.[2]

---

[1]Reprinted with permission from Erwin M. Keithley and Philip J. Schreiner, *A Manual of Style for the Preparation of Papers and Reports* (Cincinnati: South-Western Publishing Co., 1980). Erwin Keithley is Professor Emeritus—Business Administration, University of California, Los Angeles, Calif. Philip Schreiner is Professor of Speech Communication, California State University, Fullerton, Calif.

[2]See also "Selecting a Numbering System," Chapter 5, p. 81.

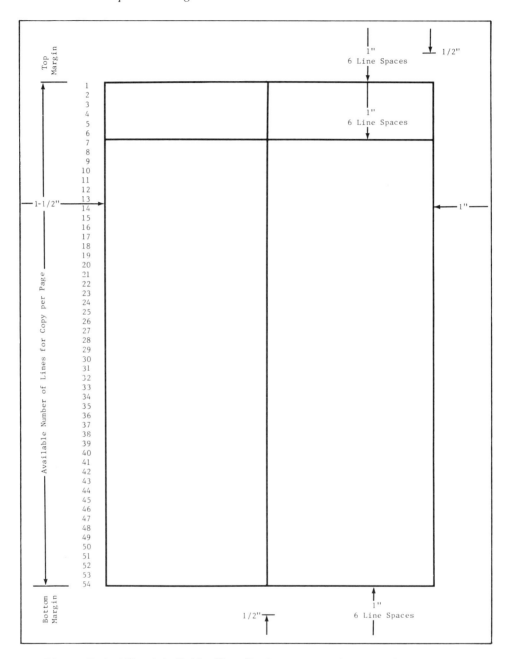

Figure 7–1. "Special Guide Sheet" (Courtesy Erwin M. Keithley, Philip J. Schreiner and South-Western Publishing Co.)

ACCOUNTING SYMBOLS AND TITLES   121

CHAPTER 1

CHAPTER TITLE

110 ALL CAPS

111 Initial Caps

     Text blocked under heading

112 Initial Caps

     112.1 Initial Caps

            Text blocked under heading

     112.2 Initial Caps

            .21 Initial Caps

                 Text blocked under heading

            .22 Initial Caps

                 Text blocked under heading

                 .221 Initial Caps

                       Text blocked under heading

                 .222 Initial Caps

                       Text blocked under heading

113 Initial Caps

     113.1 The use of headings at the section level (and below) is
            optional, but consistency is required for all sections
            in the same grouping. That is, since 113.1 has no head-
            ing, there should be no headings for 113.2, 113.3, etc.
            A section that has no heading cannot be subdivided.

120 ALL CAPS

121 Initial Caps

Figure 7–2. Typing Guide Incorporating Three-Digit Numbering System

Word Processing

In organizations equipped with word processing the task of preparing camera-ready copy is greatly simplified. The newer systems provide automatic pagination, automatic formatting, centering, justification (for even margins), and sorting, to name a few. Some of the latest equipment even provides automatic indexing using "key words," and then prints out a final index of all key words, listing every page number on which they appear.[3]

Another new trend allows typesetting organizations to convert word-processing magnetic tapes or "floppy disks" (that contain stored material) directly to phototypesetting input, thus creating professional phototypeset copy without entering the copy (or keyboarding) from scratch.

PREPARING COPY FOR THE PRINTER

Much of what has been described up to now in this chapter relates to standard short-run office duplicating. Any departure from the straightforward type of material into the realm of pamphlets, special handbooks, large quantities, and special typesetting calls for expert guidance. There are so many details to know about paper, type styles and sizes, binding, printing photos and illustrations, cover stock, and bindery operations.

The first step is to call in a printing company representative or an in-house printing consultant and explain what is needed. The printing representative can provide many valuable suggestions for proceeding as economically as possible. Once the details have been worked out with the printer, and the size and the number of pages have been decided, prepare copy for submission. Usually, there are some limits which either will determine how much copy can be given to the printer to fit within the allotted space or which will determine the size of the type to be used, if the copy is to be typeset. Two important rules to keep in mind are:

1. The draft given to the printer should be as final as possible, containing every possible anticipated correction.

2. Measure the copy before it is set in type. Do not try to expand or contract or cut things out afterwards.

All corrections made on the printer's proofs are charged to the originator rather than to the printer, unless the printer happens to make an error. Originator corrections are called "author's alterations." The charges for these are much heavier than for straight typesetting. Accordingly, go

[3]See "Advantages of Word Processing," p. 51.

over all the copy as carefully as possible before it is sent to the printer. If possible, have the copy edited independently by someone who will check it completely, not only for spelling and grammar but also for such things as uniformity of style, punctuation, capitalization, names, dates, and special style standards for technical terms.

A simple way to estimate copy measure in advance is to type it directly on guide sheets which are set up to provide the same number of typewritten characters per line as will come out of the final printed copy. This will, of course, be governed by the size and the leading of the type the printer will use.

Another technique for measuring copy to fit involves the following steps:

1. Draw a vertical line on the right-hand edge of the copy at the point where there is an average length of typewritten line. Take the count of this average line.

2. Count the number of lines of copy and multiply it by the average count of characters per line. Assume this is 60 characters per line and there are 24 lines of copy on the page; this would provide a total of 1440 characters.

3. Obtain the character count per pica of the typeface to be used as well as the measure (or width) of the printed column. (Assume, for this example, that there are 2.8 characters per pica and that there are 24 picas to the column of 4 inches.) Now multiply 2.8 by 24 and obtain 67.2, which is rounded to 67. Divide 1440 by 67 to obtain 21.5 or 22 lines.

4. To estimate how many inches in depth will be covered by the typewritten copy, find the number of lines per inch for the specific type to be used on the base on which it is to be set, whether solid or leaded. Assume, in this case, the 10-point type on a 12-point base, which would provide 6 lines per inch. Divide this into 22 and obtain 3-2/3 inches.

How to Talk Your Printer's Language

You'll be wise to familiarize yourself with the following basic printing terms and measurements: pica and point. It'll save you time and money and will simplify matters when you wish to enlarge or reduce the size of a line of type, or figure out how deep a given block of copy will be.

This line is one point thick.

■

This represents the thickness of 12 points, which equal one pica.

▬▬▬▬▬▬

This line, which is the thickness of 12 points, or one pica, is 6 picas long. It is also one inch long, which means that 6 picas equal one inch.

And, since 12 points equal one pica, 6 picas equal 72 points. Thus, a line 2 inches long measures 12 picas; 3 inches long, 18 picas.

Ordinarily, type size is specified by giving its depth only, which is measured in points. Since there are 72 points to the inch, a 6-point type is 6/72 of an inch in depth. Twelve lines of this size type set solid would take up one inch.

An effective way to increase readability is to use leading. A lead (pronounced led) is simply a measurement of the space between two lines of type. For example:

> These lines are set 6-point solid.
> These lines are set 6-point solid.
>
> These lines are set 6-point, leaded 1-point
> These lines are set 6-point, leaded 1-point.
>
> These lines are set 6-point, leaded 2-points.
> These lines are set 6-point, leaded 2-points.

Starting from 6 point up to 14 point, most type is graduated by 2 points. From 14 to 18 point, the jump is 4 points; from 18 to 48 point, the increase is by 6 points. From 48 up to 96 point, the interval is 12 points.

Not all types are available in all sizes. And some type faces are available in 7, 9, and 11 point sizes. Type up to and including 14 point in size is commonly called body type; type above 14 point is called display or headline type.

Here are a few additional suggestions to follow in preparing copy for the printer. There are reasons for all of them and careful adherence to them will result in less confusion and lower cost:

1. Type your copy, double-spaced, on one side of 8-1/2 × 11-inch sheets of paper, preferably white.

2. Allow margins wide enough for notations by the editor or the printer—at least one inch on the sides, top, and bottom of the page.

3. Number all pages consecutively on the top, preferably in the center, with the word ''end'' on the last page. Copy is sometimes given to two or more typesetters so the numerical sequence will help keep the job together without confusion.

4. Keep a copy for reference and safety.

5. Give the printer instructions on indentations, spacing, and any other unique arrangements, in addition to full typographic specifications.

The Pagination Sheet

A pagination sheet ensures that information about your publication is accurately conveyed to the printer. Figure 7-3 illustrates a typical pagination sequence form. It is helpful when you are printing material on both the front and back sides of each page (called back-to-back printing); it makes sure the printer will match the correct sets of pages as they are printed. It also serves as a guide in collating pages in the correct order.

Blank pages are indicated by an ''x.'' Odd-numbered pages should always be printed on the front side of a sheet (right-hand page when a publication is opened); even-numbered pages are printed on the back side of the sheet (left-hand side of the open publication). Special pages, such as heavy stock dividers or tabs, should also be entered on the pagination sheet to ensure that they are collated in their correct sequence.

Proof Copies

Before the printer puts your publication ''to bed'' (onto the printing press), you should get a proof copy of all your pages for final approval. This is a photographic preprint of each page in its actual printing size, incorporating typeset copy, line art, and illustrations in their appropriate relationship. The proof copy enables you to make any last-minute changes in wording, type size, or artwork.

Remember, however, that any changes at this point will be most expensive, since layout and makeup are involved as well as the basic typesetting corrections.

To ensure that final proof is properly reviewed by the responsible department, you may wish to have a ''one-final-pass'' proof copy approval form. Onan Company of Minneapolis developed a Proof Copy form (Figure 7-4) to obtain release approval for its technical documents, procedures, and policies. The form is generally sent to managers of various departments, who are in turn responsible for the document's technical accuracy, content, and merit as seen from the area of their expertise. ''The Proof Copy form,'' says the Document Administrator, ''has been very successful for Onan and is an integral part of an elaborate system of Engineering document development and control.''

CONTROL DATA CORPORATION

PAGINATION SEQUENCE

PAGE

TITLE	SECTION		PRINTING REQ. NO.
ORIGINATOR	PUB. NO.	REV.	DATE

FRONT	FRONT COVER	TITLE PAGE	TABLE OF CONTENTS	1	3
BACK	X	X	X	2	4
FRONT	5	7	9	X	
BACK	6	8	10	BACK COVER	
FRONT					
BACK					
FRONT					
BACK					
FRONT					
BACK					
FRONT					
BACK					
FRONT					
BACK					

ALL PAGES AT ______ % UNLESS OTHERWISE INDICATED.

KEY

K = KEYLINE HT/WO = HALFTONE W/OVERLAY
LA = LINE ART N = NEGATIVE SUPPLIED
HT = HALFTONE P = PLATE SUPPLIED

HALFTONES: ______________
WITH ____________ OVERLAYS

AA2453 REV 1 - –

PRINTED IN U.S.A.

Figure 7–3. Pagination Sequence Form (Courtesy of Control Data Corporation)

Proof Copy

Date _____

Route to:

Department	Name	Department	Name
_____		_____	
_____		_____	
_____		_____	
_____		_____	

The document listed below is ready to be published:

Document No. _____   Draft Date _____

Document Title _____

Please review the attached proof copy and make any necessary changes in red pencil or ink and initial all changes. Keep in mind that any change affecting content or format will seriously delay the project and require re-scheduling.

☐ A review meeting is scheduled for _____ , _____ , _____ at _____ PM in the

      Day   Month   Year   AM

_____ conference room for the purpose of discussing any changes to this document.
Please plan to attend or appoint someone to represent you at this meeting. Bring the attached proof copy along with you and be prepared to discuss any changes.
Failure to attend this meeting signifies that the attached proof copy meets your approval and will be published.

☐ No review meeting is scheduled.   Return this proof copy & letter to the RD&D Documentation Dept before _____ . If significant comments are received and a review meeting is scheduled, you will be notified.

☐ Proof OK as is   ☐ Proof OK with changes

Signature _____   Date _____
             Department Manager

Form 8B157

Figure 7–4. Proof Copy Approval Form (Courtesy of Onan Company)

8

Distribution, Updating, and Reader Feedback

The final steps to be considered in developing and publishing a managerial communication are distribution, updating, and reader feedback. The first two are vital in helping you to reach appropriate readers in a timely fashion. The third element—reader feedback—is essential in helping you to plan for future updates.

DISTRIBUTION

Even before you can print your documents, you have to know how they'll be distributed. Will it be by hand or through the mail? And how will you keep track of what's out there? When planning the distribution system, be sure to consider the following elements:

1. Names of those who receive materials.
2. Maintenance and control of your mailing list.
3. Actual delivery of the materials.
4. Control of distributed manuals.
5. Maintenance of the reserve supply.

Audience Selection

In the average organization, the variety of procedural releases makes it necessary to set up an appropriate system for distributing the releases in sufficient quantity only to those who actually use them. If they are distributed promiscuously, employees tend to disregard even those which are relevant. Most large organizations distribute releases on a ''need-to-know'' basis.

In a small organization it is probably simplest to send all general procedural materials to the same list. In a large organization, however, you may need to set up separate distribution lists for each part of a basic loose-leaf manual and for each type of circular release. If there is a separate system of orders or circulars, you might combine a standard distribution list with supplementary distributions, basing the need for additional distribution on the actual need-to-know of the intended recipients. Questions such as the following need to be answered: What is the purpose and the significance of the directive? Who is affected? Who is receiving related instructions? Who is operating under previously released instructions and now needs to know about changes? What is the technical activity and where are affected technicians located? Whose mission or function is related to this instruction?

Mailing Lists, Delivery Methods, and Reserve Supplies

Mailing lists should be checked frequently to make sure they correspond with changes in organization, personnel, and location. The need for changes can be minimized by addressing releases to organizational units rather than individuals, especially when a quantity is to be sent to the same point. Periodically, the entire list should be reviewed to detect any unreported changes.

Normal distribution channels can handle materials intended for local delivery within the organization. Field office materials can either be mailed or shipped. If large quantities of printed materials are to be sent to field offices, it may be preferable to send master copies for local reproduction. To keep track of changes in address and quantity, a return receipt addressed to the issuing office may be sent with each shipment to a field office.

Reserve supplies, over and above the mailing-list requirements, are usually maintained by a publications distribution unit. This unit also maintains a reserve stock of currently complete loose-leaf manuals and sets of circulars with which to fill special order requests. The materials for special order requests are collated before mailing, usually by the stockroom.

Improving Distribution Methods

In an effort to cut costs, companies are looking for ways to economize in distribution practices and still meet the requirements of getting information to those who need it. The following examples show how two companies have improved their distribution methods.

Union Carbide Corporation

Plagued with the problem of distributing some 75 manuals with a total of 15,000 pages, UCC devised a pilot electronic system,[1] limiting the project to manuals concerned with corporate policy, employee relations, and standard practice instructions. The final concept was to classify information into three broad categories (see Figure 8-1): (1) Major Information Area (MIA); (2) Designated Information Areas (DIA); and (3) Base Units (BU).

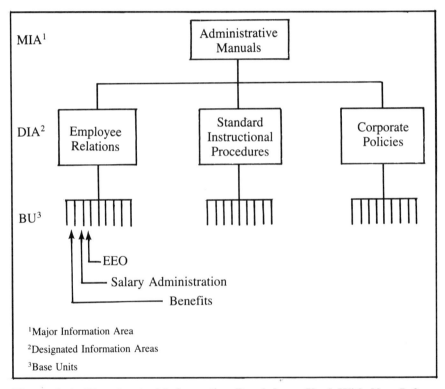

Figure 8–1. Flowchart of Information Breakdown Used With New Information System at Union Carbide Corporation (Reprinted with permission of UCC and Office Publications, Inc.)

[1]Adapted with permission from Brian M. Cluer, "Automating the Distribution of Information in Company Manuals," *The Office,* February, 1978. Mr. Cluer is the manager of Prepress Operations, Printing & Literature Distribution, UCC Marketing Services.

According to Brian M. Cluer:

"Immediate benefits were that mailing lists could be culled and restructured with information requirements. Duplicated information could be eliminated. The major payoff and key to the whole system would come in handling the base units. Under the old procedure, a request for information could be answered only by supplying the complete copy of the manual (DIA). Under the new system, each Base Unit would be supplied as an independent entity. For example, if a manager needs information on benefits, he or she can request the base unit instead of the entire employee relations section. For the next problem, which was to tell the manager what information is available, we designed an information catalog that lists subjects alphabetically. To receive a base unit, the requester marks the appropriate box and returns the catalog. With this system, preprinting manual pages is eliminated in many cases. Information for which demand is low is printed or photocopied in small quantities. Collation is eliminated.

"This, in outline, was the new approach adopted for handling the information.

"While limited in scope, this project proved that paperwork can be cut about one-third and substantial savings made in printing, binding and mailing."

Control Data Corporation

Of the more than 100 policy and procedure manuals that govern the actions of Control Data Corporation's 60,000 employees, the most important is the Corporate Policies and Procedures Manual. This 800-page document, bound in two three-ring binders, is distributed worldwide to all vice presidents and general managers.

Although it is primarily used by managers, the cost of making the total document available on such a widespread basis would be prohibitive. Thus Control Data was faced with two difficult alternatives: either require that managers use their general manager's copy—not always accessible because of meetings or others using it—or issue the complete document for all managers—a real waste of dollars because their day-to-day questions could be answered by fewer than one quarter of the total pages in the overall manual.

To solve the impasse, a third approach was selected: publishing only the most frequently used Personnel Policies and Procedures in a 250-page permanently bound book with a soft cover and updating it every six months to keep it current. What's more, with the permanently bound document, there was no problem of updating, as all the revised pages were automatically included. After incorporating this approach several years ago, Control Data has found excellent acceptance of the smaller manager's manual. And all managers have the answers to the most frequently asked questions right at their fingertips, at a fraction of the cost of the total book.

UPDATING ORGANIZATIONAL MANUALS

Because instructions need change almost from the moment they are written, a number of "housekeeping" activities are necessary to keep the system current. These include:

- Publishing checklists of current materials.
- Maintaining (1) a master set of current materials; (2) approval files on both old and current materials; and (3) an up-to-date distribution list.
- Developing training materials and programs for contributors.

Maintenance Checklists and Indexes

A *checklist* of current materials assures readers that their sets are complete as of the date of the checklist, except for missing items which can be requisitioned. The checklist should be issued through a revision notice; frequency of issuance depends upon how often revisions are released.

The checklist may include materials issued since the previous one or it may include all current materials; the latter seems preferable. The list itemizes all pages, together with their dates and the numbers of the covering transmittal memos. A circular checklist includes the number, name, and date of each current circular. The checklist must be carefully prepared and reviewed against a current set, since any error will cause every manual and set of circulars to be incorrect.

The following types of *indexes* should be maintained: (1) an index of all regulations, regardless of form of issuance; (2) an index of the basic manual itself and of any other manuals; and (3) an index of other reference materials. Indexes to the manuals and other instructions should be prepared periodically for release to holders of instruction sets. Internally, reference indexes can be maintained showing all the places in which forms, reports, or account numbers are mentioned. Then, when a change is made in any of these, you can make sure that all other instructional references are modified to the extent necessary.

Periodic Inventories (Originator-Initiated Revisions)

Originators usually keep the system current. This is more likely to be the case in organizations where the written word is enforced as law. It is less true if instructions are not observed. Accordingly, the management communications unit itself must be constantly alert to the development of changes in existing policies and practices. Inputs may come from their own procedural audits as well as from those of others within the organization. The management communications unit must be generally aware of organizational and operational changes so that it may inquire whether there have been new developments which should be reflected in the overall system.

Many companies have built-in update cycles for policies and procedures to ensure that all material is reviewed at least annually. For some, like a major Midwest department store chain, there is an annual review of policies and procedures for each of the eight major organizations of the company. (Figure 8-2 illustrates the store's policy review schedule.)

Policy Review Schedule

It is important that all policies be reviewed on a regular schedule, for updating and revision. This will be done on a yearly basis. The following schedule is the format that will be followed for a yearly organization review:

Month	*Organization*
January	Sales Promotion
February	Administration
March	Administration
April	Total Systems Development
May	Control
June	Branch Stores
July	Merchandising
August	Merchandising
September	Personnel
October	Personnel
November	Operations
December	Operations

Figure 8–2. Major Midwestern Department Store Policy Review Schedule

Control Data Corporation maintains a computer file of all policies and procedures of its four major corporate-wide manuals; every entry contains the policy/procedure title, its author, the name of the manual in which it is listed, original publishing date, last revision date, and next revision date. Once a year each entry is printed on a policy and procedure update report for author review.

Revising Loose-Leaf Pages

In some manual systems, newly revised material on a page is identified by a star or asterisk in the margin. Another method is to enclose the new material between lines (see Figure 8-3). The fallacy of such methods is that these marks remain on the page until it is replaced—which may be weeks, months, or years. If initial identification is desired, this is best done through a revision notice.

All pending revisions and all revisions being published should be noted in a master copy of the manual. Consult the master copy before making any page changes.

Revision Notices

Revision notices indicate the nature of the revision and, when identified by a serial number, assure the manual holder that all material issued has been received. A break in sequence of the numbered revision notices automatically signals missing material. The revision notice or transmittal memo should include:

1. A heading for the revision series.
2. Date of the revision.
3. Identifying serial numbers.
4. A summary explanation of each revision or insert, explaining its purpose and its effect upon existing practice.
5. Temporary information which should not become part of the basic text, including transitory instructions and background data.
6. An effective date for each item transmitted, if other than that of the revision notice.
7. The signature of the approving official.
8. A listing of pages to be removed, with a parallel listing of pages to be inserted.
9. A listing of circulars or other materials superseded or modified.

The revision date notice should be the same as the date of release printed on each page. This date automatically is the effective date unless otherwise specified in the revision notice. If the revision notice is an

Proposed procedures or suggested revisions are to be submitted to the County Administrator by the department responsible for review or further development.

The Administrative Office is responsible for approving all new content and revisions.

County Administration is responsible for the distribution of new or revised sections to all holders of the Administrative Manual.

Departments are responsible for the cost of printing all additions or revisions to the Manual. If several departments are "responsible," the major department responsible, as determined by County Administration, will be charged for the expense of printing.

MICROFICHE

All Hardware Maintenance Manuals produced after August 31, 19— must be suitable for microfiche. The source documents or diagrams submitted for microfiche cannot exceed 18 inches by 11 inches. The standard microfiche reduction is 42 to 1.

★ Overtime Requirements

Building Operations must be notified of any overtime scheduled for 12 or more employees. The Supervisor must write a memo, including his or her 8-digit responsibility code, the location of the unit, the number of employees involved, and the overtime hours scheduled.

Figure 8–3. Typical Revision Identification Marks

official part of the manual, it should carry a conspicuous notice on the bottom of the first page, worded somewhat as follows: "File this transmittal memo in the manual." This wording may limit the filing to a fixed period of time. If it is used as a return receipt, space for this must be provided.

A major Midwestern food processor involves the secretary as well as the manager in transmitting its personnel policies and procedures. Each update generally consists of four pages:

- Interoffice memo hand-delivered to the appropriate manager (Figure 8-4).
- Listing of manual section number, subject, and comments for major changes (Figure 8-5).
- Memo to the secretary indicating general instructions for updating the manual.
- Detailed instruction sheet listing specific pages to be added and pages to be removed (Figure 8-6).

For holders of the Hennepin County, Minn., Administrative Manual, revisions are sent with a pink transmittal memo that includes all of the above four elements, incorporated into a single table (Figure 8-7). Obviously, the more changes within the update, the more transmittal pages to be included.

The publishing unit may release the revisions for distribution either as they occur or at regular periods. The advantages of immediate release include satisfying the desires of the initiating office, emphasis upon a single subject, and the prompt dissemination of needed material. The advantages of periodic releases are consolidation of changes, a "breathing spell" for employees who normally react to resist change, and the fixing of regular effective dates.

The needs of the specific operating situation are also important. Information currently needed must be released as quickly as possible. However, if the information can hold, less frequent release is more convenient for the manual holder. A single series of revision notices is desirable if it is distributed as a whole to its recipients. Separate distribution for individual chapters requires specialized subseries of revision notices.

READER FEEDBACK

Reader feedback is one of the most difficult types of information to capture. It's elusive, hard to obtain, and often biased. Yet, accurate feedback is the most effective measurement of how well you're doing; it can tell you whether your message is hitting its mark.

INTEROFFICE MEMO

To Be Given Personally   Book # ▓▓▓▓▓▓▓

   TO: ▓▓▓▓▓▓▓▓▓▓

  FROM: ▓▓▓▓▓▓▓▓▓▓▓

SUBJECT: MANAGEMENT GUIDE BOOK OF PERSONNEL POLICIES AND PRACTICES REVISION #31

Attached is your copy of the 31st revision of the Management Guide
Book dated 9/1/—.

A brief summary of the revision is attached to this memo. You may
want to review the entire summary and the new pages before having
them filed in your book, but we call your particular attention to
the following sections:

     L 60   Loans
     V 5   Vacations

The attached "Dear Secretary" letter of instructions should be helpful to the individual filing these revised pages in your book.

If you have any questions, please contact me.

Attachments

Figure 8–4. Transmittal Memo for Personnel Policies and Procedures Manual Update (Part 1)

SECTION	SUBJECT	COMMENTS
Foreword		Text clarification.
Index	Vacations	New sub-topic re vacation roll-over.
D 38	Discharge	Text clarification.
D 38-2	"	Reference to banked vacation deleted.
E 30	Employee Activities	Revision of policy covering purchase of uniforms for INTER-company leagues.
E 90	Expenses, Employee	Per my earlier communication (dated 5/29/—), the mileage allowance for personally owned cars used on company business has been increased to per mile.
L 22	Leaves of Absence	Text clarification (See paragraphs A.1. and A.2. d and f).
L 60-2	Loans	NOTE: The formula for establishing the maximum loan available for transferring employees has been revised. Please read carefully section L 60-2, C. Amount of Loan, paragraph 2. a and b. Also note that the newly established maximum individual housing loan that the company will make is
M 20-5	Medical Services	Deletion of sub-section under item 4) at top of page.
R 22	Release Agreements	Text clarification throughout the entire section.
S 8-6	Salary Administration	See paragraph F - Per my earlier communication (dated 5/29/—), the temporary car allowance is increased to per month and the lump sum payment for the loss of car is increased to
S 32	Shift Differential	Per my earlier communication (dated 5/29/—), shift differentials were adjusted to /hour for the second shift and /hour for the third shift. This change was retroactive to April 3, 19—.
T 26-3	Termination of Employment	Addition of subject cross reference (Involuntary Termination).
T 72	Training and Development	Text clarification (see paragraph II. B.).

Figure 8–5. Listing of Major Update Changes for Personnel Policies and Procedures Manual (Part 2)

```
        PAGES TO BE ADDED                  PAGES TO BE REMOVED

Foreword                 9/1/--     Foreword                 1/1/--
Index U-W                9/1/--     Index U-W                2/1/--
        W (cont.) - Z    1/1/--             W (cont.) - Z    1/1/--
D 38                     9/1/--     D 38                     4/1/--
D 38-2                   9/1/--     D 38-2                   9/1/--
E 30                     9/1/--     E 30                     1/1/--
E 90                     9/1/--     E 90                     4/1/--
E 90-2                   4/1/--     E 90-2                   4/1/--
L 22                     9/1/--     L 22                     4/1/--
L 22-2                   4/1/--     L 22-2                   4/1/--
L 60                    11/1/--     L 60                    11/1/--
L 60-2                   9/1/--     L 60-2                   2/1/--
M 20-5                   9/1/--     M 20-5                   4/1/--
M 20-6                   4/1/--     M 20-6                   4/1/--
R 22                     9/1/--     R 22                     1/1/--
S 8-5                   11/1/--     S 8-5                   11/1/--
S 8-6                    9/1/--     S 8-6                   11/1/--
S 32                     4/3/--     S 32                    11/1/--
T 26-3                   9/1/--     T 26-3                   4/1/--
T 80-3                   9/1/--     T 80-3                   2/1/--
T 80-4                   2/1/--     T 80-4                   2/1/--
T 80-5                  11/1/--     T 80-5                  11/1/--
T 80-6                   9/1/--     T 80-6                  11/1/--
T 85-3                   4/1/--     T 85-3                   4/1/--
T 85-4                   9/1/--     T 85-4                   4/1/--
V 5                      9/1/--     V 5                      4/1/--
V 5-2                    9/1/--     V 5-2                    4/1/--
V 5-3                    9/1/--     V 5-3                    4/1/--
V 5-4                    9/1/--     V 5-4                    4/1/--
V 5-5                    9/1/--     V 5-5                   10/15/-
W 65                     9/1/--     W 65                     4/1/--
W 65-2                   9/1/--     W 65-2                  10/15/-
```

Figure 8–6. Detailed Instruction Sheet for Updating Personnel Policies and Procedures Manual (Part 4)

HENNEPIN

Date: February 9, 19—

To: All Holders of Administrative Manuals (DL-6)

From: Dale Ackmann, County Administrator

Subject: Additions/Changes to the Administrative Manual

Please immediately review and insert the attached material in the appropriate places in your Administrative Manual, or pull out those sections so indicated. Also, please complete the Administrative Manual Record of Updates at the front of your manual.

Section	Remove	Insert	Comments
Table of Contents	pgs. i-iv	pgs. i-iv	---
C6 - Check Cashing Policy	pg. 1	pg. 1	There is now a 25¢ check cashing fee, and the service fee charged to any employee tendering a nonsufficient-funds check has been increased to $5.00.
G2 - Grant Employees	pgs. 1-10	pgs. 1-9	A recommendation that the Personnel Department be contacted for assistance in recruiting and screening all grant position applicants, whether required by the grantor or not, has been added. For a grant program to be included as a sub-group under the County's health and life insurance programs, requests should now be made to the Personnel Department instead of Risk Management. Information concerning PERA participation has been updated. Various other minor updates to information have been made.
G5 - Grant Application and Acceptance Procedure	pgs. 1-18	pgs. 1-15	Various minor revisions have been made. The basic policy concerning review of proposed and renewal grant programs by the County Grants Coordinator and requirements for Board approval remains the same, and department heads are urged to review this policy.

(continued)

-1-

Figure 8–7. First Page of Transmittal Memo for Administrative Manual Update (Courtesy of Hennepin County, Minn.)

Reader Reply Form

The most obvious way to solicit feedback is to include a reader reply form in a document to enable readers to report suggested changes, corrections, or deletions. Figure 8-8 illustrates a major department store's method of soliciting reader feedback for its policies and procedures manuals. The drawback of this method is that readers normally use it only to report something wrong with the manual, when and if they even take the time to send it in. Response is generally poor. Here, no news is *not* necessarily good news. How else, then, can you get feedback?

Reader Questionnaire

A second method of eliciting responses on how well an organization is getting its message across is the reader questionnaire. Questionnaires of this type are difficult to construct and, depending on their length, they can be expensive and time-consuming to process. However, if properly developed for easy completion, questionnaires can provide valuable input. A major help in processing a large questionnaire is the use of computer programs which tabulate, correlate, and analyze the data.[2]

Personal Interview

A third method of obtaining reader feedback is the interview—either in person or by telephone. Both methods give you an opportunity to ask in-depth questions and the flexibility to make them as long or as short as the situation warrants. For example, the interviewer can pursue lines of questioning that provide desired, "meaty" information. At the same time, the interviewer can quickly pass over nonapplicable answers.

There are three major drawbacks, however, with the interview: (1) time required for one-on-one communications; (2) difficulties of compiling interview material into a consistent form; and (3) potential problems in obtaining unbiased information, if the interviewer is a member of the publications staff.

What's the best method? It depends on each individual situation, the size of the audience, the degree of necessity for obtaining feedback, and the funding available for such a project. If your staff continually receives phone calls about questions that are supposedly clearly explained in your documents, you've got problems. There could be similar symptoms that indicate people aren't reading the material. It just has to be a judgment call.

This chapter concludes the basic steps in publishing a management communications document. The remaining chapters deal with graphics, classification of instructional types, and examples of how-to-do it instructions.

[2]For more information on computer analysis of surveys, contact the author.

Manual Revision Recommendation

▓▓▓▓▓▓▓▓▓▓▓▓▓▓ would like to know what you think about this or any other reference manual you are using. Your comments could help us improve the manuals to better serve your needs.

Please give us your constructive criticism after you have used the manual for a time. It will be most helpful if you will be as specific as possible by indicating the subsection or paragraph numbers where the problems lie. Use the reverse side if you need more space for your comments. Please be candid with your opinions—there is no need to sign this form unless you would like us to contact you.

Manual Title	Issue Date (Month/Year)

Is there a problem with the information given in the manual? (Consider: Is it incomplete, too detailed, or out of date?)

_____

_____

_____

Is there a problem with the way the information is presented? (Consider: Is it difficult to find what you need in the manual or to determine who should carry out each procedure? Are there confusing instructions or illustrations? Are there parts that should be in another manual?)

_____

_____

_____

Is there a problem with any of the forms discussed in the manual? (Consider: Are some unnecessary, out of date, incomplete, or difficult to fill out?)

_____

_____

_____

_____

_____

If you would like us to contact you in response to your statement above, please fill in the following information:

Your Name	Your Position	Date

Address		Unit No.

Figure 8–8. Typical Manual Revision Recommendation Form

9

Graphics

Writers tend to shy away from graphics and rely, instead, on professional artists. While some companies have designers to aid these writers, many are not so fortunate. This chapter explains how to use illustrative material—either alone or integrated with the text—to help convey information or ideas.

The main use of illustrations in instruction literature is to simplify the communication of complex mechanisms or sequences. For technical manuals, this usually pertains to the assembly, theoretical principles, operation, overhaul, and maintenance of equipment and machinery. For administrative manuals, the illustrative need is for charts to trace the flow of paperwork and narrative diagrams of how to fill in and use forms. Training manuals call for a great many step sequences, showing what to do next and how.

Illustrations must reproduce with clarity of detail and with an adequate tonal range. They must be neat, clean-cut, and have a professional appearance. Poorly made drawings and fuzzy or flat photographs only confuse the reader and suggest that the instructions were not considered sufficiently worthy of a good effort.

DRAWINGS, PHOTOGRAPHS, AND COLOR

Black-and-White Drawings

Most internal publications are produced in a single pressrun using one ink, usually black on white paper. Economy is a major consideration here because the changeover from one color to another is expensive. If two colors are used, the pages must go through the printing press twice;

Figure 9–1. Line Drawing

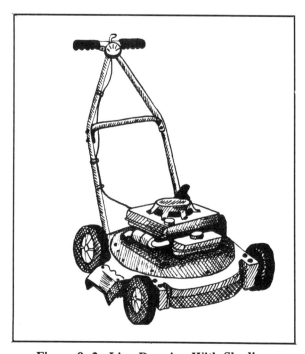

Figure 9–2. Line Drawing With Shading

three times for three colors, and so forth. There are legitimate uses for color, in spite of the extra cost, but they should be justified.

Most economical to reproduce is the "line drawing"—the ordinary pen drawing with black ink. A skilled artist can vary the monotony of line drawings through use of shading techniques, solid areas, and overlays. Through such techniques, the artist achieves tonal effects which convey a sense of depth and realism. Figures 9-1 and 9-2 illustrate a line drawing and line drawing with shading, respectively.

Figures 9-3 and 9-4 illustrate improper and proper methods, respectively, of developing a line rendering of an object. Other types of drawings include phantom effects, which show inner workings of apparatus (see page 138), and the use of enlarged details to provide easier comprehension of illustrated procedures (see Figure 9-5 page 128).

Photographs

Individually or in series, photographs are one of the best means for displaying details. Some skill is necessary, however, if the photograph is to be sharp, well-illuminated, and properly composed with respect to layout, shooting angle, and background. A common error is to have too much business in the background that confuses the reader and distracts from the details.

Illumination must be properly balanced to give depth, to avoid harsh and unsightly shadows, to reveal all necessary details, to bring out texture, and to provide snap and brilliance. Highlights need to be controlled either by dulling shiny metal parts with a spray or by retouching or both, apart from use of special light tints.

For explanatory purposes, photography is a medium of versatility. With it, multiple-image photographs can be created to make several exposures on a single negative to show movement; phantom effects can be built around the inner workings of apparatus; and macrophotographs can be made to show enlarged detail of texture and parts.

Halftones—Because printing presses apply ink with equal density (either all solid color or no ink at all), they cannot create different tones or shades. To obtain the wide range of intermediate tone values in photographs and illustrations, originals must be converted through use of the halftone process.

To create the illusion of various tone densities, continuous tone images must be divided into tiny dots. These dots are produced by photographing the image through a finely ruled line screen (or grid). (Patterned screens can be used to achieve special effects.) This screen breaks up the continuous gradations of tones into corresponding image areas of halftone dots that have uniform spacing; each dot, however, varies in

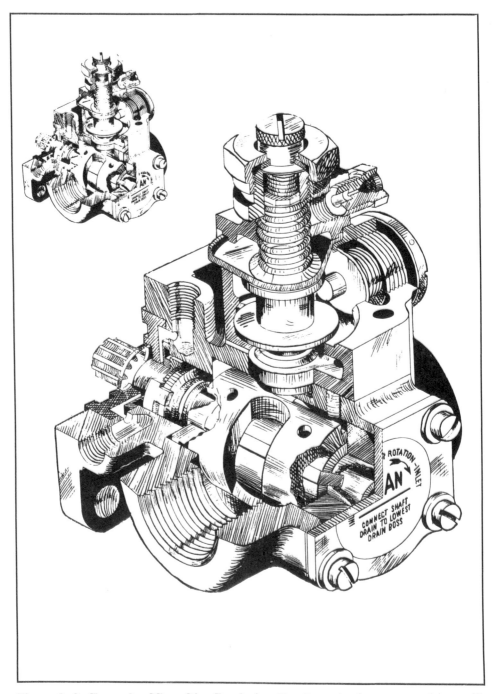

Figure 9–3. Example of Poor Line Rendering (Details are hard to separate. Lines will fill up in some places when illustration is reduced, as shown in insert. Drawing lacks character, looks amateurish, and creates impression of confusion.)

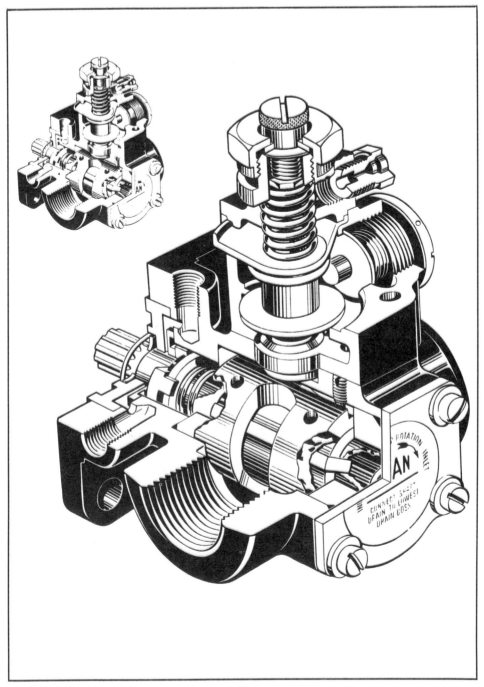

Figure 9–4. Example of Clean, Clear Shading (Drawing will reduce to any size, as shown in insert. Blacks are inked to show roundness, define shapes, and firm outlines. They give punch and solidarity.)

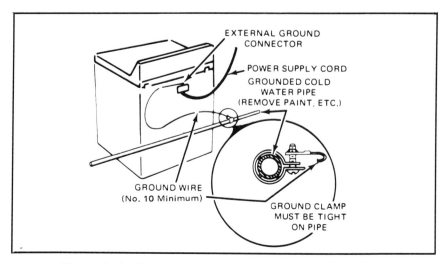

Figure 9–5. Using Enlarged Details to Illustrate a Dryer

size, according to the amount of light transmitted from the original through the screen onto the film. Then, when the printing press applies ink in each tiny dot area, the human eye translates the pattern of lighter and darker dots (as well as the unprinted areas of white paper) into a continuous black and white tone. The resulting ''screened'' photograph is called a halftone (see Figure 9-6).

Line screens can also be used to vary the intensity of ink coverage in type and illustrations. Skillful use of line screens can give the effect of additional colors without much extra expense. (See Figure 9–7.) Such screens tend to wash out the three-dimensional effect of a drawing, however, and they can reduce clarity and readability of important material.

Color

Color is another effective illustrative technique. It helps to create mood, focus attention, distinguish parts in mechanical or technical drawings, depict actual color characteristics when this is necessary, trace movement or action, or draw together otherwise unrelated sections. Color is most effective in handbooks or training materials which are to be used in conferences where focal attention is highly important.

Figure 9–6. Examples of Photograph Printed Without a Screen and With 65-, 120, and 150-Line Screens (Courtesy Russell-Manning Communications, Inc.)

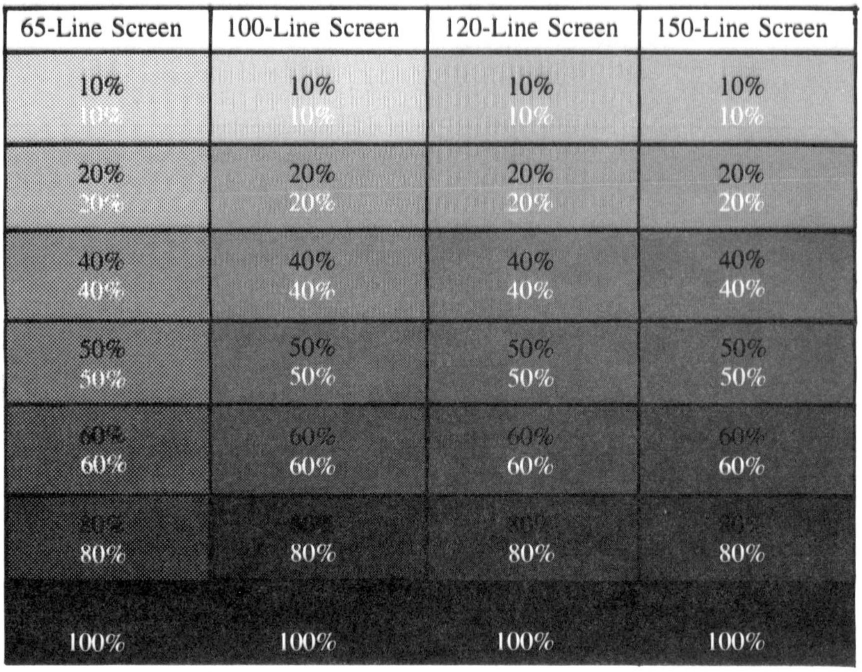

65-Line Screen	100-Line Screen	120-Line Screen	150-Line Screen
10% 10%	10% 10%	10% 10%	10% 10%
20% 20%	20% 20%	20% 20%	20% 20%
40% 40%	40% 40%	40% 40%	40% 40%
50% 50%	50% 50%	50% 50%	50% 50%
60% 60%	60% 60%	60% 60%	60% 60%
80% 80%	80% 80%	80% 80%	80% 80%
100%	100%	100%	100%

Figure 9–7. 65-Line Through 150-Line Screens (10% to 100% Values)

FORMS AND CHARTS

Forms Display

In principle, a form should be as self-explanatory as possible, taking into consideration the comprehension level of the people who are to use it. Because of the great number of people who may be called upon to fill in the form and, also, because of the need for absolute uniformity in many cases, illustrations of filled-in forms are very widely used in administrative manuals and instructional releases.

Two techniques are used: one is to fill the form in with sample entries. The other is to use side captions, keyed to the indicated entry spaces, to explain the entries. (See Figure 9-8.) Side captions used in this manner can substantially or completely replace narrative text in the body of the instructions. These side captions are most effective when they are used to explain the key points, especially if there is a possibility of misinterpretation. If too many side captions are used, the total effect may be one of confusion. To concentrate attention, sections of a form can be shown. Another technique is to shade the nonpertinent portions of a form to bring the indicated portion into sharper relief.

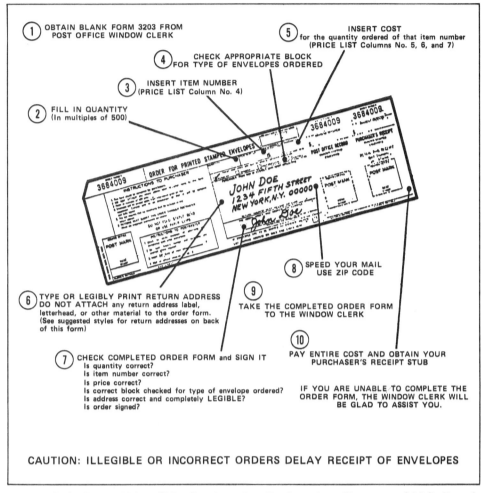

Figure 9–8. Form Using Side Captions for Explanation (Courtesy of U.S. Postal Service)

Columnar Reference Charts

The columnar chart is a highly concentrated directory. Intended to convey information in little space with little supporting text, it is self-explanatory if well designed. (See Table 9–1.) Charts can be confined to text or they can be confined to symbols. The principle, generally, is that three types of information can be combined in one chart. One series of informational items is read across the chart and another is read down the chart. To obtain information, you select a reference item from the top as well as from the side and then find the point where the two columns, vertical and horizontal, come together. Although there are variations, this is the basic operating principle which underlies all such charts.

Table 9–1. Records Control Schedule (Courtesy of U.S. Postal Service)

5. FINANCIAL MANAGEMENT			
Item No.	*Series/Description*	*Cut-Off*	*Disposal*
5–1	**Postage and Accountable Paper Requisitions and Daily Financial Reports:** Forms 17 and 1412.		
	A. Window Clerk copies		Upon completion of next audit of accountability
	B. Station and Account Book Unit Copy	FY	2 years
5–2	**Money Order Tapes:** Adding machine tapes created in the course of money order sales showing value, tour, clerk and consolidated totals.	Quarterly	2 years
5–3	**Account Book and Daily Financial Statements:** Forms 1557 and 1558		10 years
5–4	**Supporting Papers to Postmasters Account:** Copies of statements of account, vouchers, schedules and other pertinent papers.	A/P	4 years
5–5	**Government Bills of Lading (GBL):** Accountable documents used for shipping Postal Service property–except mail bags–and related papers (SF 1103).		
	A. Issuing Office Memorandum Copy (SF 1103a)		4 years
	B. All Other Copies		1 year
	C. GBLs for Mail Bag Movement		5 years
5–6	**Post Office Financial Reports (PSSR):** Used to monitor post office management practices.		3 years
5–7	**Claims for Loss and/or Damage in Transit:** Form 7343.		3 years
5–8	**Local Payroll Records:** Forms 1230–A,B,C, 1221, 1224, 1234, 2240, 3189, 3971, 3973 and 3976. (USPS 050.020)	Each PP	3 years
5–9	**Employee Claims for Personal Property Loss:** Form 2146. (USPS 200.020)		3 years

Organization Charts

The organization chart depicts the distribution of responsibilities among the component units of the organization as a whole. Naturally, it may be used to show only part of the organization as well. (See Figures 9–9 and 9–10.) Lines of authority are shown by tracing solid lines as they descend through the organization. Dash lines are used to show technical, functional, or staff relationships to components under the line of control of another officer. Staff units are usually set off to a side immediately adjacent to the principal officer to whom they report.

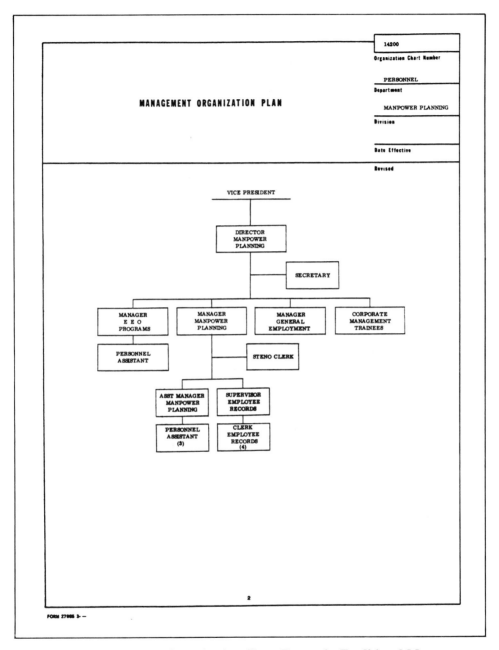

Figure 9–9. Typical Organization Chart Drawn in Traditional Manner

```
                                    RUN DATE 11/02/—        PERSONNEL DEPARTMENT        PAGE   1

VP PERSONNEL                                                D F                       14000 001
|-----DIR MANPOWER PLNG ST PAUL                             F J                       14200 007
   |-----MGR EEO PROGRAMS                                   M J                       14200 106
      |-----PERS ASST EEO                                   J E                       14200 016
   |-----MGR MANPWR PLNG                                    J A                       14212 012
      |-----A MGR MNPWR PLNG                                R J                       14212 109
         |-----PERSONNEL ASST                               P J                       14212 013
         |-----PERSONNEL ASST                               C R                       14212 104
         |-----PERSONNEL ASST                               S D                       14212 024
      |-----SUPVR EMP RECORDS                               E R                       14212 021
         |-----CLERK EMP RECORDS                            L M                       14212 022
         |-----CLERK EMP RECORDS                            I S                       14212 023
         |-----CLERK EMP RECORDS                            C L                       14212 025
         |-----CLERK EMP RECORDS                            P A                       14212 115
      |-----STENO CLERK                                     D J                       14212 006
   |-----MGR GEN EMPLOYMNT                                  R D                       14214 014
   |-----SECRETARY                                          E A                       14200 008
```

Figure 9–10. Computer-Generated Organization Chart Identical to Figure 9–9

A variation of the organizational chart is the duties chart, listing duties and responsibilities in summary form within each box on the chart. Still another variation is the staffing chart which shows all of the people assigned to all of the organizational components, with each person in the proper box.

Procedure Charts

The procedure chart is a workflow drawing. Through symbols, it shows the steps to be taken in executing a procedure and who is to perform the steps. Such charts may replace or supplement text. They are often used in fiscal manuals, in job methods manuals, and in training. (See Figure 9–11.) To assist in the drafting of these charts, various preprinted symbols are available commercially. Also available are plastic templates with conventional methods analysis symbols.

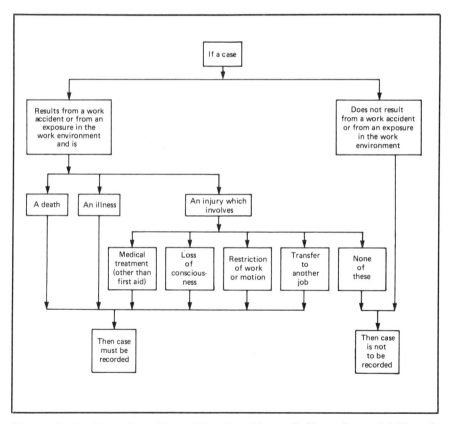

Figure 9–11. Procedure Chart That Provides a Guide to Recordability of Cases Under OSHA (Courtesy of U.S. Department of Labor)

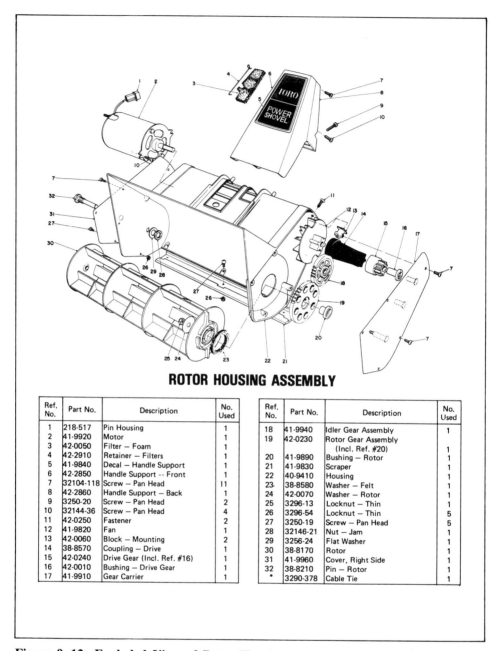

ROTOR HOUSING ASSEMBLY

Ref. No.	Part No.	Description	No. Used
1	218-517	Pin Housing	1
2	41-9920	Motor	1
3	42-0050	Filter — Foam	1
4	42-2910	Retainer — Filters	1
5	41-9840	Decal — Handle Support	1
6	42-2850	Handle Support -- Front	1
7	32104-118	Screw — Pan Head	11
8	42-2860	Handle Support — Back	1
9	3250-20	Screw — Pan Head	2
10	32144-36	Screw — Pan Head	4
11	42-0250	Fastener	2
12	41-9820	Fan	1
13	42-0060	Block — Mounting	2
14	38-8570	Coupling — Drive	1
15	42-0240	Drive Gear (Incl. Ref. #16)	1
16	42-0010	Bushing — Drive Gear	1
17	41-9910	Gear Carrier	1

Ref. No.	Part No.	Description	No. Used
18	41-9940	Idler Gear Assembly	1
19	42-0230	Rotor Gear Assembly (Incl. Ref. #20)	1
20	41-9890	Bushing — Rotor	1
21	41-9830	Scraper	1
22	40-9410	Housing	1
23	38-8580	Washer — Felt	1
24	42-0070	Washer — Rotor	1
25	3296-13	Locknut — Thin	1
26	3296-54	Locknut — Thin	5
27	3250-19	Screw — Pan Head	5
28	32146-21	Nut — Jam	1
29	3256-24	Flat Washer	1
30	38-8170	Rotor	1
31	41-9960	Cover, Right Side	1
32	38-8210	Pin — Rotor	1
*	3290-378	Cable Tie	1

Figure 9–12. Exploded View of Rotor Housing Assembly of Power Snow Shovel With Identification Numbers (Courtesy of The Toro Company)

DISPLAYING MECHANISMS AND SYSTEMS

Methods used to explain assembly, operation, maintenance, repair, overhaul, and servicing of mechanisms and systems include (1) exploded views, (2) cross-sections and cut-aways, (3) phantom views, and (4) system layouts.

The *exploded view* illustrates an entire mechanism or principal components of a mechanism. It shows all of the parts of the mechanism in the sequence in which they are physically assembled, thereby serving as a guide either for assembly or disassembly and overhaul. The exploded view also identifies parts, with the aid of indexing numbers. Exploded views may be shown through line drawings or photographs. (See Figure 9-12.)

Cut-aways and cross-sections show entire mechanisms or operations, or components of them with everything in place. The inner workings are revealed by cross-sectioning completely, by showing a three-quarter view with part of the housing cut away, or by removing an entire side, as with a doll house. This technique lends itself to photography or to the artist's brush or pen. (See Figure 9-13.)

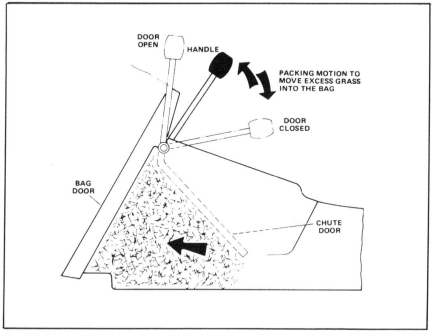

Figure 9–13. Cross-Section of Lawn Mower Bagger Mechanism (Courtesy of The Toro Company)

Phantom views are used to show a hidden part of an object or mechanism within the context of the whole. The effect is to show a ghost-like image surrounding the interior part. While this would seem to be a technique for the artist, it can also be done through photography by superimposing of negatives or by making double exposures. (See Figure 9-14.)

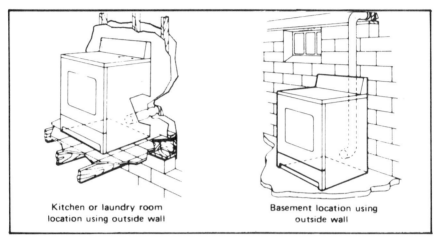

Kitchen or laundry room location using outside wall

Basement location using outside wall

Figure 9–14. Phantom Effect Shows Inner Working of Dryer Installation

System layouts are used to show all of the necessary components of a total system. This includes schematic illustrations of machine components laid out in series. Quite commonly all of the components of a plumbing system are shown interconnected, with breaks in the piping in order to crowd into the limited space on the page. Similar techniques are used for wiring diagrams. Complete systems are visualized through abstract presentation in the form of block diagrams, schematic drawings, and electrical or electronic circuits.

INTEGRATING TEXT AND ILLUSTRATIONS

Many things compete in a limited time span for the attention of the reader. Writers are therefore in a competitive market; if they want their materials to be read, they must make them interesting and understandable. Integrating illustrations in text is one means to achieve this. It is also a means whereby complex or intricate processes can be demonstrated clearly in much less space with clearer understanding than would be possible if words were used alone.

Illustrations serve various purposes: to support and amplify the text, to take the place of text, to create mood and impressions, and to break up the continuity and monotony of solid text. While each of these will be covered here, the principal concern will be with the interrelation of word and picture.

Assigning a Role to Pictures

Solid text, without illustrations, stands on its own when the ideas it contains are rather straightforward or concrete or when the reader has a compelling interest in the text. Illustrations serve a useful role when there are ideas, design concepts, or manipulative operations or sequences not readily expressed in words. It is not a question of which predominates but rather a matter to be determined for each case.

First, analyze the communication problem in the light of the informational objective and the interests and requirements of the reader. Then, develop a working outline that covers the entire presentation. This will form the basis for determining how text and illustrations will be used. Then decide what kinds of illustrations are appropriate and how to relate them to the text to achieve a natural, easy integration.

Page Layout

The simplest layout is that which uses an entire page. In this case the main problem is the internal design and composition characteristics of the illustration, especially if it is a composite illustration. Another problem is whether the illustration should be on a left-hand or right-hand facing page. The question here is what is on the facing page. Sometimes it may be additional illustration matter, in which case the two pages should be related in proper sequence or at least not in conflict.

Next in order of simplicity is the illustration that runs the entire width of the page but takes up only a part of the depth of the page. Usually, such an illustration is placed at either the top or the bottom. If there is an illustration of equivalent size on the facing page, the two illustrations usually should be matched in size and page position. An exception is if one of the illustrations is a full page and the other is a part page. If the two occupy part pages, the result appears rather awkward and off-balance unless they are of equal size.

The layout becomes more complicated if you set aside any typographic restrictions to obtain the most effective integration of text and illustration. If there are two or more columns to a page, a very simple arrangement is to break the column by inserting an illustration to fit within the column width. Another effective variation, for some purposes, is to insert an illustration that takes about one-half or less of the column width and then continue the text by its side. This is called a ''runaround.''

For maximum flexibility in page layout, visualize a page as divided into two or three columns, depending on the actual width of the page. Do this whether or not the ordinary page is divided into such columns. Now take the column length and divide it into two, three, or four sections, depending on how deep the column is. This will give you four, six, eight, or nine sections of the page in most cases. Now, you can make a layout using a series of illustrations distributed among the segments in the page diagram. For example, a simple arrangement is to divide the page into two columns, using one for text and one for illustrations. Next to each of a series of illustrations in one of the columns there might be parallel text supplementing the illustration.

Another method is to visualize the page as divided into three columns. One common arrangement is having a center column devoted to text with illustrations in the two columns on either side of it. A further variation is to arrange the illustrations in the shape of a "U." That is, in addition to the left and right columns being used entirely for illustrations, they are connected at the bottom by an illustration at the base of the center column. Still another arrangement is to arrange the illustrations in the shape of an "L."

Of course, it is not necessary to use an entire column. Sometimes, illustrations and text are interspersed in something of a checkerboard arrangement. Then, too, white space alone can be used to break up the page as well as to provide a point of pause. Remember that the variations in possible layout are almost limitless. Keep in mind, however, the need for balance. Also, avoid crowding.

Item Layout

Where a large area is covered by illustrative material, follow the general principle that the center of attention is slightly above and to the left of center. When a sequence of illustrations is ganged together, usually the action should start in the upper left corner since that is where the eye is accustomed to beginning.

On spot illustrations, such as those which depict a single point of action as demonstrated by the handling of an article or the performance of a single operation with a hand or the use of a tool held in a hand, there is no problem of layout as such. There is merely a single point of attention with all other background blotted out. More important in this type of illustration is the selection of the best angle or perspective for display of the operation, especially in photography.

Where to Locate Illustrations—Illustrations should be located as close as possible to the point of discussion in the text itself, but the layout or grouping of related illustrations may not always permit this. Then, try at least to locate the illustrations as near as the layout and text arrangement will permit. If possible, rearrange the text to permit ideal juxtaposition of illustrations. In fact, insert additional text if that helps carry other text over to the next page.

If the particular role of an illustration is to draw attention to certain text material, make sure of the physical relation of the two, no matter what juggling is required.

Small spot illustrations can be located at the margin, if it is made sufficiently wide. Smaller illustrations can be incorporated directly into the text, usually taking up about half a column width. This entails a little additional cost in setting type but it is a most effective technique since it assures very close integration.

Story Within a Story—The story within a story is a technique for amplifying something covered in the text or for supplementing it without interrupting the continuity of the text. Sometimes this is done by boxing illustrations, or illustrations and text, or even just text alone. The box is either an inset within a page taking up only part of the page width or it is the full width of a page but not its full length. A full page box is used for text alone to indicate that it is not part of the running continuity of the publication. You can dispense with a ruled box if it consists mostly or substantially of illustration material.

An entirely different technique is to rely on the text for the main line of continuity but to expand independently in free illustrations not limited by the box technique. In this technique, illustrations are referenced in the text, but they are independent of the text to a great extent.

Captions and References

Illustrations may have their captioning within the body of the text itself which refers the reader to the appropriate illustration. A preferable method is to provide an independent caption for each illustration. This assures that the reader obtains a clear understanding of the illustration's purpose. For page-turners who skip through the text, this also has an advantage in that if the illustration catches their attention, the caption may lead them into the corresponding text amplification.

If no captions are used but a descriptive reference is included in the text, place the text and illustrations as close together as possible. When they are separated, the text should make reference specifically to the page on which the illustration is reproduced.

When illustrating completion of forms and reports, a common technique is to draw balloons into the text with captions within the balloons. A variation on this technique reproduces the form or sections of it on one page with a narrative description or amplification on the facing page.

PRODUCTION OF ILLUSTRATIONS

The illustrator and the photographer are the people who will actually portray your ideas. Their performance can be no better than their understanding of your problem. If they receive instructions second-, third-, or fourth-hand, they may not understand, and work may have to be done over. To prevent this, discuss your problem directly with the artist or photographer; explain what your purpose is and what information you are trying to convey.

Some people require more specific instructions than others; some are imaginative enough to take a basic problem and suggest several treatments. Remember that any good artist or photographer has a wealth of experience. But make it clear whether instructions are to be followed literally, without change, or whether the artist is to have any personal choice or discretion—and how much.

Outside Procurement

It is even more important that instructions be quite specific when procuring illustrations from outside sources, especially if a vendor is new. Usually such procurement must go through a purchasing section—the same purchasing section that buys office materials and industrial equipment. This, however, is a different kind of procurement. Apart from the formalized procedures on issuance of the purchase order, the same kind of liaison is required with the outside agency as with an internal art department.

A large organization can afford a graphics art buyer who functions as an intermediary, with substantial responsibility for follow-through. Remember that careless instructions to the outside agency end in expensive bills because each item of rework will be a billed item outside of the original scope of work.

Review Checklist for Illustrations

1. Does the illustration aim at the comprehension level and background of the reader?
2. Is attention properly focused on the main point or points which are to be emphasized?
3. Are all unnecessary details or items eliminated, either by removal from the background, by close-ups, or by artwork?
4. Will the details reproduce clearly when reduced, including lines, outlines, shading, and index numbers?

5. Have the illustrations been checked for technical accuracy from the standpoint of content, standards of presentation and nomenclature, standards of the company, correct sequence in exploded views, conformance with specifications, and accuracy?

6. Will the illustrations be self-explanatory, with or without caption, as intended, and if with caption, has it been furnished? (Figure 9-15 is an excellent example of how *not* to incorporate a line drawing with instructions to assemble an easel. The misspellings were part of the original direction sheet that came with the easel. Overall effect: a very unclear picture of assembly.)

7. Are sequences within illustrations and from one illustration to another in correct order?

8. Have register marks been included for use when color reproduction is intended and for use with overlays?

GLOSSARY OF REPRODUCTION AND PRINTING TERMS

accordion fold—In binding, a term used for two or more parallel folds which open like an accordion.

air brush—A small pressurized gun used by artists for touching up original photographs for reproduction purposes.

alterations—In composition, changes made in the copy after it has been typeset.

art work—Drawings, sketches, photographs, etc., prepared for insertion in finished copy.

author's alterations—Changes in the original copy made by the author after it has been typeset.

binding margin—The margin on the edge of the paper where the book is to be bound.

bleeding—Placing illustrations so that they extend beyond the trim edge of a sheet or page.

blowup—A photographic enlargement of an original piece of copy.

body type—A type used for the main part or text of a printed piece.

bold face—Heavy face type used for captions and subheads; also used for emphasis in body copy.

bulk—The degree of thickness of paper.

center spread—Usually the two center pages of a book.

collating—Gathering loose printed sheets together in proper sequence.

combination line and halftone—A combination of both line work and halftones on the same page or same illustration.

composition—The process of setting and arranging type.

crop—To eliminate portions of an illustration, usually on a photograph or plate, indicated on the original by "cropmarks."

dummy—A preliminary layout showing the position of illustrations and text as they are to appear in the final reproduction.

ADJUSTABLE FOLDING EASEL

Parts List

L	LEGS	(3) E EXTENTIONS	(2)
T	TRAY	(1) TS TRAY SUPPORT	(1)
B2	BOLT 2"	(3) CE CENTER EXT.	(1)
B3	BOLT 3"	(1)W WINGNUTS	(5)
B4	BOLT 4"	(1) SH SCREW HOOK	(1)
N	NAIL		
C	CHAIN		

Instructions

ASSEMBLE AS PER DIAGRAM

PLACE LEG BOLTS IN HOLES FOR CHOOSEN

HEIGHT FOR COMPACT STORAGE: REMOVE

TRAY, LOOSEN LEG WINGNUTS AND FOLD

Figure 9-15. How Not to Prepare Assembly Instructions

elite typewriter—A typewriter that types 12 characters to the running inch.

face—The printing surface of a piece of type (typeface).

facsimile—An exact reproduction of copy.

folio—A page number.

flush paragraphs—Paragraphs having no indentation on the first line.

gutter—The blank space or inner margin from printing area to binding.

halftone—A printed ("screened") picture of a snapshot or professionally made photograph, wash, crayon or charcoal drawing. (See screening.)

halftone insert—A halftone negative to be inserted into position on the line negative.

headings—Headlines as distinguished from body type.

imposition—Laying out pages in proper position so that after printing and folding, pages will appear in consecutive order.

insert—See "line insert" and "halftone insert."

italic—The style of letters that slope forward, as contrasted with upright or Roman letters.

justified typesetting—Composition in which there are even margins on both the right- and left-hand side.

layout—The arrangement of elements to be reproduced.

letterpress—Printing from raised type.

line insert—An original, too large or too small to fit in the allotted space on a page, thus requiring an enlargement or reduction to fit in its proper position on the negative, and requiring separate photographing.

line work—Any copy composed of lines, typewritten matter, printed matter, drawings, sketches, and rules.

margins—The blank space from the edge of the printed copy to the edge of the full size sheet.

master sheet—A printed form on which copy is prepared for photographing; usually used in books with running head and tail pieces.

negative—The photographic medium from which a printing plate is made.

offset paper—A paper especially made for use on offset and lithographing presses.

opaquing—The cleaning of dirt marks or scratches on the negative with a black or red opaquing fluid. White opaque may be used to block out dark marks on white paper.

overrun—The number of impressions of a job in excess of the quantity originally ordered.

pica—Printer's unit of measurement used principally in measuring lines.

pica typewriter—A typewriter that types 10 characters to the running inch.

plate—A zinc or aluminum sheet on which the image to be printed is transferred.

proof—Printed examples of typeset material, used to insure accuracy or allow the making of corrections and changes before printing.

proofs of cuts—A proof copy taken from a cut or engraving.

reduction—Reducing photographically the size of an original piece of copy.

running head—Title or illustration repeated at the top of consecutive pages in a book.

screening—The breaking up into "dots" of a picture composed of highlights and various tones, as in a photograph; the making of a halftone.

signature—A section of a book obtained by folding a single sheet of paper so that after folding, pages will fall in consecutive order. (Consists of 4, 8, 16, 32, etc., pages.)

silhouette—A halftone from which the screen surrounding any part of the image has been removed, allowing the image itself to stand out.

stet—A proofreader's mark, written in the margin, signifying that copy marked for corrections should remain as it was.

stripping—Inserting a negative into place on a larger negative.

trim size—The overall size of a sheet including both the work or reading matter AND the margins all around; the size to which a sheet is trimmed.

type page—The area of the page that contains all the printed matter.

10

Classifying Instructional Materials

This chapter examines the various types of instructional materials. It also outlines a procedure for converting from one system of directives to another.

POLICY, PROCEDURE, AND INFORMATION

As noted in Chapter 1, the broadest division of instructional materials is into policy, procedure, and information:

Policies are guiding principles governing future courses of action, usually of a recurring nature. They constitute advance official approval of the actions which officers and employees take under certain circumstances; they are laws of conduct. Policies provide for consistency of action and assurance of support for actions taken, consistent with policy. They do not, however, contain details about policy execution.

Procedures are the actual courses of action: the methods, steps, or routines to be followed in accordance with the guiding policies or statements of principle. The statement of policy should be brief, little more than a few paragraphs or lines. The statement of procedure provides the working details which cover methods of operation. Policies tend to be stable; procedures vary more frequently in terms of paperwork, review, and routing.

Policies may be segregated from procedures and published separately, but procedures rarely can stand alone. There are systems in the Federal Government that attempt to separate policy from procedure by issuing policy directives, such as a policy manual, and by limiting its distribution to a select few. This, however, is not a widely accepted practice. In actual practice, there are disadvantages in trying to separate policy from procedure. Top management should be familiar with detailed

147

procedures to assist in improving them. Further, in separating policy and procedure, two complete sets of issuances must be maintained, and extensive reviewing and policing must be built into the system to keep them separate.

Occasionally, companies use a "purpose paragraph" in directives, with a fixed position for this paragraph in each directive. The purpose paragraph carries the policy statement while the body of the directive contains the procedure. As a result, policy statements are accessible yet separate from procedural detail.

Informational releases are statements that are important for general working knowledge, understanding of rights and privileges, or morale and sense of belonging. Ordinarily, informational releases do not require specific action by the reader. Examples include employee handbooks, brochures of organization benefits, and newsletters of all types.

OTHER CLASSIFICATIONS

These basic types of instructions can be further analyzed or differentiated by level of management, content, applicability, or form.

By Level of Management

Top policy level—In a private firm, top policy is usually determined by the board of directors or the president, while in government service it is determined by the legislature. The matters covered and the details of coverage are very broad. Top policy is usually for the guidance of the management officers or administrators who must translate and effect policy. Top policy is formulated within the scope of the operating or corporate charter of the private company and within the scope of statutes and executive orders in government service.

Operating policy level—Within the framework set by the board of directors or the legislature, the head of the organization sets operating policies without having to return for affirmation or confirmation. At this level, any procedures normally are free of detail; they simply show the major divisions of responsibility and the major lines of work flow. There ordinarily are no attempts to spell out details.

Organization-wide policies, regulations and procedures—Immediately below the top administrator's level, there is usually a general management level, although not necessarily identified as such. The position may be that of executive vice president, deputy administrator, or general manager. Here the main concern is with the more specific statements of policy, regulation, and procedure that are of general organization-wide concern, or with the relationships and work flow that tie the organization together.

Departmental policies and procedures—Within each department and subordinate unit of an organization are governing policies and procedures specific to the department's work. The amount of detail in these instructional materials increases as the unit of applicability becomes smaller. Thus, the instructions for a specific correspondence clerk are more detailed than instructions for correspondence clerks in general.

In one way or another, all of these factors interrelate and influence the planning and shaping of an organization's formal system of communicating and coordinating written instructions. As a further guide to planning, following are three different ways in which instructional materials can be classified.

By Content

Basic operating policies, regulations, and procedures govern the operating program of the organization; they include, for example, the specific technical policies and procedures necessary to accomplish the organization's objectives.

Basic administrative policies, regulations,and procedures pertain to the business management of the organization; they are consistent with its operating objectives and policies, including functions and responsibilities, personnel management, fiscal management, and housekeeping services.

Operating directives describe the objectives, responsibilities, authorities, limitations, and relationships of heads of autonomous divisions, plants, or field offices or of heads of special projects.

Office practices and routines include requisitions for personnel service, correspondence preparation, supply requisitioning, filing standards, use of telephone, and records management.

Special-purpose manuals and handbooks focus on specific technical subjects, temporary programs, or special operating programs.

Detailed job methods and performance routines apply to individual workers or units.

Informational materials are for use within the organization and are not binding as policy or procedure.

Spot announcements communicate such information as special events, important personnel changes, and reminders.

By Applicability

General instructions are applicable to all parts of the organization, both at the home office and among its branch or field offices, except as provided in individual releases. However, there may be separate forms for home and field office use.

Home-office instructions are directed only toward home-office personnel, home-office problems, or home-office treatment of field problems or activities.

Field instructions are directed toward branch or field offices for guidance, but also are for the information and guidance of home-office personnel charged with planning, reviewing, servicing, or working with field operations.

Unit instructions limit the functions and personnel under the control of the issuing unit, whether a division, department, branch, section, or field supervisory office.

By Form

The individual letter, memorandum, telex, or telegram is used for general daily communication. It is a convenient means of answering questions and stating individual rules, confidential policies, temporary instructions, exceptions to rules, and modifications of policy and procedure. It should not be used for permanent instructions of general applicability.

Circular releases or bulletins are duplicated issuances usually dealing with a single subject. Generally issued through numbered series, they are easily identified and used when ease of reference and general applicability are important factors. Sometimes they are issued prior to inclusion in a revisable manual or when they pertain to subjects not included in any manual.

The loose-leaf revisable manual houses all materials that are reasonably permanent and have a substantial reference value. The materials included should either apply generally or relate to the overall operations being described. The loose-leaf nature of the manual permits ready revision, addition, and deletion.

Nonrevisable manuals and handbooks are bound or stitched. They present materials not expected to change within a reasonable period. They are suitable for such documents as technical manuals, reference works, individual job instructions, and employee handbooks.

Any system of release is three dimensional, for in some way it must combine all of the last three elements just listed—content, applicability, and form. For example, claims adjustment instructions (content), directed toward field offices (applicability), are issued through a nonrevisable, single purpose manual (form).

DETERMINING TYPES OF NEEDED DIRECTIVES

In every system, directives are divided into two groups: permanent and temporary. Within these two broad categories there usually are several types of directives: (1) joint issuances or those developed by several organizations; (2) those from other organizations; (3) those which are urgent or rushed; and (4) those of a special nature, including telegrams and electronically transmitted messages. You should determine the types of directives to be included in your organization's system.

Permanent Directives

Permanent policies and procedures remain in effect until cancelled. Potential reference use determines whether you should issue a document as a permanent directive. A directive is considered to be permanent if it establishes a permanent organization, delegates authority, states a permanent policy, contains an approved procedure, prescribes a method, or establishes standards of operation. If the directive contains information used for reference and guidance, it should also be issued as a permanent one.

Daily communications are handled through correspondence channels. However, two factors—access and issuing level—indicate when certain memos should take the form of a permanent directive.

In terms of *access,* correspondence is normally retired to a records center after it has been retained for a specified number of years. If the subject matter is likely to be effective for a longer period, placing it in a permanent directive ensures its accessibility for as long as it is needed. The correspondence filing system frequently is not as streamlined as that of directives. If employees frequently refer to the subject, placing it in a permanent directive should make it easier to find.

In terms of *issuing level,* directives usually require approval by someone high in the organization's hierarchy. If memos are used as directives, they generally have not received the necessary clearance.

Specific names are given to permanent types to distinguish them from temporary types. The most common Federal Government permanent directives include orders, instructions, and regulations. Handbooks are another type of permanent directive. They contain policy, procedures, and instructions usually covering a complete subject area.

Temporary Directives

Temporary policies and procedures have no continuing reference value. They remain in effect for a fixed period of time such as 90 days and contain the date on which they are to be cancelled. They should be used only in emergencies to modify long-term policy or procedure and should be replaced promptly by a permanent directive.

The distinction between permanent and temporary policy or procedure reduces the volume of material retained in the system. If a directive merely changes a previous directive, it should be released as a temporary directive. Permanent changes added to the system obviously should be issued as permanent directives.

Methods of Issuance

Joint Issuances—Organizations must include any directive that has been developed by a joint effort with another organization and is applicable to both. You should identify such directives within the subject classification system and file them accordingly.

Releases From Other Organizations—It is common practice to issue policies and procedures that cross organizational lines. Of course, the ideal arrangement for handling such directives is a single intraorganizational system used by all offices and bureaus. Some organizations receive technical or functional direction from an outside source. If several units within the receiving organization can apply the content without change, you should assign the applicable subject classification number to the directive and then distribute it. If there is a possibility that the content may be misinterpreted, rewrite the directive to conform with the receiving organization's standards before distributing.

Urgent or Rushed Issuance—You should make provisions for directives requiring immediate action by simply stating the priority or by using a special marking, such as colored bordered pages. Assign priorities only when it is absolutely necessary to obtain quick action. Better still is a system so efficient and fast that there is little need for urgent or rushed directives.

Special Issuances—Policies and procedures released as telegrams, telexes, cablegrams, or other electronically transmitted messages should be identified as directives within the system. You should reissue releases sent originally as messages in the established directive format within a set period of time, such as 30 days. Reissuance of notices initially sent as wire releases is unnecessary.

Converting From One System to Another

Many times an existing directives system must be totally converted to a new system. This involves a series of expensive actions. The directives manager must incorporate all policies and procedures that employees keep and use either as mandatory reference or as recommended guides. An evaluation of all issuances collected for the inventory and a schedule or timetable for the actual conversion should be included.

The conversion process presents an excellent opportunity to offset the costs of conversion by effecting major improvements in written policy and procedure. For this reason, you should plan conversion carefully. Offices of primary interest should be told of the advantages to them and urged to devote their best effort towards streamlining the content of the directives for which they are responsible.

Gradually Converting Directives—If you are the directives manager, set a date at which time all existing policies and procedures must be reissued. This should be cleared by the proper officials. Some items collected will need revision and updating by the time an organization's issuances are converted to the new system. The time required for reproducing a large stockpile of directives delays reissuing all policies and procedures, but the conversion process must not defeat the essential point of having all policies and procedures current at all times. The complete reissuance of all directives at one time requires a special budgeting to cover costs. Therefore, conversion should proceed on a gradual, agreed-upon basis.

Schedule and Target Dates—The directives manager also sets a target date for the conversion of each directive. The size of the conversion job varies with the type of issuance and with the status of its content. Some need only slight editing. When setting the target date, determine the amount of work required in relation to the staff available. Also, consider reprinting costs. For a lengthy directive, a long-range target date, perhaps as much as 12–18 months, is best.

Converting to the New System—In developing a complete conversion plan, you should get the concurrence and approval of the top management. The final conversion plan should:

- List the issuances included.
- Point out who is responsible for rewriting each issuance.
- Give the completion date for the entire project.
- Establish target dates for incorporation of specific issuances.
- Set up controls to evaluate progress and to see that target dates are met.
- State action and timing for the conversion of all issuances at lower **organizational levels.**

11

How-to-Do-It Instructions

How can one estimate the millions of dollars lost each year through poor instructions? These are the costs of damage to consumer and industrial products resulting from the ineffective instructions often accompanying the gadgetry and mechanisms sold for home, office, industrial, and recreational use. In addition, millions of hours are lost in industry and government because of poor training of employees. This chapter examines the specialized types of materials that are included in technical manuals and training literature, and the methods used to present these materials.

TECHNICAL MANUALS

The technical manual usually covers assembling, operating and maintaining, or servicing a mechanical or electronic device. The two most frequent types of instructions are operating and service instructions issued in separate manuals or combined in one. Generally, they include parts lists and overhaul instructions. Most technical manuals are approximately 8-1/2 × 11 inches in size, although smaller sizes are often used for greater portability.

Audience requirements must be considered in determining the writing level. As a rule, technical manuals are written for an eighth-grade school level. Although readers may be technically qualified, they are not necessarily familiar with the concepts or operation of the type of equipment with which you may be dealing. In general, therefore, keep technical writing as simple as possible, even for the technical reader. Avoid technical jargon, unless there are no other meaningful words which can be substituted.

Typical Contents of a Technical Manual

A technical manual usually includes the following elements:

Theory of operation is a brief description of the operating principles and procedures in sufficient detail so that the operator has an overall understanding of the equipment.

Detailed description is a descriptive disassembly of the mechanism into all of its principal components. It describes each component's function and usually includes cut-away or exploded-view drawings. Parts lists frequently are included also.

Assembly and installation outlines special unpacking instructions; shows the steps or assembly of the item and initial mechanical adjustments; provides wiring diagrams, narrative descriptions of wiring connections, and mechanical and electrical tests for proper assembly.

Operation covers start-and-stop procedures, with particular reference to break-in and warm-up procedures; adjustments to be made in bringing equipment to optimum performance; performance tests; and special limits and precautions to be observed.

Inspection and maintenance includes normal maintenance requirements, lubrication, adjustments, inspection of operating and stationary parts, inspection tests, necessary adjustments to be made, and trouble-shooting charts.

Overhaul offers detailed instructions for disassembly, check-out of all parts, repair and replacement, and reassembly.

Safety instructions list precautions for the safety of personnel and equipment. This is a general point of emphasis and summary on precautions which ordinarily are covered throughout the text of the instruction book.

Parts lists include a list of all parts or of parts for which replacement may be needed, identified by reference to text figures and index numbers, part numbers, and narrative nomenclature. The identifying numbers must correspond to the index numbers shown in the exploded view and cut-away drawings.

How to Describe Processes

The general rules for clear writing, discussed in Chapter 3, are applicable here except that it is even more critical that precise instructions, such as the following, be given:

- Identify the process by its correct name and description.

- State the basic principle or theory involved in the operating process.

- Describe what is to be accomplished or what the product of the operation is to be, giving some general criteria.

- List each step in order of actual operator performance, omitting nothing, no matter how minor it may seem.

- Explain what to do, how to do it, and when to do it for each step.

- Use active verbs in the second person whenever possible.

- Be clear as to cause and effect.

- Identify symptoms of error or failure, and state corrective action for each type of situation.

- State any precautions to be taken.

- Identify special hazards or dangers.

- Provide instructions for maintenance of any equipment used.

- Tell what to do with the completed work.

- Tell what to do about situations not covered by the instructions.

Production of a Technical Manual

The first element to consider in producing a technical manual is the overall cost analysis. Before separating the job into cost units, however, you should have an idea of the effort needed and the nature of the end product. Determine the following:

1. What specifically must be done to satisfy the requirements of the company or of the contracting agency?

2. How much of the source material is presently available and in what shape is it?

3. What effort is needed to obtain the remainder of the source material?

4. Is travel required?

5. How many and what kinds of illustrations are needed?

6. Are there design changes which require re-do of the work?

7. How many drafts are anticipated?

8. What is the probable size, the number of pages, and the method of reproduction?

Having made this preliminary analysis, prepare a budget which includes cost estimates for the following:

Writing time (if charges are applicable)—time spent in research, conferences, preparation of outlines and drafts, planning and layout of illustrations and tables, travel time, required supervision, and overhead assistance.

Illustrations and photographs—actual photography, retouching, opaquing, and drawing in of index references. For line drawings, roughly estimate lay-out costs, inking, and shading. On all illustrations, figure checking costs.

Editing—at least two complete passes through.

Editorial production—at least three complete typings with additional page changes and corrections. Allow for proofreading of each complete typing as well as for page revisions. Also allow for proofreading of galley proofs and page proofs from the printer, if the document is typeset.

Preparatory reproduction—any preliminary illustration setups, blueprints, photostats, and photographic work.

Printing and reproduction—marking copy for printer, conferences with printer, pasting up dummy, obtaining cost estimates, and actual physical estimates of printing and binding.

Miscellaneous charges—transportation and subsistence. Allow pro rata overhead charges for use of plant, facilities, and general clerical assistance.

To organize the writing job:

1. Make a list of all the specifications of what to include in the final instruction manual.

2. Gather all the available source material, including the original project proposal, interim reports, and all applicable drawings and specifications.

3. Study the equipment to become acquainted with its purpose, theory of operation, functioning, major components and inter-relationships, starting-and-stopping procedures, and any other features which add to preliminary knowledge.

4. Make an overall schematic diagram of the entire assembly; do the same for the subassemblies.

5. Make lists of all parts, such as accessory equipment, test equipment, special service tools, and connecting cables.

6. Prepare a brief overall outline and then expand it into a more detailed complete outline; check this with the product or project engineer for completeness and for technical accuracy but not necessarily for presentation.

7. Prepare a first draft; have it reviewed by the project personnel.

8. Prepare final or semifinal drafts which include the working in of all illustrative materials.

Throughout the preparation of the manual, technical writers should consult frequently with the project engineers to keep abreast of constant refinements. The technical writer must recognize that drafts are subject to change. Adjustments are made more easily in written drafts and drawings than at the very end of project engineering.

TRAINING LITERATURE

While almost any kind of instructional or explanatory literature is used for training, better results are obtained by using especially prepared literature. Different techniques are required if the object involves attitudes, ideas, knowledge, and skills rather than policies, procedures, step-by-step job sequences, and reference information.

When developing training literature, seek various ways to overcome resistance to learning. Organize your material into "learning units" which build progressive understanding:

Avenues to Learning—To write for readers, find out how much they know about the subject, what the conceptions and misconceptions are, the related kinds of information or skill the typical reader has, and the best learning sequence.

Building and Maintaining Interest—People learn most and best about those things in which they are interested or "what's in it for me?" Some training materials are naturally important to the trainee, such as job instruction material which must be studied to learn a new procedure or new skill. This self-evident reason for learning carries with it a very high motivation as a basis for sustaining interest. In many other situations, however, the material focuses on the building of working attitudes, the improvement of the quality of performance, or the acquisition of ideas where the immediate benefit to the employee may not be self-evident. Arrange the material, then, so that the learner can realize what the accomplishments are and understand what that means. This is particularly important when the training material is self-administering, so that the trainee is not under the discipline of a classroom situation.

Structured Ideas—The stream of information given to readers must have a logic which enables them to see each idea in relation to a total pattern or plan. This logic usually consists of a description of a goal and a departure point followed by a presentation of the steps necessary to achieve the goal. Each type of idea presentation has its own logical solution. For example, material might be organized into a general treatment of most conditions to be encountered, followed by the treatment of major variations or trouble-shooting categories.

Building on the Familiar—New concepts, techniques, or processes are more readily understood and learned if they are related to familiar things or experiences. Preferably, these should be within the specific field. But if this is not feasible, seek parallel situations within the readers' experiences. Remember that the reader feels uncomfortable in the face of the unknown.

Active Learning—An important phase of the learning process is implementation. If equipment is to be used, use the training literature as a preparatory and review aid. If no instructor is present, present a safe sequence which enables readers to test understanding of the instruction through actual practice.

If the instruction focuses on specific paperwork, the written material together with illustrations can depict each step in filling out the forms. However, if the instructions are built around ideas or concepts, the emphasis should be on discussion stimulation or on current application to reinforce the learning process. Instruction manuals should incorporate questions, discussion topics, problem assignments, and writing exercises, all intended to induce practice in order to intensify the acquisition of learning.

The Attention Span—Most people understand one idea at a time. There is no fixed rule as to this; usually, the higher the level of intelligence, the more one can grasp and the more which can be added to the store of knowledge. Other influences which expand or limit the attention span include:

- Effectiveness of presentation.
- Extent of reader's motivation or interest.
- Complexity or simplicity of the information.
- Logic of the presentation.
- Familiarity of the readers with the subject matter.
- Conditions under which the readers are expected to study the material.
- Reader morale.

The training manual should be limited to one subject or one group of related subjects. Individual sections should each present portions of the overall subject, with further subdivisions to the point of readily assimilable units of learning. This principle also applies to the illustrations incorporated in the training material.

Repetition and Review—The subdivision of ideas into digestible portions enables you to spread the learning out over a period of time. Note, however, that while spaced learning has the advantage of intensifying learning, there is some danger of forgetting. There is a great amount of memory fall-off which occurs immediately after initial learning. For this reason, each lesson unit needs to make reference to the original learning.

Design of Training Manuals and Instructions

The following suggestions may be adapted to fit your readership and training requirements:

The Introduction—Before launching into the actual sequence of ideas or training instructions, ease the reader into the subject by providing a preface or an introductory chapter. This background discussion or statement of importance clarifies benefits to the company as well as to the employee. It can include an explanation of the relationship of training operation.

Contents of Training Manuals—Training manuals cover every conceivable phase of work. Popularly, they are built around standard job sequences and duties, but they also run the gamut from training in the performance of complex paperwork to the understanding of broad management and behavioral principles.

A major manufacturer uses training manuals in its assembly line operations. Because the complex electronic and mechanical assemblies involve precision work, highly detailed assembly line manuals are prepared. The first step in preparation is to conduct a job analysis by a qualified methods engineer who draws also on the skills of experienced workers. The result is a step-by-step sequence which serves as a guide.

Photographs together with captions are mounted in a loose-leaf book; under each photographic print is a short caption of two or three lines. Thus, instruction is presented through the photographs themselves. These are more quickly grasped than the lengthy text which they replace. A mechanical sequence is ideally suited to this type of treatment.

Learning Units—The concept of the learning unit, as previously explained, is that the trainee absorbs and retains only a limited amount of new information. The amount absorbed varies according to the complexity and range of the subject. Therefore, you should organize it in three stages: an introduction, the body, and the conclusion. The introduction serves as a transitional recall and review of earlier material as well as an introduction or preview of the new material. The conclusion does not serve merely as a summary; rather it brings out key points that have been made. Also, it gives a brief preview of the next lesson unit, although this is not necessary.

Auxiliary Aids to Learning—While illustrations and charts have a very definite value in training literature, they must satisfy at least one of two criteria: either they contribute information on their own or they contribute to the communication of the ideas embodied in the written text. Do not include them merely for the sake of artistry. Illustrations can be included legitimately, however, when they contribute a sense of mood or tone. Auxiliary devices which aid the reader include checklists, references to other sources of information and assistance, and bibliographies or reading lists.

Leaders' Guides—A specialized form of the training manual is a leader's guide—also called a meeting guide or meeting manual—for the use of the discussion leader. Typically, a leader's guide includes information which the leader needs to prepare for the meeting, a duplicate of the information which is distributed to the discussion participants or trainees, and advisory notes to the leader to assist in managing each step of the discussion.

A very effective form of display of the conference leader's notes is to divide the page into two columns. The right-hand column is either for the leader's outline or actual remarks. The left-hand column then is used for special notes and cues. These tell the leader what to emphasize, what kinds of questions to address to the group, reminders to pass out material, remarks pertaining to charts which are to be used, reminders to tell certain stories or anecdotes, reminders about elapsed time up to that point, and anything else which helps the discussion leader. Some leaders' guides are quite elaborately prepared, even to the point of including miniature sketches of materials to be put on the blackboard or an easel pad.

A typical leader's guide is one prepared by the staff of a pharmaceutical manufacturer designed for experienced managers who are able to discuss practical problems of organization. The course explores in detail the executive's responsibility for clarifying jobs, for delegating, for planning, for decision-making, and for generally improving habits of personal efficiency. The course consists of seven sessions. For each one, the participants receive one or more reading handouts. The discussion leader has these as well as each of the outlines for each of the discussion sessions. While some leaders' guides contain the full, literal text of the speaker's remarks, others are in outline form so that the leader can project personality and ingenuity into the discussion itself.

Appendix A

Union Carbide Corporation Style Manual for Corporate Policies and Procedures*

*Reprinted with permission of Union Carbide Corporation, New York, NY

STYLE
MANUAL
FOR CORPORATE POLICIES
AND PROCEDURES

UNION
CARBIDE

UNION CARBIDE — STYLE MANUAL FOR CORPORATE POLICIES AND PROCEDURES

SUBJECT	DATE	NUMBER	PAGE
INTRODUCTION	12/1/	1	1

PURPOSE/BACKGROUND

This Style Manual provides guidelines to writers and publishers in the preparation of policy and procedure manuals at Union Carbide. The content, organization, physical characteristics and maintenance of a manual are presented with illustrations. Application of these guidelines will help to provide uniformity of approach in the presentation of policy and procedural material.

The development and communication of written policies and procedures which achieve agreed upon objectives through uniform action and efficient management are essential elements of the Union Carbide Management System.

Over the years, the growth and complexity of business activity and management's increasing span of control combined with newly developing external requirements of regulatory agencies clearly demonstrate the need to establish clear and concise policies and procedures which:

- Clarify organizational accountability and limits of authority.
- Provide consistency in performing repetitive transactions.
- Provide a means for uniform instruction and performance evaluation.
- Facilitate auditing and control.
- Demonstrate compliance with the law.

UNION CARBIDE — STYLE MANUAL FOR CORPORATE POLICIES AND PROCEDURES

SUBJECT	DATE	NUMBER	PAGE
TABLE OF CONTENTS	12/1/		1

UNION CARBIDE

STYLE MANUAL FOR CORPORATE POLICIES AND PROCEDURES

SUBJECT	DATE	NUMBER	PAGE
INTRODUCTION	12/1/	1	3

• Category II - Policies and Procedures

Policies and procedures issued by managers of the functional components of Union Carbide to define and implement their delegated line, coordinating, and service roles.

Category II Policies and Procedures are:

- Generally applicable to the organization as a whole on either a worldwide or on a United States and Puerto Rico only basis.

- Intended to be important elements in achieving worldwide or United States and Puerto Rico integration and consistency of approach.

- Expected to contain more detailed procedures in order to meet the objective of providing ground rules for day-to-day operation.

- Usually included in manuals designated and associated with a particular function, for example, Accounting, Purchasing, Employee Relations.

Examples of Category II Policies and Procedures Manuals include those such as Corporate Accounting, Purchasing, Employee Relations, International Procedures, Corporate Planning & Budgeting, Financial & Related Policies, etc.

• Divisional/Departmental/Area Policies and Procedures issued by operating divisions to support their delegated line roles.

RESPONSIBILITY

The responsibility for maintenance and issuance of this manual and for providing a service role to Categories I and II, and Division/Area/Department policy manual writers is delegated to the Financial Policies, Procedures & Consulting Department, Tarrytown, NY 10591.

SUBJECT	DATE	NUMBER	PAGE
INTRODUCTION	12/1/	1	2

SCOPE

The Style Manual applies to the following areas:

• Category I - Policies

Standing decisions of the Chairman of the Board and the President of UCC that are applicable worldwide or to the United States and Puerto Rico.

- Functional line roles delegated by the Chairman or President—generally through corporate officers to corporate departments. These functional services are supplied on a worldwide or United States and Puerto Rico basis as specified in the policy. Delegation of such line roles results in a monopoly right to provide the functional services and restrains other component managers from providing their own.

- Coordinating roles delegated by the Chairman or President to component managers or corporate departments that are worldwide or United States and Puerto Rico in scope. Coordinating roles carry the right to make recommendations to the organization as a whole that cannot be ignored. The means of coordinating are the policies, procedures, or objectives which are issued by the coordinator for compliance by the organization as a whole. These policies, procedures, or objectives can and should be challenged but they cannot be ignored.

- Statements which define the basic mode of management. These include such things as the Employee, Social and Information Commitments in the Corporate Charter, the Policy Statement on Business Integrity and Ethics, etc.

Category I policies are intended to be the apex of corporate policies and procedures from which all others are derived and with which they must not conflict. The Corporate Policy Manual is comprised of Category I Policies.

Left page (Page 4)

UNION CARBIDE — STYLE MANUAL FOR CORPORATE POLICIES AND PROCEDURES

SUBJECT	DATE	NUMBER	PAGE
INTRODUCTION	12/1/	1	4

DEVELOPING A CATEGORY II PROCEDURES MANUAL

The publication of a manual is a formidable assignment; a number of tasks are involved in its planning and creation and they entail a substantial investment in managerial, technical and clerical effort.

When planning to establish a new manual or substantially revise one or several manuals, it is suggested that a detailed action plan be developed at the outset. A well thought-out plan will identify the essential tasks which must be undertaken and provide management with an understanding of the work involved and engender their support.

An illustration of an Action Plan for developing a Category II procedures manual (See Exhibit 1-A) describes an objective, standards, needed program steps, accountabilities and dates essential to the orderly development of a manual.

Right page (Page 5)

UNION CARBIDE — STYLE MANUAL FOR CORPORATE POLICIES AND PROCEDURES

SUBJECT	DATE	NUMBER	PAGE
INTRODUCTION	12/1/	1	5

EXHIBIT 1-A

ILLUSTRATION OF AN ACTION PLAN FOR DEVELOPING A CATEGORY II PROCEDURES MANUAL

OBJECTIVE

To provide the Controller's Group with an integrated system for developing, publishing and maintaining Category II procedures which support the line, coordinating and service roles delegated to the Controller.

STANDARDS

A. Procedures developed are consistent with, and supportive of, the Corporate Policy Manual.

B. Accountable managers are delegated to develop, recommend, integrate and issue procedures.

C. The format, style, cataloging and scope are established and standardized.

D. Procedures are written clearly, briefly, accurately and serve the needs of recipients.

E. A system for reviewing, clearing, approving, publishing and distributing is established.

F. Procedures promote auditability.

DESIGN OR STUDY PHASE

• Inventory and analyze existing Procedure Manuals to be integrated.

• Review and define users "real" needs.

• Determine appropriate content for procedures.

• Determine alternate approaches and combinations for effective publishing and maintenance of Prodcedure Manual(s).

• Determine effective style and format for Procedure Manual(s).

IMPLEMENTATION PHASE

• Scheduling, priorities, writing concepts.

• Approval, Authorization and Publication.

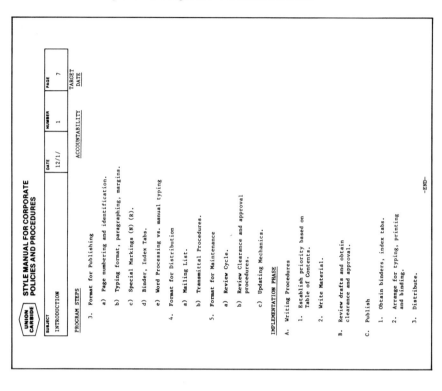

UNION CARBIDE — STYLE MANUAL FOR CORPORATE POLICIES AND PROCEDURES

SUBJECT: INTRODUCTION | DATE: 12/1/ | NUMBER: 1 | PAGE: 7

PROGRAM STEPS | ACCOUNTABILITY | TARGET DATE

3. Format for Publishing
   a) Page numbering and identification.
   b) Typing format, paragraphing, margins.
   c) Special Markings (N) (R).
   d) Binder, Index Tabs.
   e) Word Processing vs. manual typing

4. Format for Distribution
   a) Mailing List.
   b) Transmittal Procedures.

5. Format for Maintenance
   a) Review Cycle.
   b) Review Clearance and approval procedures.
   c) Updating Mechanics.

IMPLEMENTATION PHASE

A. Writing Procedures
   1. Establish priority based on Table of Contents.
   2. Write Material.

B. Review drafts and obtain clearance and approval.

C. Publish
   1. Obtain binders, index tabs.
   2. Arrange for typing, printing and binding.
   3. Distribute.

—END—

SUBJECT: INTRODUCTION | DATE: 12/1/ | NUMBER: 1 | PAGE: 6

PROGRAM STEPS | ACCOUNTABILITY | TARGET DATE

A. Inventory and Analyze existing procedures.
   1. Objective, content, style, scope, format, distribution and maintenance.
   2. Review user needs.

B. Review alternate approaches, develop and recommend standards for format, publishing, distribution and maintenance.
   1. Determine Table of Contents, Scope of Manual, Criteria for Inclusion of Material.
   2. Determine format for writing (presentation/organization of content).
      a) Writing Style
         – Narrative
         – Outline
         – Playscript
         – Combination
      b) Introduction to Manual (Establish uniform editorial captions) for example:
         – Purpose
         – Scope
         – Delegation
         – Style
         – Location of Material
         – Maintenance of Procedures
      c) Manual Sections (establish uniform editorial captions) for example:
         – Purpose
         – Policy
         – Scope
         – Responsibility
         – Overview/Synopsis
         – Critical Considerations
         – Procedure
         – Appendix

SUBJECT	DATE	NUMBER	PAGE
CONTENTS OF A MANUAL	12/1/	2	2

GLOSSARY OF TERMS

Provides a definition of terms used throughout the manual to assure uniform meanings for commonly used words or abbreviations.

(For illustration of Glossary of Terms - See Exhibit 2-C)

POLICY STATEMENTS

A policy statement is a continuing directive applying to recurring questions and problems important in setting the limits and directions of managerial actions through which objectives of the enterprise are to be reached.

Illustration of Policy Statements

Records Retention And Protection

Records are to be retained and protected as long as they are needed for normal business operations and for such period as is necessary to fulfill the Corporation's obligations to its stockholders, customers, employees, governmental agencies and to the public. Records are to be retained for the periods of time specified by retention policy and at the end of this time are to be promptly destroyed.

Chart of Accounts

There will be a single Chart of Accounts to provide a logical approach to classification and definitions for all asset, liability, equity, revenue and expense accounts

PROCEDURAL STATEMENTS

Procedures are standardized methods of performing specified work. Procedures implement policies and they explain the "how" by which objectives are obtained.

Illustration of a Procedural Statement

Custodians will be notified by the Corporate Records Center 30 days before their records are destroyed. Upon receipt of the notification form, custodians will sign and return form to the Center.

UNION CARBIDE — STYLE MANUAL FOR CORPORATE POLICIES AND PROCEDURES

SUBJECT	DATE	NUMBER	PAGE
CONTENTS OF A MANUAL	12/1/	2	1

This section describes the principal parts of policy and procedure manuals, including: Table of Contents, Introduction and Glossary of Terms, Policy Statements, Procedural Statements, Exhibits, Subject Index.

The Table of Contents, Introduction, Exhibits and Subject Index facilitate the location of material. Procedural statements comprise the bulk of most manuals. Policy statements are usually brief and take up a small portion of the volume (except in those instances where the entire manual is devoted to the exposition of policy, e.g., Corporate Policy Manual, Financial & Related Policies Manual).

TABLE OF CONTENTS

Includes the title of the manual, a listing of the general subject matter treated in each section, and within each section the specific subject with its beginning page number.

• Usually located at beginning of manual.

• May be supplemented by a more detailed table of contents for each section or index.

(For illustration of Table of Contents - See Exhibit 2-A)

INTRODUCTION

The introductory part of a manual includes:

• The purpose of the manual.

• Its scope and authority.

• Information relative to preparation, distribution and maintenance.

• Instructions on using the manual.

• Cross references to other related policy and procedure manuals.

(For illustration of Introduction - See Exhibit 2-B)

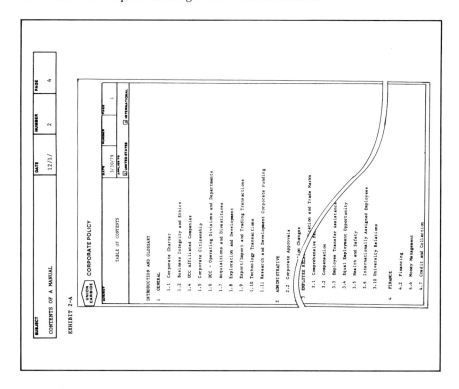

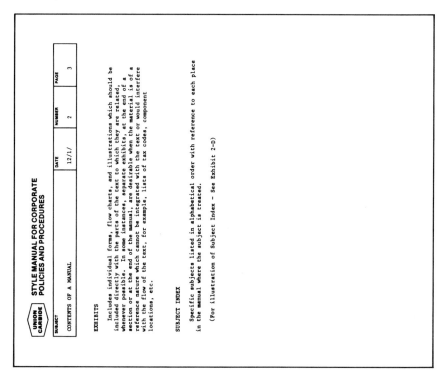

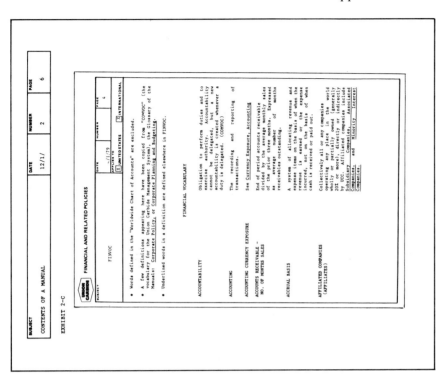

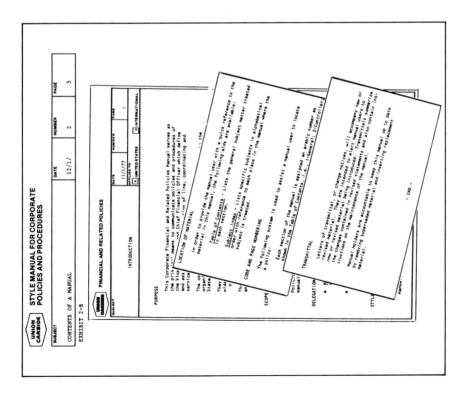

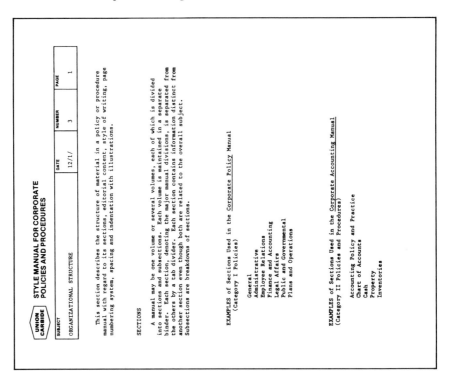

UNION CARBIDE — STYLE MANUAL FOR CORPORATE POLICIES AND PROCEDURES

SUBJECT	DATE	NUMBER	PAGE
ORGANIZATIONAL STRUCTURE	12/1/	3	1

This section describes the structure of material in a policy or procedure manual with regard to its sections, editorial content, style of writing, page numbering system, spacing and indentation with illustrations.

SECTIONS

A manual may be one volume or several volumes, each of which is divided into sections and subsections. Each volume is maintained in a separate binder. Each section, denoting the major manual divisions, is separated from the others by a tab divider. Each section contains information distinct from another section even though both are related to the overall subject. Subsections are breakdowns of sections.

EXAMPLES of Sections Used in the Corporate Policy Manual (Category I Policies)

    General
    Administrative
    Employee Relations
    Finance and Accounting
    Legal Affairs
    Public and Governmental
    Plans and Operations

EXAMPLES of Sections Used in the Corporate Accounting Manual (Category II Policies and Procedures)

    Accounting Policy and Practice
    Chart of Accounts
    Cash
    Property
    Inventories

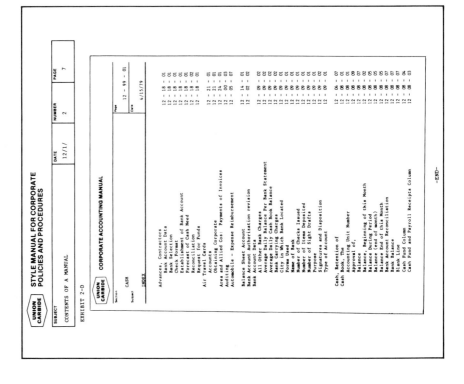

UNION CARBIDE — STYLE MANUAL FOR CORPORATE POLICIES AND PROCEDURES

SUBJECT	DATE	NUMBER	PAGE
CONTENTS OF A MANUAL	12/1/	2	7

EXHIBIT 2-D

UNION CARBIDE — CORPORATE ACCOUNTING MANUAL

Section
Subject: CASH

Page: 12 - 99 - 01
Date: 4/15/79

INDEX

—END—

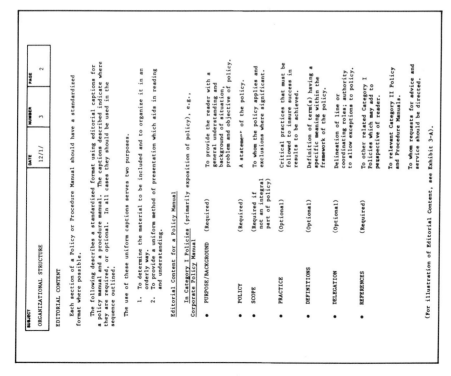

SUBJECT	DATE	NUMBER	PAGE
ORGANIZATIONAL STRUCTURE	12/1/	3	3

Editorial Content for a Procedures Manual

In Category II Procedures (Primarily procedurally-oriented manuals), e.g., Corporate Accounting Manual, Employee Relations Manual, Purchasing Manual, Corporate Planning and Budgeting Manual etc.

- PURPOSE (Required) — Why the procedure is there. What the user is expected to do. What the procedure is expected to accomplish.

- POLICY (Required) — Restatement of the policy which authorized this procedure. (Refer to appropriate policy manual)

- SCOPE (Required) — To whom the procedure applies and significant exclusions.

- RESPONSIBILITY (Required) — Who is responsible for application and interpretation; authority to allow exceptions to the procedure.

- OVERVIEW/SYNOPSIS (Optional) — Treatment of the overall subject of the procedure to provide readers with a general understanding and interface with other procedures and functions. This could be narrative, flowchart or diagram.

- CRITICAL CONSIDERATIONS (Optional) — Critical actions required to implement procedure. Early warning intent.

- PROCEDURE (Required) — Provides the instructions for implementation of a policy and is arranged sequentially.

- APPENDIX (As Needed) — Location of forms, tables or charts which, if included in above elements, would detract from the flow of narrative. Includes also definition of term(s) having specific meaning in this procedure.

(For illustration of editorial content - See Exhibit 3-B)

SUBJECT	DATE	NUMBER	PAGE
ORGANIZATIONAL STRUCTURE	12/1/	3	2

EDITORIAL CONTENT

Each section of a Policy or Procedure Manual should have a standardized format where possible.

The following describes a standardized format using editorial captions for a policy manual and a procedure manual. The captions described indicate where they are required, or optional. In all cases they should be used in the sequence outlined.

The use of these uniform captions serves two purposes.

1. To determine the material to be included and to organize it in an orderly way.
2. To provide a uniform method of presentation which aids in reading and understanding.

Editorial Content for a Policy Manual

In Category I Policies (primarily exposition of policy), e.g., Corporate Policy Manual

- PURPOSE/BACKGROUND (Required) — To provide the reader with a general understanding and background of situation, problem and objective of policy.

- POLICY (Required) — A statement of the policy.

- SCOPE (Required if not an integral part of policy) — To whom the policy applies and exclusions where significant.

- PRACTICE (Optional) — Critical practices that must be followed to insure success in results to be achieved.

- DEFINITIONS (Optional) — Definition of term(s) having a specific meaning within the framework of the policy.

- DELEGATION (Optional) — Delineation of line or coordinating roles; authority to allow exceptions to policy.

- REFERENCES (Required) — To other related Category I Policies which may add to perspective of reader. To relevant Category II Policy and Procedure Manuals. To whom requests for advice and service should be directed.

(For illustration of Editorial Content, see Exhibit 3-A).

UNION CARBIDE — STYLE MANUAL FOR CORPORATE POLICIES AND PROCEDURES

SUBJECT	DATE	NUMBER	PAGE
ORGANIZATIONAL STRUCTURE	12/1/	3	5

Illustration of Page Numbering System (Corporate Accounting Manual)

Each page number is composed of three segments: The Section Number, Subject Number, and the individual Page Number of the particular subject.

The numbering system is as follows:

```
20 _____   Section Number (Property)
   03 _____   Subject Number (Acquisitions)
      01 _____   Page Number
```

ARRANGEMENT

The physical arrangement of printed material is important:

- Headings draw attention to the content of paragraphs.
- A solid page of typewritten material is monotonous without headings and indentations.
- Uniformity of arrangement is an orderly way of doing things.

HEADINGS

Headings are guideposts to the subject matter of a paragraph. Their position or the use of capitalization and underlining develop subordinate relationships of sections and subsections.

SUBJECT	DATE	NUMBER	PAGE
ORGANIZATIONAL STRUCTURE	12/1/	3	4

STYLE OF WRITING

A variety of writing styles is available to the publishers of manuals. The material being presented and the user determine which style is most suitable. The style of writing and format should be consistent throughout the sections of a manual.

The most commonly used writing styles include:

- Narrative – This style presents material in story form. It is most commonly used in writing policies.

- Playscript – This style is used to specify the duties of personnel involved in the accomplishment of sequential tasks. It is similar to the script of a play and is used most effectively in presenting detailed procedures.

- Outline – This style arranges material into a formal structured outline. It makes extensive use of capital letters, arabic numerals and lower case letters. It serves the function of dividing an overall procedure into its component parts.

While policies are always written in the narrative style, procedures are usually written using a combination of all styles.

PAGE NUMBERING

The development of an indexing and page numbering system is the responsibility of the writers and publishers of manuals.

Illustration of Page Numbering System (Corporate Policy Manual)

Each section of the manual is assigned an arabic number: General 1, Administrative 2, Employee Relations 3, Finance and Accounting 4, Legal Affairs 5, Public and Governmental 6, Plans and Operations 7.

Each policy statement in a section, filed in order of sequence, is also assigned an arabic number, e.g., 3.6 Employee Relations section, policy statement on internationally assigned employees.

The pages of each policy statement are numbered separately. At the conclusion of each section, the word END is recorded.

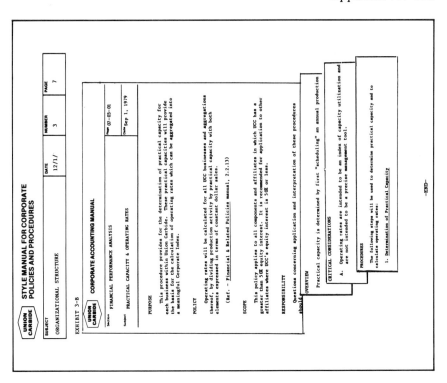

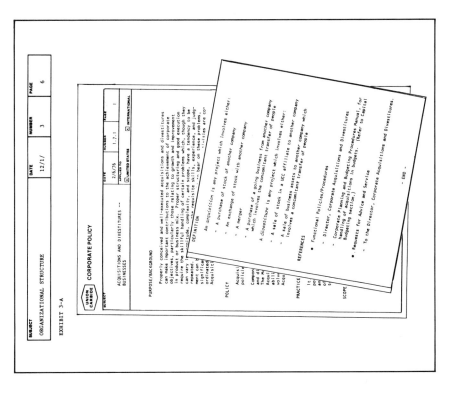

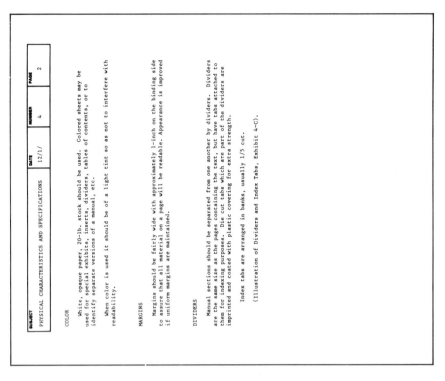

UNION CARBIDE — STYLE MANUAL FOR CORPORATE POLICIES AND PROCEDURES

SUBJECT	DATE	NUMBER	PAGE
PHYSICAL CHARACTERISTICS AND SPECIFICATIONS	12/1/	4	1

This section describes the physical characteristics of a manual including binder cover construction, page type and size, dividers and index tabs.

BINDER

Type – looseleaf.
Construction – three ring supports.
Material – vinyl cover.
Size (outer dimensions) – 11 3/4 X 10.
Capacity – up to 2-1/2 inches of sheets and dividers.
(Illustration of Binder type and Construction, Exhibit 4-A)

PAGE SPECIFICATIONS

Size standard 11 X 8-1/2 inches, 3 hole perforations, straight corners. Where a larger sheet size is required, it can be folded to conform to standard size.

PAGE DESIGN

Pages should be printed on both sides for economy and for minimal bulk in manual.

The masthead should include space for the following information:

The "Union Carbide" hexagon.
The name of the manual.
Section title or description.
Subject of the section.
Page number.
Publication date.
If required the effective date should be in the text of the section

(Illustration of Page Design and Masthead, Exhibit 4-B)

SUBJECT	DATE	NUMBER	PAGE
PHYSICAL CHARACTERISTICS AND SPECIFICATIONS	12/1/	4	2

COLOR

White, opaque paper, 20-lb. stock should be used. Colored sheets may be used for special exhibits, inserts, dividers, tables of contents, or to identify separate versions of a manual, etc.

When color is used it should be of a light tint so as not to interfere with readability.

MARGINS

Margins should be fairly wide with approximately 1-inch on the binding side to assure that all material on a page will be readable. Appearance is improved if uniform margins are maintained.

DIVIDERS

Manual sections should be separated from one another by dividers. Dividers are the same size as the pages containing the text, but have tabs attached to them for indexing purposes. Die cut tabs which are part of the dividers are imprinted and coated with plastic covering for extra strength.

Index tabs are arranged in banks, usually 1/5 cut.

(Illustration of Dividers and Index Tabs, Exhibit 4-C).

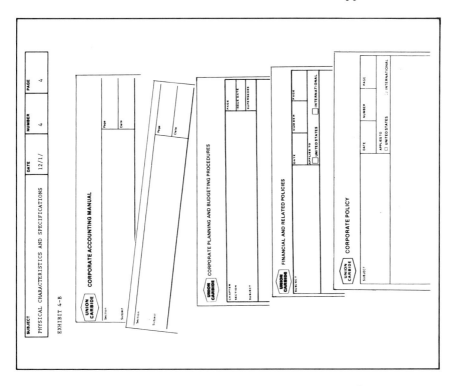

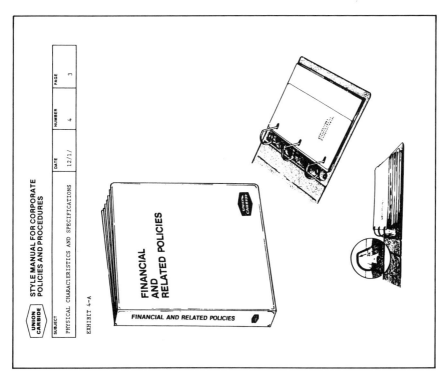

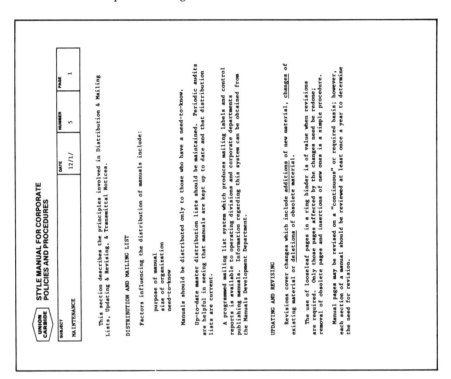

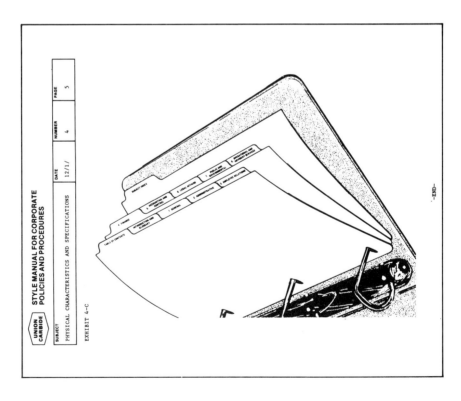

EXHIBIT 4-C

SUBJECT	DATE	NUMBER	PAGE
MAINTENANCE	12/1/	5	3

UNION CARBIDE — STYLE MANUAL FOR CORPORATE POLICIES AND PROCEDURES

Form of Transmission

The material transmitted for review should be typewritten with double spacing and ample margins for written comments.

A distinctive Clearance Document should be used with space for the following:

- Addressee name and address
- Identification of material being transmitted
- Reasons for proposing material, synopsis of material, material to be superseded, etc.
- Deadline for returning material
- Clearance action and signature

(Illustration of Clearance Document, Exhibit 5-A)

TRANSMITTAL NOTICE

Transmittal notices should accompany new or revised manual pages. They alert manual users to new or additional material being introduced.

A transmittal should identify:

- date of revision.
- specific page, subject, paragraph being revised.
- summary explanation of each revision or insert, explaining its purpose and effect on existing practice.
- an effective date for each item transmitted, if different from the transmittal date.
- a listing of pages to be removed with a parallel listing of pages to be inserted.

(Illustration of Transmittal Notice, Exhibit 5-B)

SUBJECT	DATE	NUMBER	PAGE
MAINTENANCE	12/1/	5	2

The following suggestions are made as to a revision procedure:

Clearance and Review

Relates to the development of an efficient process for getting policies and procedures ready for publishing.

Clearance means agreement by interested parties and has as its objectives:

- To refer policy/procedural material to interested parties whose comments contribute to the formulation of effective proposals.
- To coordinate viewpoints and resolve differences.
- To assure management that full staff work is represented in materials submitted for approval.
- To submit to management for resolution unresolved differences.

Selection of Points of Clearance

Clearance should only be obtained from those having a bonafide interest in the material, such as:

- They take some form of action as a result.
- They would be affected materially by the adoption of the proposed policy or procedure.
- They are technical authorities.
- They are administratively accountable for making the review.

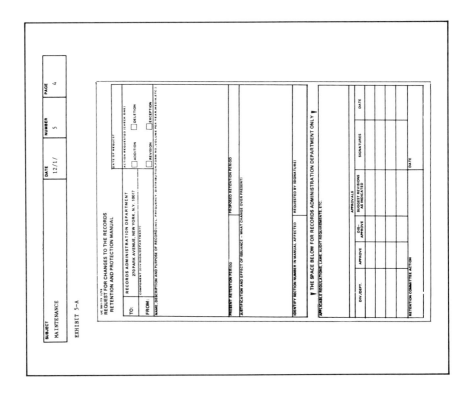

UNION CARBIDE

STYLE MANUAL FOR CORPORATE POLICIES AND PROCEDURES

SUBJECT	DATE	NUMBER	PAGE
MAINTENANCE	12/1/	5	5

EXHIBIT 5–B

UNION CARBIDE

CORPORATE ACCOUNTING MANUAL   TRANSMITTAL

INSTRUCTIONS: In order to communicate the policy/procedural material forwarded with this transmittal and to keep your manual up-to-date, the following steps should be taken.

1. Please review this material prior to inserting it in the manual.
2. Follow the filing instructions in the sequence outlined below.
3. Please bring this change(s) to the attention of your personnel who have a need to know.

EXECUTIVE SUMMARY

FILING INSTRUCTIONS

REMOVE & DESTROY   REPLACE WITH   COMMENTS

December 1, 1979

—END—

SUBJECT	DATE	NUMBER	PAGE
MAINTENANCE	12/1/	5	4

EXHIBIT 5–A

REQUEST FOR CHANGES TO THE RECORDS RETENTION AND PROTECTION MANUAL

DATE OF REQUEST

ACTION REQUESTED (CHECK ONE)
- ADDITION
- DELETION
- REVISION
- EXCEPTION

TO: RECORDS ADMINISTRATION DEPARTMENT
     270 PARK AVENUE, NEW YORK, N.Y. 10017

FROM: COMPONENT (DIVISION/DEPARTMENT)

NAME, DESCRIPTION AND PURPOSE OF RECORD (INCL. FREQUENCY, DISTRIBUTION FORM NO., VOLUME PER YEAR INDIC.ATE)

PRESENT RETENTION PERIOD   PROPOSED RETENTION PERIOD

JUSTIFICATION AND EFFECT OF ISSUANCE – WHAT CHANGE OVER PRESENT)

IDENTIFY SECTION NUMBER IN MANUAL AFFECTED   REQUESTED BY (SIGNATURE)

▼ THE SPACE BELOW FOR RECORDS ADMINISTRATION DEPARTMENT ONLY ▼

APPLICABLE REGULATIONS, LAWS, AUDIT REQUIREMENTS, ETC.

APPROVALS

DIV./DEPT.	APPROVE	DIS-APPROVE	SUGGEST REVISIONS AS INDICATED	SIGNATURES	DATE

RETENTION COMMITTEE ACTION   DATE

—END—

Appendix B

Writing in Plain Language (With Mini Writing Guide)

COMPLYING WITH PLAIN LANGUAGE LAWS*

As more and more states approve and enforce plain language laws all affected organizations should learn how to comply with them. Moreover, the Federal Government has become increasingly interested in quality assurance practices, including literature which relates to products and services. Although this is especially true in the defense, aerospace, food and drug, nuclear, automotive, and computer industries, no organization is now exempt. The following section, which examines the coverage and the readability tests of Connecticut's general and insurance plain language laws, illustrates how one state's legislation influences writing practices.

What Do the Connecticut Plain Language Laws Cover?

The general plain language law purposely limits coverage to the more common consumer transactions, in which a consumer is not represented by a lawyer and must accept the printed form as he or she finds it. Under this law, you are a consumer if you are acting as an individual and enter into an agreement for personal, family, or household purposes. The agreement must be in plain language if it relates to any one of these three transactions:

- You borrow money or receive credit of up to $25,000 from a person or organization who is acting in the ordinary course of business; or

- You buy or lease personal property or services of up to $25,000 from a person or organization acting in the ordinary course of business; or

- You lease a residential dwelling.

Excluded from the coverage of the law are mortgages, real estate deeds, insurance policies, and documents relating to securities transactions. No consumer can bring an action on a contract if (1) the consumer prepared it, or (2) the consumer was represented at the closing by an attorney and this fact is shown in the contract.

*Adapted with permission from John O. Morris, "Plain Language Is Here—Are You Ready?" *Connecticut Law Tribune*, October 1, 1979.

The insurance plain language law requires that the policy form be in plain language if the coverage of the policy is designed primarily for personal, family, or household needs. The exclusions from the law are technical and are not drafted in plain language.

What Are the Plain Language Tests?

The general plain language law offers the drafter or issuer of a form two choices: to follow the subjective plain language tests of Section 2(b), or to follow the objective "alternate" tests of Section 2(c). The objective tests, and the detailed and carefully drafted procedures for meeting them, are the most pioneering features of this law. Because the tests are wholly objective, there is virtually no room for the kind of disputes or personal judgment that leads to lawsuits. Most creditors, sellers, and lessors will be well advised to design their plain language forms to meet these tests.

The subjective tests are designed for the creditor, seller, or lessor who is occasionally involved in a consumer transaction covered by the law. These tests are easier to follow and, if the drafting is done carefully, the risk of lawsuit should be slight. The subjective tests are also available if a redrafted form unavoidably misses one of the objective tests but appears to comply fully with the subjective tests.

The insurance plain language law contains both objective and subjective tests. The tests of the two laws cover the following plain language principles:

- Prefer everyday words and active verbs.
- Avoid unnecessary polysyllabic words.
- Keep sentences and paragraphs short.
- Use personal pronouns ("we" "you") to name the parties.
- Use headings, and be sure they stand out from the text.
- Use a readable layout with adequate white space.
- Organize a contract logically and carefully.
- Avoid obscure or misleading constructions.
- Use a table of contents, if the contract is long enough.

Objective Tests for Readability—General Plain Language Law

The first five objective tests of the general plain language law relate to readability: (1) The average number of words per sentence must be less than 22; (2) no sentence may exceed 50 words; (3) the average number of words per paragraph must be less than 75; (4) no paragraph may exceed 150 words; and (5) the average number of syllables per word must be less than 1.55. These five readability tests are the most important of the objective tests. Where do they come from and what is their validity?

If you measure the length of sentences and paragraphs and the syllable count per word in mass circulation newspapers and magazines, you will find certain well-established norms which writers ignore at their peril. Editors of these publications have long since learned that circulation drops off if they allow their writers to use sentences and paragraphs that are too long, or words that are unnecessarily polysyllabic. The readability norms of these newspapers and magazines therefore represent a level at which most people find it comfortable to read.

On the other hand, if you measure the length of sentences, paragraphs, and syllables per word in insurance policies, bank loan forms, government regulations, and other legal documents, which we as consumers must deal with regularly, you will find scores that materially exceed the newspaper and magazine norms. These legal documents are simply not written at a reading level which most readers find comfortable.

That, in a nutshell, is what readability tests are all about. Although these tests cannot guarantee clear writing or plain language, they do provide a means of pinpointing and measuring a prime cause for difficult writing.

Readability Tests of the Two Laws: A Comparison—Test 1 of the Connecticut insurance plain language law requires a minimum score of 45 on the Flesch reading ease test. As noted earlier, the Flesch test scores only two items— average words per sentence and average syllables per word—and then combines the two scores to produce an overall rating. The pattern in the insurance industry is to use the Flesch test, with minimum scores varying from state to state. The Connecticut general plain language law intentionally does not use the Flesch test. Instead, it uses the five tests described in this section, for these reasons:

1. These five tests are expressly designed for measuring readability in legal documents and in other forms of complex, analytical writing. They have been tested for this purpose hundreds of times in the past 10 years. No other readability test has been so designed or tested. The Flesch reading ease score is one of two tests Flesch designed in the 1940s to measure readability in general writing.

2. One test measures average paragraph length. The Flesch test does not. Complex legal rules written in long paragraphs are difficult for any reader; the conversion to shorter paragraphs forces a desirable discipline on the writer. Paragraphs can and should be shorter in rule writing than in general expository writing.

3. Two of the tests prescribe maximum lengths for any sentence or paragraph. The Flesch test does not. Only one overly long, structurally difficult, or disorganized sentence or paragraph can create enormous readability and comprehension problems. This is less true in general writing.

4. The five test scores are considered separately. The validity of combining the average-words-per-sentence count and the average-syllables-per-word count into one overall score has simply not been established, particularly

for analytical writing. No one really knows what this score means. All
we know and can prove is that mass circulation newspapers and magazines have measurable norms for each of these tests. The allowable
limits for the five tests are based on these norms.

5. The tests include carefully drafted procedures for counting syllables,
   sentences, and paragraphs. Again, rule writing is not general writing.
   The flexibility which Flesch encouraged in this counting process has
   been carried out in the insurance industry's use of the Flesch test. It is
   not satisfactory, particularly in the defining of a sentence as a unit of
   words ending with a period, semicolon, or colon. This allows sentence
   fragments, without verbs, to be counted as sentences.

The procedures used for counting in Section 8 of the Connecticut general plain
language law strongly encourage the drafter to list and, in listing, to write in
full sentences, not sentence fragments. The sentence-fragment-style of listing,
in rule writing, often leads to exceedingly difficult writing.

Other Objective Tests of the General Plain Language Law

The objective tests not related to readability are largely self-explanatory.
Test 6 requires the use of personal pronouns or actual names, when referring to
the parties to the contract. The ''we''-''you'' style of drafting is a most desirable
change that immediately leads to a simpler, more readable style. Test 7 requires
that no typeface be less than 8 point; test 10 requires captions, of at least 10
point (or underlined, if typewritten). Tests 8 and 9 require 3/16 inch of white
space between paragraphs and sections; and at least 1/2 inch of white space at
all borders of the page. Test 11 requires an average length of line of no more
than 65 characters.

Subjective Tests of the General Plain Language Law

The subjective tests largely parallel the objective tests, except that they
omit specific numerical limits. The drafter has more flexibility but faces the
possibility of lawsuits in which the court will decide if a particular contract does
or does not meet a specific test.

The subjective tests include requirements for the following: (1) short sentences and paragraphs, (2) everyday words, (3) personal pronouns, (4) simple
and active verb forms, (5) readable type size, (6) contrasting ink, (7) section
headings which stand out, (8) use of white space to separate paragraphs and
sections from each other and from the paper border. Test 9 is a catch-all that
requires that the contract be ''written and organized in a clear and coherent
manner.'' This is a worthwhile test; unfortunately, the opportunities for valid
differences of opinion are obvious.

Readability Tests of the Insurance Plain Language Law

This law has seven readability tests. Test 1, and its limitations for the
measuring of rule writing, has been fully discussed previously.

Test 2 requires at least 10-point type, one point leaded. Test 3 requires layout and spacing which separate paragraphs from each other and from the borders. Test 4 requires section headings which stand out. Test 5 requires the policy to avoid the use of unnecessarily long, complicated or obscure words, sentences, paragraphs, or constructions. This test gives the commissioner broad discretion. Test 6 says that the policy must give no undue prominence to any portion of the text, by style, arrangement, or overall appearance. Test 7 requires a table of contents if the policy is over a stated length.

MINI WRITING GUIDE

The following mini writing guide,[1] which appears in an introductory chapter in a manual system for a large corporation, is an example of a clear, readable format and layout. The guide summarizes and illustrates the use of basic principles for writing efficient procedures in plain language.

STANDARD OPERATING GUIDE

MS-4: HOW TO WRITE PROCEDURES

TABLE OF CONTENTS

---

[1]Reprinted with permission by John O. Morris, noted author, president of John O. Morris Associates, and management communications expert, West Hartford, Conn. 06107.

4.1 PURPOSE

This Guide summarizes and illustrates basic principles for
writing procedures for the Policy and Procedure (P&P)
Manual System.

4.2 POLICY

Procedures shall be user-oriented, carefully organized,
written in plain language, and shall follow a standard
format.

4.3 SCOPE

This Guide applies to all procedures in the P&P Manual
System.

4.4 BACKGROUND

  A Well-written procedures are efficient. They save
     everyone's time and help avoid misunderstanding and
     error. When procedures form part of a manual system,
     it is desirable to follow a standard format and to
     consistently use accepted basic principles for writing
     efficient procedures. This Guide presents and illustrates
     these principles and the standard format for the P&P
     Manual System.

  B The sections in this Guide cover 3 topics -

     4.1 through 4.5 provide preliminary information,

     4.6 through 4.10 relate to planning before you write,

     4.11 through 4.13 relate to the writing process itself.

4.5 DEFINITION

As used in this Guide, a "procedure" is a written communication
that tells someone to do, not to do, or how to do, something.
It may be labelled a guide, instruction, order, rule, regulation,
directive, etc.

4.6 PLAN BEFORE YOU WRITE: KNOW YOUR AUDIENCE

  A Who is the audience for your procedure? How many
     different groups are there in this audience? What are
     the needs and levels of interest of each group, as
     related to this procedure? Are they subject-matter
     experts or do they know little about the subject of
     your procedure?

  B As you start to plan the writing of a procedure, ask
     yourself these questions. You do not write a procedure
     for yourself and seldom do you write it solely for
     those who are the experts in the subject matter. Usually,
     you write for a broader audience of non-experts whose
     interests and knowledge may vary widely from yours.
     Look at the procedure from their viewpoint, not yours,
     if you want to succeed.

  C It takes only a few words to say "Know Your Audience"
     and to explain what this means; but it may take considerable
     thought on your part, as procedure writer or reviewer,
     to be sure you have considered carefully the questions
     in paragraph A. Take the time now for this step; it's
     an important one.

4.7 PLAN BEFORE YOU WRITE: GET THE FACTS

A Do you have all the facts you will need to write this
procedure? Here are some questions to ask yourself on
this topic:

1 May I take at its face value the information I
have collected, or should I look behind for hidden
problems that will interfere with the acceptance
of this procedure?

2 Do I need to do further research? Do I need to
meet with anyone else who might be affected by the
procedure? Is there anyone who might oppose this
procedure that I should clear it with?

3 What other procedures will be affected? How does
that affect this procedure?

B An important part of fact-gathering, before starting
the procedure, often involves meeting with people from
each functional area that will be affected and reviewing
the outline of the procedure (not necessarily the
detailed draft). This process avoids the unexpected
problems that can come up later, if preliminary meetings
have not been held.

4.8 PLAN BEFORE YOU WRITE: USE STANDARD OPENING SECTIONS

Begin each Guide, Instruction, or other procedure with the
standard opening sections. Use only the headings that are
appropriate for the particular procedure. Listed below are
the section headings, and a summary of content for each:

TABLE OF CONTENTS

If the procedure is longer than four pages, include
here a table of contents, listing section headings in
order. Do not number or letter the table of contents.

PURPOSE

State the subject of the procedure here, and its purpose.
This heading is mandatory; start every procedure with
it. Give this section and each following one the appropriate
letter or number.

POLICY

State briefly the Corporate, Department or Division
policy that is covered by this procedure. Keep this
section short; don't clutter a policy statement with
procedural details.

SCOPE

Summarize here who the procedure applies to; and what
subject matter it covers.

BACKGROUND

Include here key background facts that will help the
reader who is not a subject matter expert to understand
the procedure better. If there is no table of contents,
consider here a road map paragraph summarizing the
content of the procedure.

DEFINITIONS

Include as few formal definitions as possible. Most
readers find them difficult. Don't put substantive
material into the definition. If the defined term is
used throughout the procedure, include the definition
here; otherwise, define it in the section where it is used.

4.9 PLAN BEFORE YOU WRITE: KNOW THE STANDARD FORMAT

A How To Use Coding System

1   Use the standard decimal/alpha-numeric coding system shown below, as you plan or write your procedure.

2   Use the appropriate code in front of each section or subdivision of a section. Exception: You may omit the code in front of a short introductory paragraph or a series of items (not action steps) in a short list.

3   Refer to a provision in another procedure by using the full code reference.

    For example, if this paragraph is referred to in another procedure, the reference is to "SOG/MS-4.9A3". This is a complete and unique reference, which cannot be confused with any other reference.

4   Refer to a section or subdivision within the same procedure by showing section and subdivision code only.

    For example, if this paragraph is referred to elsewhere in this procedure, the reference is to "4.9A3" or "4.9A3 of this Guide".

5   The coding system is as follows:

Tier	Part	Chapter	Section	first subdivision	second subdivision	(third subdivision)	(fourth subdivision)
SOG/	MS-2	.1	A	1	(A)	(1)	

4.10 PLAN BEFORE YOU WRITE: PREPARE YOUR OUTLINE

A well-written procedure requires a careful outline first. After you have collected the facts, proceed as follows:

A Identify the major topics you plan to cover.

B Write a descriptive heading for each topic.

C Arrange the headings in an order logical for the user.

    Note: This may be a work flow or process order; a functional or subject matter order; or a first things first order. Use the process order, if possible.

D Add subheadings under each section heading.

E Assign code numbers or letters to each section or subdivision. If sections are too long, break them up.

F Consider reviewing your outline with those who will be affected, before you start to write the detailed procedure.

4.11 WRITE AN EFFICIENT PROCEDURE: USE PLAIN LANGUAGE

A <u>Prefer</u> <u>Everyday</u> <u>Words</u>

Prefer the shorter, simpler, everyday words that are
familiar to everyone in your audience. Avoid gobbledygook,
pompous polysyllables and in-house jargon.

> For example, substitute "use" for "utilization",
> "begin" for "commence", and "help" for "facilitate".

B <u>Prefer</u> <u>Active</u>, <u>Action</u> <u>Verbs</u>

The verb is the most important word in the English
sentence. Let it carry the weight of the sentence.
Avoid the passive voice.

> For example, don't say "Consideration should be
> given...". Instead, say "Consider..." or "You must
> consider..." or "You should consider...", depending
> on the meaning.

C <u>Prune</u> <u>Unnecessary</u> <u>Words</u>

Vigorously prune your writing of unnecessary words that
clutter the writing and slow down the reader. (But
don't cut out helpful explanatory material.)

> For example, "We are in the process of obtaining
> permits..." can be cut to "We are obtaining permits...".

4.12 WRITE AN EFFICIENT PROCEDURE: USE LISTS

The basic structure of any procedure is usually an introductory
statement, followed by either a series of action steps for
the user or a series of conditions. Always use a list for
the action steps or conditions. Follow these guides as you
write a list:

A Prefer a full sentence for the introductory statement
   and for each item in the list.

> - In a long list, sentence fragments are confusing.

B List each item separately.

> - If you combine two items in one sentence, the
>   reader may miss the second one.

C List the items in a logical sequence for the reader.

D Be parallel in style throughout the list.

E Be consistent in word choice.

F Avoid the passive voice.

G Separate the action steps in the list from explanatory
   material.

> - Each of these guides is illustrated in this
>   section.

4.13 WRITE AN EFFICIENT PROCEDURE: KEEP SENTENCES AND PARAGRAPHS SHORT

Long sentences and paragraphs do not belong in procedures.
Follow these guides:

A Do not exceed 25 words per sentence, on the average.

B Do not exceed 75 words per paragraph, on the average.

C To estimate the length of sentences and paragraphs,
   proceed as follows:

   1   Assume an average of 10 words per line, for material
        typed in one column on a standard 8½" x 11" sheet.

   2   Count the number of lines per sentence. If the
        sentence exceeds 3 lines, examine it carefully to
        see if it is too long and needs to be broken up.

   3   Count the number of lines per paragraph. If the
        paragraph exceeds 8 lines, examine it carefully to
        see if it is too long and needs to be broken
        up.

Appendix C

Specialized Manual Outlines

The primary directives of virtually all organizations are provided in the general policies and procedures manual. Other specialized directives, however, are also vitally important, such as the organization manual, the sales manual, the employee handbook, and the purchasing manual. This chapter provides a detailed analysis of each of these specialized manuals.

THE ORGANIZATION MANUAL

An organization manual spells out the distribution of authority and responsibility among the components of an organization. The descriptions of the duties and responsibilities of each component are called functional statements, which often contain some of the worst prose imaginable. One reason for this is that vague and ambiguous language is used to cover up or avoid settling organizational or jurisdictional conflicts. Functional statements also tend to be overwritten to lend to the function an air of impressiveness and prestige.

The principal purpose of a functional statement is to fix authority and responsibility, thereby establishing a base of accountability. A collateral purpose is to clarify responsibilities and "settle arguments" among related activities.

The organization manual may be used in program budgeting to relate expenditure programs to officially assigned responsibilities. Also, it may be used to review position classification or other individual duty statements of employees to make sure they are not claiming responsibilities not authorized for their units.

Contents

The organization manual contains statements of policy governing the interrelationships and manner of general operation of organizational components. It does not, however, prescribe policies for actual work performance and routing. Some organization manuals include general operating creeds, expressed as policies, but anything more specific is out of place. The organization manual contains:

1. The purpose, authority, and manner of use of the contents of the organization manual, signed by the appropriate officer.
2. The organization's general operating goals and creed.

191

3. A statement of the organization's operating principles.
4. A statement of responsibilities common to all organizational components.
5. Individual functional statements for each component of organization.
6. Organization charts.
7. Committee assignments.
8. Glossary of terms.
9. Procedure for changes in organization.

Statements of Common Responsibility

All organizational components have certain common duties and responsibilities which they exercise in greater or lesser degree, consistent with their status and the character of their work. These responsibilities need not be repeated in each functional statement; instead, they may be covered by a standard statement of common responsibilities included in the organization manual. The following paragraphs represent the common responsibilities of a typical manufacturing company:

COMMON MANAGEMENT RESPONSIBILITIES

Within the scope of their responsibilities, executive and supervisory officers shall:

1. Carry out the responsibilities assigned to them within the overall framework of the policies and procedures of the parent corporation and within the scope of law. Such officers shall assure observance of governing law, policy, and procedure by those for whom they are responsible.
2. Budget resource requirements and assure their most effective and economical utilization in achieving goals.
3. Carry out responsibilities in accordance with established schedules, reporting progress against such goals.
4. Provide guidance to and supervise the performance of assigned employees.
5. Provide necessary support services to other components of the organization.
6. Provide general advance information about major workloads to other components of the organization.
7. Maintain equipment in good order; assure that personnel safety practices are observed; enforce observance of the requirements of military and of company security.
8. Represent the company to the best advantage with the customer specifically and the public generally.

Using this common statement eliminates repetitious language, which otherwise is included in most of the individual functional statements.

A medium-sized organization uses this format:

1. APPLICATION OF COMMON RESPONSIBILITIES

   There are certain common responsibilities which all executive and supervisory personnel assume to a certain degree, depending on the character of their work. To avoid repeating these responsibilities in each individual's Authority and Responsibility Statement in the manual, they have been included in this section.

2. SPECIFIC RESPONSIBILITIES
   a. Program Planning
      (1) Plans, directs, and coordinates the activities, as assigned, to insure efficient utilization of personnel, materials, and equipment.
      (2) Plans and schedules production or other work programs and sees that such programs are carried out effectively.
      (3) Plans personnel requirements and sees that necessary personnel are available and properly assigned to meet work requirements.
      (4) Plans supply and material requirements to insure that adequate supplies are available for all operations.
      (5) Coordinates plans with other organizational units as required to insure a coordinated approach in carrying out interdepartmental functions.
      (6) Revises plans as necessary to cover revision of work schedules, shutdowns, irregular or special work assignments, or rush periods.
      (7) Keeps other individuals or units concerned acquainted with plans or changes which affect their operations.
   b. General Management
      (1) Delegates sufficient authority to subordinates to carry out assigned responsibilities.
      (2) Assigns supervisory authority and responsibility to others during absence or unavailability.
      (3) Assumes responsibility for maintaining a high level of morale within an assigned organizational unit.
      (4) Conducts periodic meetings with subordinates to discuss matters which are of general interest, such as new policy, procedure or method changes, production, personnel, or safety.
      (5) Cooperates with other organizational units in the development of plans, policies, and procedures, the exchange of ideas and information, or in carrying out programs in which more than one organizational unit is interested.
      (6) Anticipates problems wherever possible and takes steps to meet such problems before they arise.
      (7) Sees that all rules, regulations, policy, and procedures are properly carried out.

   c. Personnel Management
      (1) Guides personnel in carrying out their assigned responsi-
         bilities and trains them to assume more important respon-
         sibilities, including the training of understudies to fill positions
         in case of absence or promotion.
      (2) Continuously strives for the improvement of working con-
         ditions and the maintenance of sound employer-employee
         relations; investigates and settles employees' complaints where
         possible.
      (3) Initiates and carries out measures in accordance with com-
         pany personnel practices and policies to recognize and com-
         mend individual merit and performance as well as to correct
         any laxity or breaches of discipline.
      (4) Requests investigation of absent personnel when necessary.
      (5) Reports through proper channels to the appropriate industrial
         relations department any surplus personnel available for
         transfer or other appropriate disposition.
   d. Property Management
      (1) Sees that equipment, tools, and other company property are
         properly protected and maintained.
      (2) Promotes orderliness, cleanliness, and good housekeeping
         practices.

Contents of Functional Statements

   Items to include. A functional statement conveys clearly the following
information and precisely defines the extent of responsibility in each case:

   1. Action responsibility for policy formulation or development as distin-
      guished from determination, which also requires specific assignment.
   2. Review responsibility, if any, regarding matters for which other units
      have action responsibility.
   3. Performance responsibility for specifically assigned duties.
   4. Continuing or occasional relationships with other units or other orga-
      nizations, when mention of the relationship is necessary for clarity.
   5. Limits on discretion to decide or commit.

   If an organization is highly integrated, you should give special attention to
preparing functional statements delineating responsibilities between separate
components; this shows the relationship between units. This is not a serious
problem in an organization in which the separate components or divisions do
not tie in with each other to any appreciable extent.
   The terms "action" and "review" determine degree of responsibility. Action responsibility means taking all steps either directly or indirectly to assure
the accomplishment of the mission of the organizational component. This responsibility includes obtaining the review of other organizational components
which have a defined responsibility of related nature. It also means obtaining a
resolution of differences through administrative channels in such cases.

Review responsibility is given to those who are interested; however, giving a review responsibility also means giving a right to insist on participation in a decision.

Functions of supervisory levels. The normal assumption is that the superior level simply is inclusive of its component units and their stated responsibilities.

Although the superior level has responsibility for all work assigned to its component units, its own working responsibilities serve as a channel of communication to and from superior and parallel levels of authority. In some cases, supervisory levels retain specific operating responsibilities without assignment to a subordinate unit. In these cases, in addition to specifying the overall statement of responsibilities assigned to that officer, it is also necessary to prepare a functional statement covering duties performed by units or individual officers within the immediate ''office of the (title of officer).''

Arrangement of items. Arrange the items or paragraphs in a functional statement according to any logical and useful sequence, such as order of importance or order of operational sequence. If relationships require definition, include them as part of the item to which they pertain. Number the items within a single functional statement in a simple arithmetic or alphabetic series—1, 2, 3, etc., or a, b, c, etc. Do not include a separate preamble or purpose paragraph for each functional statement. The list of duties and responsibilities defines and clarifies the purpose of the unit. You do not need to include a paragraph on who reports to whom since organization relationships are shown in the charts.

Statements of Organization Principles

A typical research organization manual includes the following statements of organization principles for guidance of all personnel:

LINE OF EXECUTIVE DIRECTION

From the Parent Corporation—The line of executive direction from the parent corporation extends from the President through the Executive Vice President and General Manager to the Executive Vice President. The channel for communications upwards is the same in reverse.

From the Executive Vice President—The line of executive direction extends from the Executive Vice President to principal officers reporting directly to him or her as shown on the organization chart. The supervisory line continues from each of these officials to Department Directors and Section Heads and so on down through the last supervisory official and individual employees reporting to them. The same line of relationship is followed for upward communication and reporting.

Authority and Accountability—The line of executive direction is significant because it constitutes the means to delegate authority and responsibility. Supervisory officials and employees are responsible and accountable for performance according to the pattern of accountability established through the line of executive direction. Higher officers are responsible for communicating instructions so as not to impair the performance accountability of intermediate officials.

Bypassing of Channels—On technical matters it may occasionally be expedient for superior officials to communicate directly with subordinate technical or administrative personnel without proceeding through intermediate officials. If it is to obtain service, the superior official assumes the role of the ordinary claimant for service. If the matter is more than routine, both the superior official and the employee have a responsibility for reporting the incident as soon as possible to the next subordinate or next higher official, as the case may be. This preserves the pattern of accountability established through the line of executive direction. An official or supervisor who is not informed of instructions given to a subordinate is not held accountable for performance unless it is of a routine character. The same principle applies when channels are bypassed in an upward nature.

DISTRIBUTION OF RESPONSIBILITY

Basis of Organization

a. Responsibility is distributed to maximize performance. This recognizes the variation in operating problems and priorities characteristic of several areas. Thus, activities such as long-range studies and procurement engineering are concentrated along with other duties under a Vice President for Development.

b. This enables the Vice President, Operations, to concentrate solely on meeting contract commitments for development projects within financial and time constraints.

c. The establishment of a Department of Administration is intended to relieve engineering personnel from having to administer details. It also clarifies the uniform service responsibility of the Department of Administration to the several technical components, each reporting to the Executive Vice President.

d. A Quality Assurance Department reports separately to the Executive Vice President to assure independence of review and control.

Integration of Responsibility—Although management makes every effort to assign responsibilities on a clearly delineated basis, there probably is some overlapping. Because this company is an integrated organization, components rarely have exclusive responsibility. The latter is vested solely in the Executive Vice President.

Lateral Coordination

a. Companies should have official communication across organizational lines. Subordinate personnel should not in all cases have to proceed upward through their line of executive direction to communicate with personnel in other areas. The main factor determining whether to proceed through formal channels is the extent of involvement of a new policy or a new course of action.

b. If one component exercises its responsibility, it must obtain participation, review, and concurrence of other affected components. If such others do not act in a timely fashion, the principal component must complete the matter even though this means referring it to a higher level.

DELEGATION OF AUTHORITY

Chain of Delegation—The highest officer in the chain of command has the authority to carry out the mission of the organization. This is usually the Executive Vice President. The Executive Vice President subdivides and delegates all aspects of his or her authority to immediate subordinates as deemed necessary. This authority, in turn, is subdivided and redelegated to other subordinates. In this manner, authority and accountability are established down through the chain of command.

Nature of Delegation—Delegation grants a license to perform duties and take action under specified conditions; this may be very broad or quite restricted.

Review of Performance—Subordinate officials are accountable for performance within the delegations and criteria of performance established. This is subject to review by higher authority and also subject to redirection. Reciprocally, the higher official has a responsibility for providing guidance or criteria which enables subordinates to discharge their duties.

Use of Organization Charts

Organization charts should be used to show the relationships among the separate activities within an organization. There should be one organization chart for the entire organization showing as much detail down to subdivisions as necessary to give a picture of the entire organization. Each major component of the organization should also have its own organization chart in the manual adjacent to the group of functional statements to which it is related. Also, organization charts may be used for subordinate levels of the organization. Some cut-off point must be established at a level of diminishing utility. Otherwise, there will be too much chart review activity each time there is a change in organization or even a change in nomenclature. A slight change in title may require review not of one chart but of a series of them.

THE SALES MANUAL

A fictional corporation had embarked on an intensive sales promotion campaign, including redesign and packaging, national and local advertising, sales incentives, and sales training. One of the key elements in sales training was a sales manual. This is a hypothetical case study of how such a manual was planned and produced.

Planning Factors

The corporation operated through its own field selling organization, dealing both with local distributors and direct-factory dealer accounts. Each field sales group was under a regional sales manager, with each sales person assigned a geographic territory. The regional sales manager reported to the Sales Vice President at the home office.

The company carried a multiple product line, selling both goods and services. Competition in its line was growing increasingly sharp.

Product and price information was subject to change on a moderate basis. Sharpening of competition had forced out marginal producers among the sales personnel and turnover continued at a moderate pace. Local, independent distributors had been pressing for selling aids for their own sales representatives.

The Sales Vice President recognized the need for inspiring the sales force, for bridging the long-distance gap between them and the company, and for giving them every possible help in promoting and making sales. From another standpoint, the Vice President recognized that improvement of customer relations depended in part on the adequacy, understandability, and uniformity of the product. It also depended on the service and business information furnished to the sales representatives.

Basic Plan of the Manual

The geographic dispersion of the sales force, coupled with the need for uniformity, made written instructions important. The training aspect of the manual loomed large alongside of its reference use, in view of the turnover situation and the number of new recruits to the sales force.

Some members of the sales department were in favor of issuing the manual in bound pamphlet form; it would be simplest and would not require continuous attention in the department as would be necessary for a loose-leaf manual. They argued, moreover, that a busy sales rep would not take the time to keep a loose-leaf manual current with all the changes. On the other side of the argument, it was said that current information had to be sent out in some form. If there were no means for automatically correcting the manual, it would soon become full of obsolete or conflicting information. The weight of the argument was on the side of a loose-leaf issuance.

Subsequent discussions reinforced this decision when it was brought out that portions of the manual could be made available to local distributors for use by their own sales representatives. A loose-leaf format permitted this to be done on a selective basis, without the expense of separate printings.

Management recognized that a simple and direct style would be desirable since the training and educational backgrounds of the sales personnel varied widely. It was decided to include subject-matter background information pertaining to the company and its products, particularly for the orientation of new sales personnel. By no means would the manual include or cover all of the required visual or reading equipment needs. Other items of equipment, some of which were already in the field, included special sales portfolios of suggested dealer display arrangements, testimonials, and slides.

Physical Format

The size selected for the manual was 8-1/2 × 11 inches. Before this decision was reached, however, there were some who argued briefly in favor of a pocket-size manual, on the theory that the salespeople are more likely to carry their manuals with them. This idea was dropped when it was realized that a pocket manual in this case would be too bulky and that, since the sales personnel carried most of their supplies in briefcases, they would slip the manual in, too. In addition, the 8-1/2 × 11-inch format tied in conveniently with the page size most readily run off on the office duplicating equipment, without requiring special cutting or trimming of the page or readjustment of the machine settings.

Preparation of the Manual

When it came time to prepare the manual, there was great reluctance to be involved with the actual work. The manual could be prepared by:

- The advertising department or its outside agency
- The public relations department
- The training branch in the personnel department
- The systems and procedures staff in the management planning department
- The sales department itself

Recognizing that all of these sources might have to assist, the head of the sales department decided to assign the manual's basic job of planning and developing to a member of her own staff, with assistance drawn from within the department. These people were most intimately acquainted with the communication needs of the sales force. Before the manual was completed, all these departments did assist, as well as the controller's department and the various product departments.

One of the sales staff, Ralph Thompson, a man who had shown aptitude for organizing and presenting ideas in writing, was assigned the responsibility of planning, coordinating, and following through on production of the new manual. Since he had no prior experience in designing loose-leaf manuals, he consulted texts, periodicals, and other reference sources on sales management. His colleagues had samples of sales manuals produced by other companies.

With this general background, Thompson began developing the sales manual. Informational sources included (1) the results of the market survey and analysis, (2) files of correspondence with the field sales force, (3) correspondence with customers, (4) catalogs, (5) advertising and promotional campaign materials, (6) previously issued relevant instructions of the sales department and other departments, and (7) the experience and ideas of key personnel.

His central problem, he soon learned, was to find out what the field sales force needed most to know, both from their standpoints and that of the home office management. When he understood this problem, he developed a tentative master outline for discussion with the key people in the situation. After his discussions, he collected more materials—some he had missed—and made modifications in his outline.

When the outline was completed, he recommended a writing assignment plan for personnel of the sales department as well as several of the other departments. At this juncture, other priorities loomed large in everyone's mind. The head of the sales department listened patiently, then told all concerned to do the best they could. She took upon herself the task of enlisting the cooperation of other department heads.

Thompson had prepared a writing guide sheet and actual written samples to assist the various writers in working up their assignments. This was followed by conferences and meetings to clear up working problems. One by one, the pieces came back and were fitted into the master outline. They required varying amounts of editing, both for editing's sake and for the sake of uniformity of style. There were arrangements with the plant print shop, artwork to be done, binders to be ordered, and a myriad of other details. At last the manual was issued and distributed. Thompson's work was complete only for the moment, however, for now he had to prepare the first revisions.

Content of the Manual

The purpose of the manual was to provide instructions to sales personnel— instructions which both management and employees believed were necessary. Occasionally, a return to principle was necessary, because people wanted to include material of limited applicability, or of interest to home office personnel only.

Thompson's initial research evolved into an outline built in successive stages by subdivision and expansion of topics. While the final working outline was quite long and detailed, the following gives a representative view of its coverage and shows varying stages of topical development.

Chapter 1—Company Information

110   Products and Services Sold (General Description)
120   Organization of Company
    121   Corporate Organization
    122   General Department Organization and Personnel
    124   Sales Department Organization and Personnel
130   History of Company
    131   Early Beginnings
    132   Company Growth
    133   Current Scope of Operations
    134   Company Trends and Outlook
140   Manufacturing and Selling Policies

Chapter 2—Products and Services

210 Classification of Products and Services (Specific Descriptions)
220 Product Uses and Markets
230 Manufacturing and Design Features
240 Typical Installations

Chapter 3—Selling Procedures

310 Sales Equipment
   311 The Sales Manual
   312 Auxiliary Sales Equipment
   313 Obtaining Special Sales Equipment
320 Market Analysis
   321 Use of Company Market Surveys
   322 Local Territory Analysis
   323 Prospect Analysis
330 Advertising and Sales Promotion
   331 National Campaigns
   332 Local Advertising and Promotions
   333 Advertising and Promotion Budgets
   334 Exhibits and Displays
   335 Customer Sales Meetings
340 General Selling Principles
   341 Self-Analysis and Improvement
   342 General Relationships with Prospects
   343 Planning to Sell a Prospect
   344 Effective Negotiations
   345 Follow-Ups
   346 Competition
350 Applied Sales Presentations

Chapter 4—Servicing Customers and Products

410 After-Sale Relationships
420 Service and Repairs
430 Helping Dealers
440 Consumer Relationships
450 Building General Good Will

Chapter 5—Business Terms and Adjustments

510 Credit Policies
520 Quotations and Discounts
530 Trade-In Allowances
540 Claims and Returns
550 Shipping
560 Laws and Public Relations

Chapter 6—Sales Administration

Chapter 7—Personnel Information

Chapter 8—Sales Meetings

It was decided that while price information might conceivably be part of the chapter on products and services, it might more appropriately be included in an appendix or as inserts to separate catalogues.

Selling the Sales Manual

As far back as when he found out what the field sales force would like to have in the manual, Thompson began merchandising it. He made them part of the developmental effort and thus had opened the threshold of their acceptance at least a little bit. He knew, however, that he would have to merchandise the manual to the sales personnel—to get them to look upon it as a tool which would help them do their jobs better, getting more return for their effort and assisting them in their home office relationships. He made a start in this direction through the initial distribution control system which required numbering each copy by entering names on it, having the sales personnel sign a receipt, and explaining the periodic audit of the manual. This, of course, merely let the sales personnel know that the manual was regarded as important by the company.

Continuing, he set up a schedule of initial meetings at which the manual as a whole would be discussed, with subsequent meetings covering each of the chapters. These meetings were carefully staged to bring out maximum participation by each of the sales personnel. Then, to draw further attention to the manual, it was put on the agenda for the national convention of the company's sales personnel.

Apart from the meetings, references to the manual were incorporated into the field bulletins, correspondence, and supervisory discussions. Similar practices were set up for introduction of new or revised material for the manual. Each release automatically became a topic for a local sales meeting.

THE EMPLOYEE HANDBOOK

The employee handbook is the most common of all instructional forms. For the new employee, it relieves some of the early bewilderment of a strange environment. For employees generally, it is a useful compendium of information about the organization, its products, its facilities for employees, its personnel rules, and its benefits.

From a management standpoint, it assures that employees have essential information. As a matter of administrative control, the distribution of the employee handbook establishes that employees are made cognizant of the rules and regulations by which they abide. From a more positive standpoint, however, a well-planned and executed employee handbook helps set a tone of cordiality between management and employees.

Organizations with multiple facilities may consider developing a basic text with variable inserts to accommodate local requirements. Even though personnel rules and regulations may conceivably be identical, the actual facilities arrangements—such as cafeterias, parking lots, and location of health center—can vary from plant to plant.

Checklist of Subject Matter

I. The Company
  A. Brief history: How established, when, where and by whom
  B. Products and services and general policies pertaining to them
  C. Organization: Stockholders, directors, and management
  D. Physical scope: Size of company and location and identification of plants
  E. Customers, public relations, and future prospects

II. Employment Regulations and Procedures
  A. Hiring policies and procedures
  B. Identification of employees
  C. Personal records and forms that must be completed
  D. Hours of work, time clocks and time cards, tardiness, rest periods
  E. Holidays
  F. Vacations
  G. Time off for jury duty, illness, emergencies, and military duty
  H. Lunch periods
  I. Probationary employment
  J. Termination of employment
  K. Performance evaluation

    L. Promotion and transfer
    M. Seniority
    N. Union membership, dues and collective bargaining
    O. Military security regulations

III. Financial Compensation
    A. How payment is made and when
    B. Payroll deductions
    C. Bonuses and profit-sharing
    D. Overtime payments and shift premiums

IV. Employment Benefits
    A. Pension and retirement plans
    B. Company insurance plans
    C. Hospitalization plans, and sick-and-accident benefits
    D. Social Security, Unemployment Insurance, Workmen's Compensation
    E. Credit union, employee association, or facilities for emergency aid
    F. Severance pay
    G. Savings and stock purchase plans
    H. Discounts on company products
    I. Company store

V. Safety and Health
    A. General safety regulations
    B. Medical facilities: first aid room, first aid kits, company doctor, restroom
    C. Rules about returning to duty from illness
    D. Periodic physical examinations
    E. How to report an accident on the job
    F. Miscellaneous health aids provided by the company

VI. Plant Facilities and Services
    A. Map or diagram of plant
    B. Eating facilities, schedules
    C. Parking facilities and regulations
    D. Lost-and-found service
    E. Lockers and showers
    F. Company transportation facilities
    G. Bulletin boards, posting of items by employees

VII. Training and Education
    A. On-the-job training policy
    B. Outside courses supported by company
    C. Library facilities and usage
    D. Correspondence courses
    E. Company publications

VIII. Operating Policies, Regulations, and Procedures
   A. Personal calls, mail, and visitors
   B. Carrying packages in and out of building
   C. Attention to duties: idling, quitting work early, horseplay, disorderly conduct
   D. Gambling and drinking on premises
   E. Smoking in plant or restricted areas
   F. Solicitations, political canvassing, unauthorized personal activities
   G. Authority of supervisors, insubordination, discipline
   H. Furnishing false information for records
   I. Bad debts, borrowing on the job, and wage garnishment
   J. Conduct unbecoming an employee
   K. Abuse, destruction or waste of equipment, facilities, materials

Photographs, charts and drawings may be included. They should be selected from the standpoint of what they contribute to the employees' knowledge or impression of the company, its operations, and its facilities. Typically, illustrations may include plants, products being made, products in use, plant facilities in which employees may be interested, floor plans, employee activities, and company organizational charts.

Preparation and Distribution

Style—Most employee handbooks are prepared in an informal style. The degree of informality and the kind of language used depends upon the type of employees addressed. Sometimes, if there is too wide a disparity among the employee groups, it is better to issue individual versions of the handbook. This will accommodate differences in the governing regulations and practices.

Cartoons and other light illustrative materials are used in employee handbooks to soften the presentation of difficult text. One way to present delicate rules is to "kid" about them in a cartoon while allowing the text to be presented seriously.

Format—Most employee handbooks are about 6 × 9 inches in size. Usually, they are bound with wire staples through the center fold so that the handbook will open and remain flat. Wire or plastic file bindings may be used and, in some cases, loose-leaf binders are provided so that changes can be accommodated. The more frequent practice, however, is to reprint the entire pamphlet intermittently.

Covers range from a simple captioning and identification to an elaborately illustrated publication. The simple title "Employee Handbook" may be acceptable, but many organizations use titles suggesting "Introduction to . . . ," "Your Job with . . . ," "Getting Acquainted at . . . ," among others. To brighten the publication and induce reading, many employee handbooks use color both in the text and on the cover. Headings are used generously to provide a self-indexing guide to the subject matter. Often the headings are worded rather informally as compared to the text.

Distribution—When a new handbook is released, it is usually distributed to all employees, generally on the premises, although sometimes through the mail to the employee's home. New employees are given copies when they report ⸲ for duty. The distribution of a new handbook or a substantially revised one may be an opportunity to hold group meetings with employees.

To establish the responsibility for reading the contents of the handbook, a great many companies require that employees tear out a receipt page from the pamphlet and return it to the personnel department. The receipt may simply state that the employee has carefully read the stated publication and that the employee expects to abide by its rules and regulations. A typical receipt is worded as follows:

> "I have received an ABC Company Employee Handbook. I certify that I have read this handbook, that I fully understand the rules and regulations contained in it. I accept responsibility for following them faithfully in all respects."

THE PURCHASING POLICY MANUAL

Purchasing departments operate with the guidance of heavily detailed paper work and accounting procedures. On a higher level than mere documentation, however, lies the whole range of purchasing policy embodying company operating policy in this sensitive area, relations with other departments, and relations with customers.

While it is difficult to conceive of a thoroughly prepared procedure manual without policy interlaced within it, companies should have a policy manual which serves as a broad operating control for all levels of management.

Checklist for a Purchasing Policy Manual

Guides to the selection of material to make up company policy on purchasing may come from issuances of the National Association of Purchasing Agents, miscellaneous trade literature, issuances of other companies, as well as the history of one's own company's policy and practices. The following is a suggested checklist:

1. **Management Letter**
   Obtain a letter from top management which serves as the official sanction of the policy and endorses it as being consistent with overall company policy.
2. **This manual is written for:**
   - Purchasing employees
   - Employees of other departments
   - Vendors
   - Customers

     (Can one document serve for all four; or, should more than one be written?)

3. **This is how we are organized:**
   (This probably isn't policy as such, but is this manual a logical place to clarify an organization?)

4. **Our department head reports to** _____ :
   - We are given a full voice in management decisions.

5. **We purchase the following:**
   - Raw materials consisting principally of:

     _____
     _____
     _____

   - Production parts, consisting principally of:

     _____
     _____
     _____

   - Subcontracted parts, consisting principally of:

     _____
     _____
     _____

   - Supply items, consisting principally of:

     _____
     _____
     _____

   (This isn't really policy, perhaps, but should it be in such a manual?)

6. **We do not purchase the following:**
   - Insurance
   (This comes close to policy. Shouldn't a manual say who IS responsible for these purchases?)

7. **We are responsible for:**
   - Vendor selection
   - Contract form selection
   - Expediting
   - Handling of rejections and complaints
   - Disposal of scrap and surplus
   - Auditing invoices
   - Determining order quantities
   - Inventories
   - Standardization
   - Stores
   - Finding new products and services
   - Studying forward markets
   - Governmental priorities and regulations
   - Terminations
   - Reporting leadtimes
   - Value analysis
   - Traffic
   - Receiving

8. We are not responsible for:

- Such items in 7 as are specifically assigned to another department
  (How candid should the manual be about responsibilities that are split by management decisions, or by long-standing precedence? Aren't there specific areas where management, production personnel, engineering personnel, or even clerical personnel definitely dictate the vendor from whom items are purchased?)
- Selection of contract form
  (Doing business with the government dictates a definite influence on the form of contracts; or, there may be management or controller direction or influence.)
- Expediting orders
- Handling rejections and complaints
  (How about direct contacts from the inspection department? Isn't that condoned sometimes?)
- Finding new products and services
  (Aren't there other departments who make direct contact with the vendors?)

9. In dealing with a vendor, we will be:

- Courteous
- Honest
- Fair
- Open
- Impartial
  (These are always made as very positive statements. Would anybody like to be a little more candid and admit people are human and may, at times, seem cantankerous?)

10. Our goal is:

- To get maximum value for our money
- To purchase for the best interests of the company

11. In selecting a vendor we consider:

- Ability to meet schedules
- Capacity
- Integrity
- Financial status
- Geographic location
- Rejection record
- Cost reductions, received
- Guarantees

12. In evaluating a quotation, we consider:

- Quality
- Service
- Price
  (Could the manual be more specific as to how these will be weighed?)

13. **It is good buying to have:**
    - More than one active source
    - All the sources we can find
    (Will Purchasing be willing to specify the areas where it will be perfectly satisfied with a single source? Or, other areas where too many sources are just a nuisance?)

14. **But:**
    - We will not play one supplier against another
    - We will not be opportunists of the moment
    - We will not reveal competitive prices
    - We want to be sure that our suppliers make a profit

15. **We believe in competition, so we:**
    - Get three bids on everything
    - Get as many bids as seem practical
    (Same question as 13. Is Purchasing willing to go on record as to single source areas or areas where too many sources are already available and quotations are limited?)

16. **For your sales personnel:**
    - We will see all who call
    - We will see sales personnel at certain hours only
    (Is Purchasing willing to make a statement with respect to the bothersome sales personnel who take too much time on the wrong things at the wrong time?)

17. **With respect to new ideas or materials:**
    - We welcome all those with constructive ideas to offer
    - We are interested in any new materials or equipment which result in a saving to our company
    (Is there a more candid statement that acknowledges that other people have to be sold? Or, that Purchasing is sometimes biased against an idea but will still get it to the right people in the best possible light?)

18. **With respect to cash discounts:**
    - They are always considered as a cost element
    - We prefer to do business with companies who give cash discounts
    - Invoices that allow discounts are given preferential treatment

19. **With respect to speculative purchases:**
    - We do not purchase speculatively
    - We may buy against known markets or price changes
    - Any advance buying requires management approval.
    (This appears in most manuals. What is its real significance?)

20. **Our policy objectives on inventory are:**
    - To carry minimum quantities of goods necessary to protect the continuity of our operations
    - To place orders consistent with good order quantity practice

21. As to inspection:
- Goods are inspected on receipt and at the point of use
- We try to arrive at a complete written understanding regarding inspection methods

   (For the first item, how about the goods that aren't used until months after receipt?)

22. For other departments:
- All vendor contracts are to be made through Purchasing
- No one outside of the Purchasing department is authorized to commit the company with respect to a vendor
- The Purchasing department will arrange all vendor interviews with other departments

   (Would you consider a more candid statement asking vendor cooperation when other departments of the company do commit the company, whether you like it or not?)

23. In case of emergencies:
- Occasional emergency departure from plan requires vigorous support
- Unforeseen emergencies shall be mutually interpreted and satisfactory action mutually decided

24. Blanket orders:
- Are sometimes placed for a year's supply of a commodity
- Contain a provision for downward negotiation of price

   (Upward negotiation of price is usually not mentioned. What do you really do? Is this the place to suggest that annual calls are adequate on such items?)

25. With respect to gifts from suppliers:
- Our employees are forbidden to accept gifts or gratuities in any form from any seller at any time for themselves or their families
- We prohibit ''immoderate'' gifts or entertainment
- We prohibit gifts, except those which would in no way cause the company to be embarrassed or obligated
- Our buyers are instructed to refuse gifts or other factors which might give rise to doubts concerning their impartiality
- We prefer that the social-business entertainment be paid by our own employees and prefer that commercial gift-giving be discontinued

   (Can Purchasing's policy be defined more specifically? Are employees really encouraged to participate in the ''social-business'' aspect of business to the point of giving them expense accounts? Is Purchasing really concerned about them being influenced, or more about the psychological effects of being on the receiving end all of the time?)

26. Employee interest in vendor companies:
- Personal financial interest in any vendor company must be revealed
- Personal financial interest in any vendor company is prohibited
- ''Substantial'' interest in the ownership or management of any vendor company is prohibited

(How far should Purchasing go with such a statement or with such a policy? Does this just apply to Purchasing or to ANY employee?)

27. **With respect to reciprocity:**
    - Reciprocity will be considered only when all factors are equal
    - If you feel you're not being treated fairly, see the head of Purchasing
    (Would anyone like to be more specific?)

28. **Buying for employees:**
    - Only with department head approval
    - No purchase orders will be issued
    - We buy only for our company's requirements
    (Most purchasing departments do some buying for some people. Could Purchasing define this more specifically?)

29. **Contract form:**
    - The standard contract form will be used on the great percentage of our purchases and exceptions must be negotiated
    (Is this the place to make a clear statement on the matter of acknowledgment copies?)

30. **Vendor visitation:**
    - We encourage our buyers to visit vendor plants frequently
    - We insist that our buyers visit important vendors periodically
    (No one comes out and says that they are limited as to budget on this sort of thing. What is Purchasing's policy on vendor-paid visitation?)

31. **Membership in associations:**
    - We encourage members of our purchasing department to become active in associations that are allied with their line of endeavor
    (What is Purchasing's policy with respect to financial support of this sort of activity?)

32. **Government regulations:**
    - It is our intention to comply with all local, state and federal laws in the conduct of our business
    - In the handling of contracts for the government, it is necessary that we comply with certain provisions as directed by the cognizant authorities.

Appendix D

A Case Study

Examining the publications of other organizations is an excellent way to gain ideas during the development of any document. Hennepin County, Minn., has provided such a resource by graciously permitting the reprinting of selected pages of its administrative manual. A single-volume three-ring binder, the manual is an outstanding example of a well-organized, easy-to-read policy and procedure publication. It is printed on 8-$\frac{1}{2}$ × 11-inch stock and features abundant white space and good use of playscript. The following description of the manual was prepared by the Hennepin County Office of the Administrator.

The Hennepin County Administrative Manual

County government relies on a volume of official policies and procedures to function smoothly and to achieve the most basic goals in government. Hennepin County has more than 7,000 employees working in 48 divisions of some 25 major departments. Policies affecting these departments and their employees are diverse and include such topics as preparing payroll checks, record storage, and vacation policy.

The Administrative Manual's 70 sections are marked by alphabetical tabs; sections themselves are divided by numbers. Material following a section letter is in numerical, not alphabetical, order.

A Table of Contents provides an efficient way to find the correct section. An Index at the back of the manual lists topical items such as "Cash, Loss or Suspected Theft" or "Public Records, Destruction of."

The information is written in playscript, which tells the reader what department is involved and what steps each involved person is responsible for. Whenever possible, subject matter is divided into short, readable paragraphs. When a form must be filled out as part of the correct procedure, a sample is included in the manual.

Policies and procedures change frequently and require constant updating. Individual departments are responsible for revisions or additions to the manual. Proposed changes are sent to Administration for approval. If approved, the changes are printed and paid for from the individual department's budget allocation and circulated to holders of the manual by Administration.

An Administration staff member, who is primarily responsible for supervision of the manual, also monitors action taken by the county Board of Commissioners for possible entry into the manual. Cross-referencing within the manual refers to sections rather than to specific page numbers, to avoid complications when changes are made. Several times a year, the index is changed to keep entries up to date.

Approximately seven months after the Administrative Manual was distributed to county departments, a questionnaire was sent out to determine employee reaction. Of the 190 surveys sent, 105 were returned. The response was a positive one: 91 persons said they could find information easily in the manual and 93 said the manual helped them in their jobs.

Following are some of the ways the manual helps county employees:

1. A new employee or a person taking over a new position can learn correct procedures simply by looking them up in the manual. He or she can find helpful, concise information about the interdepartmental mail service, retirement, or preparing budget forms, among others.
2. A department head can use the manual as a source of information about another department's responsibilities.
3. The manual helps employees avoid costly mistakes. A payroll form that is completed incorrectly, for example, could possibly demand action on the part of the accounting department, data processing computer time, and additional work by a keypunch operator. Doing it correctly the first time, as explained step by step in the manual, saves effort.
4. Telephone calls and memo-writing are minimized by first checking for an answer in the Administrative Manual. Administration staff have noted a distinct decrease in the number of telephone calls requesting information concerning areas described in the manual.
5. The manual improves the image of Hennepin County when working with outside companies or agencies. By following information in the manual, contracts and other official documents are handled in a consistent manner.
6. As a central repository for safety information, the manual assists the county in its compliance with an Occupational Safety and Health Act (OSHA) directive that all employees be cognizant of OSHA rules and regulations.

Government at any level has a recognized propensity for paperwork. All county governments at one time or another face the challenge of organizing such information and making it accessible to employees. The Administrative Manual allows Hennepin County to meet that challenge in a particularly noteworthy way.

Sample pages include:

- Introduction
- Manual Format
- Table of Contents (first page)
- Miscellaneous Page A1
- Section A9 (pages 1 through 5)
- Index (first page)

MANUAL FORMAT

The sections of the Administrative Manual are placed in alphabetical/numerical order. For example, if the topic heading in the Table of Contents or the Index refers to Section A3, look for the third section behind the A tab. Each individual section behind an alphabetical tab has a divider sheet noting the section number to distinguish one section from another.

The Table of Contents is listed in alphabetical order by topic for easy reference instead of listing by sequence of sections.

The department or departments listed at the top of each page are responsible for the material presented in that section. If there are any questions regarding the material, contact those department(s) listed.

Rev. 7/17/—

INTRODUCTION

The Administrative Manual provides a source for Countywide policies, procedures, and general information which is readily available to County personnel.

Sections within the Administrative Manual are prepared by departmental personnel most knowledgeable about a given topic. These departments are responsible for planning and preparing initial content and initiating revisions for their sections and will be charged the printing costs for new sections or changes to present sections.

Procedures and policies require constant review and updating. Proposed procedures or suggested revisions are to be submitted to the County Administrator.

The County Administrator's Office is responsible for review, further development, and approval of new material and revisions and for the distribution of the new material and revisions to those holding Administrative Manuals.

Employees are urged to contribute suggestions for the improvement of existing policies and procedures.

Rev. 7/17/—

ADMINISTRATIVE MANUAL	POLICY GENERAL INFORMATION PROCEDURE

SECTION A1
PAGE 1

Administrative Manual

RELEASE DATE: July 17, 19—

REPLACES ISSUE DATED: November 15, 19—

DEPARTMENT RESPONSIBLE: Administration Rev.

Introduction

The concept of the Administrative Manual is to provide a single repository for information regarding countywide procedures, policies, and general information which will be readily available to County personnel.

It is intended that the content of the Manual be prepared by those persons most knowledgeable about a given topic. For example, the Personnel Department would prepare the procedural instructions and explain the applicable policies and procedures pertaining to the Certification Process.

Procedures and policies are dynamic and will require constant updating. The departments listed after "Department Responsible" on all of the forms are the departments responsible for or involved in that section.

Management personnel should encourage employees to contribute to the improvement of existing procedures.

 Rev.

Proposed procedures or suggested revisions are to be submitted to the County Administrator by the department responsible for review or further development.

The Administrative Office is responsible for approving all new content and revisions.

County Administration is responsible for the distribution of new or revised sections to all holders of the Administrative Manual.

Rev.

Departments are responsible for the cost of printing all additions or revisions to the Manual. If several departments are "responsible," the major department responsible, as determined by County Administration, will be charged for the expense of printing.

Table of Contents

July 17, 19—

ADMINISTRATIVE MANUAL	POLICY GENERAL INFORMATION PROCEDURE	SECTION A9 — PAGE 1

Automobile Use and Assignment - County-Owned Automobiles [Rev.]

RELEASE DATE: July 2, 19—

REPLACES ISSUE DATED: February 12, 19—

DEPARTMENT RESPONSIBLE: Administration and Property Management

Policy
Unmarked County automobiles shall be assigned on a permanent basis to the County Attorney and the Sheriff. County automobiles shall also be assigned on a permanent or seasonal basis to the Sheriff's Department and the Transportation Department as is necessary for the pursuit of official County business. At the discretion of the County Administrator, unmarked automobiles or vehicles bearing the insignia of Hennepin County may be assigned on a permanent-use basis to County employees depending on conditions such as frequency of use, requirements for transportation availability outside the normal working hours, geographical dispersion of work sites, or terms of employment.

Responsibility for Compliance with Policy
Each department head shall be responsible for assuring compliance with this policy.

The Sheriff, County Attorney, and Director of Transportation shall be responsible for filing with the County Administrator a policy statement governing the use of unmarked cars by their respective employees. Any subsequent revision of the department policies shall also be filed with the County Administrator.

General Information
The Central Operations Office of the Property Management Division operates a car pool for the Bureau of Public Service from the Government Center. A limited number of cars are available for County-related business use by employees based in the Downtown Minneapolis area subject to the provisions outlined in this policy.

Reservations
Employees may not call ahead to reserve a pool car.

(continued)

ADMINISTRATIVE MANUAL	POLICY GENERAL INFORMATION PROCEDURE	SECTION A9 — PAGE 2

Automobile Use and Assignment - County-Owned Automobiles

RELEASE DATE: July 2, 19—

REPLACES ISSUE DATED: February 12, 19—

DEPARTMENT RESPONSIBLE: Administration and Property Management

General Information (continued)

Lengthy Trips
Pool cars are not to be used for lengthy, out-of-state or out-of-town travel. If a County automobile is needed for such a trip, arrangements should be made through the Central Mobile Equipment Division of the Bureau of Public Service.

Overnight Use
The Government Center Central Operations Office is staffed 24 hours a day, and pool car keys may be returned to that office at any hour. Overnight use of pool cars is discouraged because departments are charged for every hour that the keys are out of the Central Operations Office, business hours or not. The hourly rate is $1.50.

Gasoline [Rev.]
Gasoline is available from the service station run by the Bureau of Public Service at 2556 Blaisdell Ave. So. in Minneapolis. The hours of operation are 7:30 a.m. through 4:00 p.m., Monday through Friday. Pool car users are responsible for filling County automobiles if it is needed after use.

Accidents
If involved in an accident while driving a County vehicle:

1. Do not admit liability in any case as the County's insurance carrier will handle the legal aspects.

2. Refer the other party to the Hennepin County Equipment Division, 935-3381, ext. 404.

3. Report the accident as soon as possible to the Equipment Division, 935-3381, ext. 404, so the County's insurance carrier can be informed.

(continued)

ADMINISTRATIVE MANUAL	POLICY GENERAL INFORMATION PROCEDURE

SECTION __A9__
PAGE __4__

Automobile Use and Assignment –
County-Owned Automobiles

RELEASE DATE: July 2, 19—
REPLACES ISSUE DATED: February 12, 19—
DEPARTMENT RESPONSIBLE: Administration and Property Management

Procedure (continued)

Employee (continued)

9. After use:

   a. fill automobile with gas if needed,

   b. park car on D Level of Government Center Garage, and

   c. remove all personal and business material from car.

10. Return keys immediately to Central Operations Office window on A Level.

   Note: Departments will be charged for every hour that pool car keys are out of the Central Operations Office.

Central Operations

11. Record date returned, time returned and lapsed time on card.

Central Mobile Equipment Division

12. Submit accumulated Pool Car Authorization cards weekly to the Central Mobile Equipment Division.

13. Compute charges by department and bill monthly through Unified Accounting System.

ADMINISTRATIVE MANUAL	POLICY GENERAL INFORMATION PROCEDURE

SECTION __A9__
PAGE __3__

Automobile Use and Assignment –
County-Owned Automobiles

RELEASE DATE: July 2, 19—
REPLACES ISSUE DATED: February 12, 19—
DEPARTMENT RESPONSIBLE: Administration and Property Management

General Information (continued)

Breakdowns

If mechanical problems disable a County vehicle, call 935-3381, ext. 405, to arrange for a tow truck or the dispatching of a mechanic.

Procedure

Employee   [Rev.]

1. Fill out the left side of Pool Car Authorization card (HC 51) (see Exhibit A). A supply of these cards is available from the Building Office of the Property Management Division, or departments may have a supply printed for themselves.

2. Submit card to department head or authorized personnel for signature.

Department Head/ Authorized Personnel

3. Fill in organization and program codes on card.

4. Sign card authorizing use of automobile.

Employee

5. Present card at Central Operations Office window on A Level of Government Center.

Central Operations

6. Issue set of keys for automobile if available.

7. Record automobile number, date taken and time taken on card.

Employee

8. Locate car on D Level of Government Center Garage. Number on keys will match number on side of automobile.

(continued)

Exhibit A

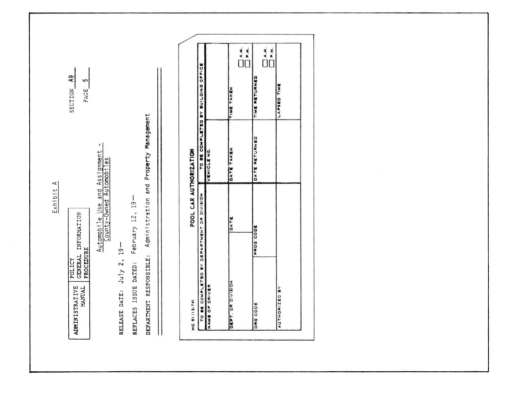

Appendix E

Training and Consulting Services

One comment invariably raised at procedural writing seminars is the obvious need for writer training. Those who are assigned to prepare policies, procedures, and other how-to documentation generally have little or no formal training. This appendix describes six current educational programs being offered, with the organizations listed alphabetically. Their inclusion does not constitute endorsement either by this manual's author or by the publisher, nor has there been any attempt to evaluate their effectiveness. All courses have been offered at least since 1978; some have been offered since 1965.

American Management Associations (AMA)

AMA holds its three-day seminar, "Preparing Administrative Manuals," in key cities throughout the United States. According to the Associations' brochure, the course shows participants how to produce simple, clear, orderly, user-oriented administrative manuals. After examining objectives, students learn how to pinpoint their audience, then gear the language, layout, and format to the people who will use the manual.

The seminar will help writers anticipate the problems they are likely to encounter, such as how to win support from top management, prepare a realistic work schedule and operate within the budget, overcome resistance to change, get sufficient manpower to complete the job within time limitations, and cope with any mechanical and technical snags that may crop up. It will also teach them how to use the Clear River Test to measure the readability of their manuals. For more information, course schedules, and cost, write to:

American Management Associations
135 West 50th Street
New York, N.Y. 10020

Information Resources, Inc.

"Developing Instructional Materials and Procedures" is an intensive five-day Information Mapping* Seminar on structured writing offered by Information Resources, Inc.

As the firm's brochure explains, virtually all information has a structure,

*Trademark of Information Resources, Inc., Lexington, Mass.

or topography, with main ideas forming the peaks, and details forming the valleys. "Our structured writing method," states the firm, "graphically points up the main ideas on the information terrain—making them easy to identify and understand—and puts supporting information in its proper place."

Structured writing helps writers organize their material efficiently and effectively, by replacing the paragraph with new analytic units called Information Blocks. Attendees learn how structured writing enhances modern instructional methods such as behavioral objectives, programmed instruction, feedback, and simulations. For more information, course schedules, and costs, write to:

Information Resources, Inc.
133 Massachusetts Avenue
Lexington, Mass. 02173

Manuals Corporation of America (MCA)

MCA offers three basic seminars: "Manuals Orientation" (3 and 4 days); "Layout Planning and Writing" (2 days); and "Advanced Development Workshop" (2 and 3 days). The seminars train personnel how to develop, design, write, and maintain effective manuals—policy, procedure, administrative, user, operating, and other internally required manuals.

Manuals Orientation and Development Seminar

This seminar describes the many facets of development—design, organization, writing, and maintenance. Students learn standards and practices for developing and maintaining a wide variety of manuals required by today's organizations. The seminar considers not only conventional manuals but also booklets and guidebooks, microfiche, panels, filmstrips, slide charts, and computer-stored documentation. Students also learn about the effects that word processing, advanced documentation techniques, and metrication will have on manuals.

Layout Planning and Writing Seminar

This course concentrates on layout planning, writing styles, word usage, and writing principles as they apply to manuals. In-class writing problems and exercises provide practice in use of caption and playscript layout techniques, and in understandable writing.

Advanced Manuals Development Seminar

This special advanced program is for manuals managers who are looking for in-depth problem-solving opportunities. The program is a mix of lectures, discussions, and workshops. The discussion sessions are recorded and transcribed; each participant receives a complete set of edited transcripts of these sessions. The workshop sessions give each participant an opportunity to test and apply selected principles and techniques. For more information, course schedules, and costs, write to:

Manuals Corporation of America
P.O. Box 247
Setauket, N.Y. 11733

John O. Morris Associates

Since 1965, John O. Morris Associates has provided consulting services in written communications. The firm focuses on clear thinking, orderly structure, and writing for a particular audience. John O. Morris emphasizes plain language and efficient, reader-oriented communications, including such complex communications as proposals, reports, regulations, contracts, insurance policies, and manuals.

Plain Language Workshops

These workshops are tailored to fit specific needs of clients and usually include three phases: preparation, workshop, and follow-up. Participants' written materials are first reviewed; then program objectives are drawn up. Workshops are highly participative; a typical session runs two days and is built around participants' written materials and specific needs. The follow-up includes individual critique of materials which participants have written since the workshop and a mini workshop to discuss progress and problems.

Writing Regulations and Procedures for Public Understanding

Offered primarily for federal employees under the auspices of the Office of Personnel Management, this three-day seminar shows participants how to write plain language procedures, directives, manuals, and regulations. Objectives, measurable standards and principles for efficient writing are particularly emphasized.

Specific objectives of the course include:

- Reviewing and evaluating existing standards for writing this material.
- Defining the audience for specific material.
- Showing participants the basic principles for writing this material.
- Applying these principles and practicing writing and editing this material.

For more information, course schedules, and costs, write to:

John O. Morris Associates
40 Wood Pond Road
West Hartford, Conn. 06107

University of Connecticut, Management Development Program

"How to Prepare Executive Summaries" and "How to Prepare Procedures and Manuals" are intensive one-day workshops offered regularly in Connecticut. For more information, course schedules, and costs, write to:

University of Connecticut
Management Development Program
Storrs, Conn. 06268

University of Minnesota, Continuing Management Education

"Writing Effective Administrative Manuals and Directives" is the title of a two-part seminar that shows participants how to produce policies, procedures, and "how-to" instructions. During Part 1 (two days in length), students learn to analyze their audience and recognize the appropriate style, structure, and sequence of information for their readers. This session also teaches students about efficient methods of maintaining, revising, and purging manuals and publications. Part 2 (two half-days) concentrates on writing policies and procedures. Both parts are taught by James W. Jacoby.

Each student receives a complete "how-to" manual that includes sample pages from procedure manuals of many organizations. Participants are requested to bring examples of their own work to ensure a practical approach that will center on their needs. The seminar is also offered on a customized basis for in-house presentation.

For more information, course schedules, and costs, write to:

University of Minnesota
Continuing Management Education
107 Armory, Church Street SE
Minneapolis, Minn. 55455

Selected Bibliography

ADMINISTRATIVE PUBLICATIONS/
POLICIES, PROCEDURES, DIRECTIVES

Andrews, A. James. "Preparing and Using Administrative Manuals," Parts 1, 2, and 3. *Journal of Systems Management* (March, April, and May 1980): 14–20, 6–17, and 6–11.

Berry, Elizabeth. "How to Get Users to Follow Procedures," *Journal of Systems Management* (July 1981): 15–19.

Campbell, Robert B. "Standardizing Procedure Documentation." *Journal of Systems Management* (June 1976): 15–19.

Cluer, Brian M. "Automating the Distribution of Information in Company Manuals." *The Office* (February 1978): 37–43.

Cobaugh, William B. "When It's Time to Rewrite Your Personnel Manual." *Personnel Journal* (December 1978): 686–89.

Cowan, Paula. "Establishing a Communication Chain: The Development and Distribution of an Employee Handbook." *Personnel Journal* (June 1975): 342–49.

Davis, Keith. "Readability Changes in Employee Handbooks of Identical Companies During a Fifteen-Year Period." *Journal of Business Communication* 6 (1968): 33–40.

Diamond, Susan Z. *Preparing Administrative Manuals*. New York: American Management Associations, 1981.

Driscoll, Marilyn D. "How Do You Produce Company Training Manuals?" *Supervisory Management* (October 1974): 16–22.

Dunlap, Donald P. "A Guideline for Developing Administrative Manuals." *Best's Review* (Life/Health Edition) (January 1973).

Famularo, Joseph J. *Organizational Planning Manual*. New York: American Management Associations, 1971.

Hill, James W. "Look It Up—Or Can You? (A Proposal for a Management Communications Index)." *Business Horizons* 20 (1977): 61–68.

Huegli, Jon M., and Tschirgi, H. D. "An Investigation of Communication Skills Application and Effectiveness at the Entry Job Level." *Journal of Business Communication* 12 (1974): 24–29.

IFM Guide to the Preparation of a Company Policy Manual, The. Old Saybrook, Conn.: Institute for Management, 1978.

Ilett, Frank, Jr. "Flow Charts—Origin of Procedures Manuals." *Management Services* (November-December 1970): 31–38.

Jackson, Clyde W. "Functional Manuals and Formats." *Journal of Systems Management* (May 1976): 6–13.

Jones, Don E. "The Employee Handbook." *Personnel Journal* (February 1973): 136–41.

Lawson, J. W., and Smith, B. *How to Develop a Personnel Policy Manual.* Chicago: Dartnell Corp., 1980.

Matthies, Leslie H. "Task Outlines: Work Instructions for One Person." *Journal of Systems Management* 29 (1978): 28–32.

McNairn, William N. "Three Ways to Wake Up Procedures Manuals." *Management Advisor* (May-June 1973): 26–33.

Ross, John H. *How to Make a Procedure Manual.* Longwood, Fla.: Office Research Institute, 1974.

Seltz, David D. and Radlauer, Marvin I. *How to Prepare an Effective Company Operations Manual.* Chicago: Dartnell Corp., 1982.

Spencer, Hollister. "Task Definition and Exposition: The Catalyst in the Matching Process." *Personnel Journal* 53 (1974): 428–34.

Sticht, Thomas G.; Caylor, John S.; Kern, Richard P.; and Fox, Lynn C. "Maybe They Can't Read the Manual." *Research* (June 1974): 36–37.

U.S. Department of Defense. *Defense Standardization Manual 4120.3M: Standardization Policies, Procedures, and Instructions.* Washington, D.C.: Government Printing Office, 1966.

Vardaman, George T., and Vardaman, Patricia B. *Communication in Modern Organizations.* New York: John Wiley & Sons, 1973.

Zaiden, Dennis. *Dartnell's Cost Cutting Paperwork Simplification Manual.* Chicago: Dartnell Corp., 1974.

WRITING

Fleischhauer, F. W. "Apply Logic to Your Procedure Writing." *Journal of Systems Management* (January 1970): 27–30.

Flesch, Rudolf. *How to Be Brief.* New York: Harper & Row, 1962.

———. *The Art of Plain Talk.* New York: Macmillan, 1962.

———. *The Art of Readable Writing: 25th Anniversary Edition.* New York: Harper & Row, 1974.

———, and Lass, A. H. *A New Guide to Better Writing.* New York: Popular Library, 1977.

Fruehling, Rosemary T., and Bouchard, Sharon. *Business Correspondence,* 2d ed. New York: McGraw-Hill, 1976.

Gunning, Robert. *New Guides to More Effective Writing in Business and Industry.* Boston: Industrial Education Institute, 1964.

Hogan, Patricia. "A Woman Is Not a Girl and Other Lessons in Corporate Speech." *Business and Society Review* (1975): 34–37.

Horn, Robert E. "Information Mapping." *Datamation* (January 1975): 85–88.

———. "Information Mapping." *Training—The Magazine of Human Resource Development* 11 (1974): 27–37.

Kahn, Charles. "Psycho-linguistics and Business Communications." *Journal of Systems Management* (June 1975): 22–25.

Kalt, Neil C., and Barrett, Katherine Merlo. "Facilitation of Learning From a Technical Manual." *Journal of Applied Psychology* 58 (1973): 357–61.

Kimes, J. D. "The Need for Clarity in Business Writing." *Financial Executive* (January 1979): 17–23.

Lybbert, E. K. "Making Policy Readable." *Administrative Management* (February 1978): 31–33.

Matthies, Leslie H. *The New Playscript Procedure.* Stamford, Conn.: Office Publications, 1977.

———, and Matthies, Ellen. "Converting a Procedure to Playscript." *The Office* (March 1977): 96–98.

Morris, John O. *Make Yourself Clear. (Improving Business Communication)* New York: McGraw-Hill, 1980.

———. "Plain Language Is Here—Are You Ready?" *Connecticut Law Tribune* (October 1, 1979).

———. "Plain Language Is Winning." *Connecticut Law Tribune* (December 15, 1980).

Pearsall, Thomas E. *Audience Analysis for Technical Writing.* Encino, Calif.: Glencoe Publishing Co., 1969.

———, and Cunningham, D. H. *How to Write for the World of Work.* New York: Holt, Rinehart, and Winston, 1978. Reviewed by Norman B. Sigband in *Journal of Business Communication* 15 (1978): 57.

Pickens, Judy E.; Rao, Patricia Walsh; and Roberts, Linda Cook, eds. *Without Bias: A Guidebook for Nondiscriminatory Communication.* San Francisco: International Association of Business Communications, 1977.

Roget, Peter M. *Roget's International Thesaurus.* 4th Ed. New York: Thomas Y. Crowell, 1977.

Schindler, George E., Jr. "Why Engineers and Scientists Write As They Do—Twelve Characteristics of Their Prose." *Standards Engineering* (October 1976): 106–10.

Todd, Alden. *Finding Facts Fast: How to Find Out What You Want to Know Immediately.* West Caldwell, N.J.: William Morrow & Co., 1974.

U.S. Environmental Protection Agency. *Be a Better Writer: A Manual for EPA Employees.* Washington, D.C.: Government Printing Office, 1980.

Walsh, Ruth M., and Birkin, Stanley J., eds. *Business Communications—An Annotated Bibliography.* Westport, Conn.: Greenwood Press, 1980.

ORGANIZATIONAL/ADMINISTRATIVE MANAGEMENT

Allen, Richard K. *Organizational Management Through Communication.* New York: Harper & Row, 1977. Reviewed by Norman B. Sigband in *Journal of Business Communication* 15 (1978): 61.

Allen, T. H. "Communication Networks: The Hidden Organizational Chart." *Personnel Administrator* (September 1976): 31–35.

Anastasi, Thomas E., Jr. *Desk Guide to Communication*. Reading, Maine: Addison-Wesley Publishing Co., 1974.

Bromage, Mary C. "Bridging the Corporate Communications Gap." *SAM Advanced Management Journal* 41 (1976): 44–51.

Burns, J. Christopher. "Evolution of Office Information." *Datamation* (April 1977): 60–64.

Danko, D. E. "A Perspective on Corporate Communications." *Public Relations Journal* 30 (1974): 10–13.

D'Aprix, Roger M. "The Believable House Organ. *Management Review* (February 1979): 23–28.

Demers, Robert W. "Ask and Ye Shall Receive." *Supervision* 38 (1976): 18–19.

Deutsch, Arnold R. "Does Your Company Practice Affirmative Action in Its Communications?" *Harvard Business Review* 54 (1976): 16, 186–88.

"Disclosing Information." *Management Today* (September 1976): 113.

Falcione, Raymond L., and Greenbaum, Howard H. *Organizational Communication: Abstracts, Analysis, and Overview*. Vol. 5. Beverly Hills, Calif.: Sage Publications, 1980.

Famularo, Joseph J. *Modern Personnel Administration*. New York: McGraw-Hill, 1972.

Gelfand, L. I. "Communicate Through Supervisors." *Harvard Business Review* 48 (1970): 101–104.

Goldhaber, Gerald M. *Organizational Communication*. 2d ed. Dubuque, Iowa: William C. Brown Co., 1977.

Harriman, Bruce. "Up and Down the Communication Ladder." *Harvard Business Review* 50 (1974): 143–51.

"How to Keep Employees Well-Informed." *Personnel Management* (July 1977): 13.

James, Vaughn E. "Encouraging Use of Reference Documentation." *Journal of Systems Management* (October 1975): 32–33.

Johnson, H. Webster. *How to Use the Business Library*. 4th ed. Cincinnati: South-Western Publishing Co., 1972.

Kintisch, R. S., and Weisbord, Marvin R. "Getting Computer People and Users to Understand Each Other." *Advanced Management Journal* 42 (1977): 4–14.

Lewis, Phillip V. *Organizational Communications: The Essence of Effective Management*. 2d. ed. Columbus, Ohio: Grid Publishing, 1980.

Maedke, William O.; Brown, Gerald F.; and Robek, Mary. *Information and Records Management*. Encino, Calif.: Glencoe Publishing Co., 1974.

Neidt, Charles, and Sears, Eugene. "Increasing Employee Understanding of Company Policies and Operating Philosophy." *Personnel Journal* 42 (1963): 276–80.

Schneider, Arnold E.; Donaghy, William; and Newman, Pamela. *Organizational Communications*. New York: McGraw Hill, 1975. Reviewed by Lawrence D. Brennan in *Journal of Business Communication* 12 (1975): 47–49.

Smith, Robert M., ed. "MAS (Management Advisory Services)." *The Journal of Accountancy* (July 1975): 70–74.

Walton, Thomas F. *Communications and Data Management*. New York: John Wiley & Sons, 1976.

Whitehouse, Frank. *Documentation: How to Organize and Control Information Processes in Business and Industry*. Chicago: Business Books, 1971.

EDITING, STYLE, AND USAGE

Andrasik, Frank, and Murphy, William D. "Assessing the Readability of Thirty-Nine Behavior Modification Training Manuals." *Journal of Applied Behavioral Analysis* 10 (1977): 341–44.

Baker, Sheridan. *The Complete Stylist*. 2d ed. New York: Thomas Y. Crowell Co., 1972.

Barzun, Jacques, and Dunbar, Georgia. *Simple and Direct*. New York: Harper & Row, 1976.

Bass, Bernard, and Klauss, Rudi. "Communication Style, Credibility and Their Consequences." *Personnel Administrator* (October 1975): 32–36.

Chicago Manual of Style, The. 13th ed. Chicago: University of Chicago Press, 1982.

Flesch, Rudolf. *How to Test Readability*. New York: Harper & Bros., 1951.

———. *Look It Up: A Deskbook of American Spelling and Style*. New York: Harper & Row, 1977.

Guidelines for Equal Treatment of the Sexes in McGraw-Hill Book Company Publications. New York: McGraw-Hill, 1974.

Keithley, Erwin M., and Schreiner, Philip J. *A Manual of Style for the Preparation of Papers and Reports*. Cincinnati: South-Western Publishing Co., 1980.

McNaughton, Harry H. *Proofreading and Copyediting: A Practical Guide to Style for the 1970's*. New York: Hastings House, 1973. Reviewed by Norman G. Shidle in *Journal of Business Communication* 11 (1974): 56–57.

Powell, Eileen A., and Angione, Howard. eds. *The Associated Press Stylebook and Libel Manual*. New York: The Associated Press, 1980.

Strunk, W., Jr., and White, E. B. *Elements of Style*. 2d Ed. New York: MacMillan, 1972.

U.S. Government Printing Office Style Manual. Washington, DC: Government Printing Office, 1976.

GRAPHICS

Environmental Research Information Center, U.S. Environmental Protection Agency, *Handbook for Preparing Office of Research and Development Reports*, Washington, D.C.: Government Printing Office, 1978.

Pocket Pal—A Graphics Arts Production Handbook. New York: International Paper Co., 1981.

Selby, Peter H. *Interpreting Graphs and Tables*. New York: John Wiley & Sons, 1976.

Stevenson, George H. *Graphic Arts Encyclopedia*. New York: McGraw-Hill, 1979.

WORD PROCESSING

Anderson, Thomas, and Trotter, William R. *Word Processing Users' Manual*. New York: American Management Associations, 1976.

Goldfield, R. J. "The New Text Editors: Smarter and Easier to Use." *Administrative Management* (June 1978): 36–60.

Greenwood, Dr. F. "Word Processing Primer." *Journal of Systems Management* 29 (1978): 36–38.

Konkel, G. J., and Peck, P. J. "Word Processing Requires a Basic Knowledge of English." *The Office* 84 (1976): 524.

Lederer, Victor. "Word Processing: It's More Than Faster Correspondence." *Administrative Management* (April 1978): 60–66.

McCabe, Helen, and Popham, Estelle. *Word Processing: A Systems Approach to the Office*. New York: Harcourt Brace Jovanovich, 1977. Reviewed by Gretchen N. Vik in *Journal of Business Communication* 15 (1978): 63.

Rosen, Arnold, and Fielden, Rosemary. *Word Processing*. Englewood Cliffs, N.J.: Prentice-Hall, 1977.

Williams, L. K., and Lodahl, Thomas M. "Comparing WP and Computers." *Journal of Systems Management* 29 (1978): 9–11.

"WP: A Special Management Update." Special Report. *Administrative Management* (April 1978): 59–103.

Index

About the Author

James W. Jacoby has more than 25 years' experience in writing, editing, communications management, consulting, and teaching. For the past 15 years he has been managing communications departments for Control Data Corporation in Minneapolis, Minn.—a multi-billion dollar Fortune 500 company. He is currently manager of marketing communications and employee communications for the five-division Systems and Services Company of Control Data, and is a member of the Corporate Employee Communications Committee.

He also owns his own company—Management Communications Consultants—which provides communications seminars and consulting to scores of Midwest and Canadian organizations. He serves on the faculty of the University of Minnesota's Continuing Management Education program, where he developed and teaches a seminar on "Writing Effective Organizational Manuals and Directives." He has also been a faculty member of Inver Hills College in the Twin Cities, where he taught Business Communications from 1974 through 1980.

Mr. Jacoby's educational background includes a bachelor of arts degree cum laude in journalism from The Pennsylvania State University, plus advanced courses at Harvard University, the University of Michigan, the University of Minnesota, and New York University. He is a member of the American Society for Training and Development and the American Business Communication Association.